THE TSARNAEV BROTHERS

Masha Gessen is an acclaimed Russian-American journalist and the author of several books, including bestsellers *The Man Without a Face* and *Words Will Break Cement*. Her work has appeared in *The New York Times, Slate, Vanity Fair*, and many other publications, and has received numerous awards. A longtime resident of Moscow, she now lives in New York.

ALSO BY MASHA GESSEN

Dead Again: The Russian Intelligentsia After Communism

*Ester and Ruzya: How My Grandmothers Survived
Hitler's War and Stalin's Peace*

*Blood Matters: From Inherited Illness to Designer Babies,
How the World and I Found Ourselves in the Future of the Gene*

*Perfect Rigor: A Genius and the
Mathematical Breakthrough of the Century*

The Man Without a Face: The Unlikely Rise of Vladimir Putin

Words Will Break Cement: The Passion of Pussy Riot

Gay Propaganda: Russian Love Stories (editor)

THE
TSARNAEV
BROTHERS

the road to a modern tragedy

MASHA GESSEN

SCRIBE

Melbourne • London

Scribe Publications
18–20 Edward St, Brunswick, Victoria 3056, Australia
2 John St, Clerkenwell, London, WC1N 2ES, United Kingdom

First published by Scribe 2015

This edition published by arrangement with Riverhead Books, an imprint of
Penguin Random House LLC, 375 Hudson Street, New York, New York 10014

Book design by amanda dewey
MAPS © 2015 by DARYA Oreshkina

Typeset in Caslon 540 9.75 / 16.5pt
Printed and bound in the UK by CPI Group (UK) Ltd, Croydon CR0 4YY

National Library of Australia
Cataloguing-in-Publication data

Gessen, Masha, author.

The Tsarnaev Brothers: the road to an American tragedy / Masha Gessen.

1. Tsarnaev, Tamerlan, 1986-2013. 2. Tsarnaev, Dzhokhar, 1993-
3. Boston Marathon Bombing, Boston, Mass., 2013 4. Terrorists–Biography.
5. Refugees–Social aspects–United States. 6. Refugees–Cultural assimilation–
United States. 7. Terrorism–United States.

363.325092

9781925106619 (Australian edition)
9781922247506 (UK edition)
9781925113884 (e-book)

scribepublications.com.au
scribepublications.co.uk

The pain inflicted by the Boston Marathon bombing was one of the few aspects of that act of terror that were immediately evident and certain. Such is the nature of the crime that hundreds of individuals and families will suffer loss and trauma for many years to come. This book, however, is not about that pain. It is about something that, whatever evidence is unearthed, will never be entirely certain: it is about the tragedy that preceded the bombing, the reasons that led to it, and its invisible victims.

CONTENTS

PART THREE

AFTERMATH

CAST OF CHARACTERS

THE TSARNAEV FAMILY

The Brothers: Tamerlan, wife Karima (formerly Katherine Russell), daughter Zahira; and Dzhokhar (later Jahar)

Parents: Anzor and Zubeidat

Paternal grandparents: Zayndy and Liza

Paternal uncles, aunts, and cousins: Ayndy; Malkan and son Husein; Maret; Alvi, wife Zhanar, children Aindy and Luiza; Ruslan, first wife Samantha Fuller, father-in-law Graham Fuller

Sisters: Bella, husband Rizvan, son Ramzan; Ailina, husband Elmirza, son Ziaudy

Cousin: Jamal Tsarnaev

KYRGYZSTAN

Friends and neighbors: Semyon and Alladin Abaev, Anzor's closest friends; Badrudi and Zina Tsokaev, neighbors and advisors; Alaudin and Aziz Batukaev, organized-crime bosses; Raisa Batukaeva, next-door neighbor and unofficial Chechen community leader; Ruslan Zakriev, owner of amusement park and official leader of Chechen community; Yakha Tsokaeva and Madina, friends in Bishkek, the capital

School personnel: Lubov Shulzhenko, Tamerlan's principal; Natalya
    Kurochkina, Tamerlan's grade-school teacher

DAGESTAN

Gasan Gasanaliyev, imam of Makhachkala's Kotrov Street mosque
Magomed Kartashov, Tamerlan's second cousin, head of Union
    of the Just
Mohammed Gadzhiev, Kartashov's deputy
Kheda Saratova, human rights advocate

BOSTON AREA

Other Chechen immigrant families: Khassan Baiev (sambo champion,
    plastic surgeon, author), wife Zara Tokaeva, children Islam and
    Maryam; Makhmud (Max) Mazaev (owner of an elder-care
    center), wife Anna, son Baudy (Boston University student);
    Hamzat Umarov, wife Raisa
Joanna Herlihy, the Tsarnaevs' landlady
Nadine Ascencao, Tamerlan's girlfriend
Brendan Mess, Tamerlan's best friend, murdered in 2011 along with
    Erik Weissman and Raphael Teken
Donald Larking, home-care client of Zubeidat and later Karima
Norfolk Street neighbors: Rinat Harel, Chris LaRoche
At Cambridge Rindge and Latin: Larry Aaronson, retired history teacher
    and photographer; Steve Matteo, English teacher; Lulu Emmons,
    former classmate of Jahar's; Luis Vasquez, Tamerlan's friend
Abdulrahman Ali Alharbi, marathon bombing victim who was an early
    suspect
Other early suspects: Sunil Tripathi, Salaheddin Barhoum, Yassine
    Zaimi
Boston-area law enforcement: Sean Collier, murdered MIT campus
    security officer; Richard Donohue, wounded transit cop;

Jeff Pugliese, Watertown policeman; David Earle, Essex County police detective also on the Joint Terrorism Task Force; Timothy Alben, Massachusetts State Police superintendent; Farbod Azad, Kenneth Benton, Scott Cieplik, Michael Delapena, Richard DesLauriers, Dwight Schwader, John Walker, Sara Wood, all FBI; Douglas Woodlock, federal judge; Carmen Ortiz, U.S. Attorney; Scott Riley and Stephanie Siegmann, Assistant U.S. Attorneys
"Danny," owner of the SUV hijacked by Tamerlan and Dzhokhar
Khairullozhon "Kair" Matanov, taxi driver, refugee from Kyrgyzstan, friend of Tamerlan; attorney Edward Hayden
Michael Dukakis, former governor of Massachusetts

UNIVERSITY OF MASSACHUSETTS DARTMOUTH AND NEW BEDFORD

Robel Phillipos, Jahar's friend, also from Cambridge Rindge and Latin; friend Elohe Dereje (Maryland); attorney Derege Demissie
Dias Kadyrbayev, from Kazakhstan; girlfriend Bayan Kumiskali
Azamat Tazhayakov, from Kazakhstan; father Amir Ismagulov; attorneys Nicholas Wooldridge and Arkady Bukh (New York)
Andrew Dwinells, Jahar's roommate
Other friends and classmates of Jahar's: Pamela Rolon; Alexa Guevara; Tiffany Evora; Lino Rosas; Quan Le Phan, Robel's former roommate; Jim Li, Quan's roommate
Brian Williams, teacher of class on Chechnya

OTHERS

Almut Rochowanski, founder of legal aid organization for Chechen refugees (New York)
Musa Khadzhimuratov, Max Mazaev's paralyzed cousin; wife Madina, son Ibragim (later Abraham), daughter Malika (Manchester, New Hampshire)

Ibragim Todashev, Chechen immigrant killed during questioning by
FBI agents and Boston police in 2013 (Orlando, Florida); wife
Reni Manukyan, born Evgenia (Nyusha) Nazarenko (Atlanta), her
mother, Elena Teyer (Savannah, Georgia), and her brother, Alex
(Atlanta); girlfriend Tatiana Gruzdeva (Orlando); father Abdulbaki
Todashev (Chechnya); best friend Khusein Taramov (Orlando;
later Russia); lawyer Zuarbek Sadokhanov
Yerlan Kubashev, with the consulate of Kazakhstan in New York

PART ONE

DISLOCATION

THE TSARNAEVS' JOURNEY

Every few years the Tsarnaevs traveled thousands of miles in search of a better life.

1985 > Anzor and Zubeidat from Novosibirsk to Tokmok
< 1986 Anzor and Zubeidat from Tokmok to Kalmykia
1986 > Anzor, Zubeidat, and Tamerlan from Kalmykia to Tokmok
< 1992 Tsarnaev family from Tokmok to Chiry-Yurt
1994 > Tsarnaev family from Chechnya to Tokmok
< 2000 Tsarnaev family from Tokmok to Makhachkala
< 2002 Dzhokhar and parents from Makhachkala to Cambridge
2002 > Tamerlan and sisters from Makhachkala to Almaty
< 2003 Tamerlan and sisters from Almaty to Istanbul
< 2003 Tamerlan and sisters from Istanbul to Cambridge
2012 > Anzor from Cambridge to Dagestan
2012 > Zubeidat from Cambridge to Dagestan

One

LOVE

YOU CAN BE PROUD OF BEING A DAGESTANI, proclaim the billboards lining the highway from the airport to Makhachkala.
It is the spring of 2013. The billboards picture, by way of argument, the recently appointed head of Dagestan, Ramazan Abdul-
atipov, speaking with Russia's president, Vladimir Putin. Both look
unhappy, but the photo op, apparently a one-time occurrence,
seems not to have generated a better option.

The highway to the capital, like so much of Dagestan, is an
object of pride and an embarrassment at the same time. It was
built recently, and well; it is by far the best road in Dagestan, so
good that at night young men race their souped-up Lada Priora
sedans here. The Lada Priora is a bad, Russian-made car, but its
twentieth-century technology lends itself to quick fixes. Which is
a good thing, because as the road enters the city, turning into the
main avenue, the smooth surface gives way to potholes that can
cost you your tire or your life.

Outside the city, the highway is lined with unfinished houses,
scores of them. They betray modest ambition—small two-story
structures along a highway—and yet even this dream has gone
unfulfilled. Rectangular openings stare at the highway where

windows should be. Cows graze in between these carcasses and wander lazily onto the highway.

People you meet in Dagestan will tell you where else they have been. They have rarely ventured very far, but they have invariably found any other place to be remarkably different. Several drivers tell me that in Moscow or Saint Petersburg or even provincial Astrakhan, three hundred miles to the north of Makhachkala, people do not drive into natural-gas fueling stations (almost everyone in Dagestan seems to drive a car retrofitted for natural gas) with a lit cigarette in their mouths. In Astrakhan, one man tells me, they get all the passengers out of the car before refueling. This kind of regard for human life awes and baffles him. Astrakhan is no hub of bourgeois humanitarianism, but then, compared with Dagestan, almost anyplace is.

The Russian Federation includes eighty-three nominally self-governing regions, districts, autonomies, and republics; the republics differ from the rest of the convoluted federation's members in that they have the right to choose their own state language—mostly because the republics are, by and large, populated by non-Russian ethnic groups. Dagestan, a republic, sits on the edge of the Russian empire, a mere two and a half hours by plane south-southeast from Moscow but as culturally remote as the far northeast, where Russia borders the United States, or the far east, where it seeps into China. Dagestan borders Azerbaijan and Georgia to the south and war-torn Chechnya to the north. Throughout its history as a part of Russia, Dagestan has been one of the poorest parts of the empire, and one of the most embattled. It has also always been the most diverse, with dozens of distinct ethnic groups living in various states of war and peace. Each group has a fiercely defined identity, but no single ethnic group claims the region as an ersatz nation-state, and a Dagestani identity per se can hardly be said to exist. So the billboards seem to be calling on people to take pride simply in living in Dagestan. But why would anyone want to live here?

This is where the story begins.

FIRST, Zubeidat ran from Makhachkala. In May 1985, she was walking in the outskirts of Novosibirsk, terrified of getting into trouble, though most people back home would have said she was asking for trouble just by being in Novosibirsk. She had graduated from high school in Makhachkala a year earlier, and she wanted to go to college. Worse, she wanted to go to Moscow. One of her older brothers lived there, and from what she could tell, this brother was an important person. He worked in retail, which in the Soviet Union meant access to all sorts of nice things and influential people, and she had kept calling him, begging him to take her out of Makhachkala.

Makhachkala is a hard place to love. In the 2010s, a pair of journalists who set out to compile an oral history of the city, a coffee-table book with lots of nostalgic sepia-colored photographs, were repeatedly told by the residents they interviewed how unlivable Makhachkala had always been, what a misunderstanding of a city it was. A locally prominent artist called it "a town without a legend" that was "unsuited for normal life." A fort reconstituted as a town in the mid–nineteenth century, it felt like a haphazard and temporary agglomeration of more than a hundred ethnic groups, each of which maintained its own language and used variously simplified and mangled Russian to communicate with one another and the outside world. Streets bore the names of the ethnic groups that had originally settled there: Armenian Street crossed Persian Street. Soviet authorities renamed the streets in the spirit of internationalism and Communist ideology, but the old designations remained in the vernacular. Each group made its own living arrangements, usually unaided by the Communist state that had assumed the obligation for sheltering and feeding all citizens but failed consistently, and failed worse the farther from the center the citizens resided. People lived in barracks, in rehabbed fort structures, in sheds and other temporary dwellings, and well into the late twentieth century, indoor plumbing and cooking facilities remained the stuff of dreams.

Neighborhood borders were inviolate: a male outsider who tried to date a neighborhood girl would be knifed. The single unifying culture of the city was that of the prison. There were eight prison camps within the city limits before Stalin's death in 1953; once released, many of the inmates stayed on in the city. In at least one case, a camp was abolished and the barbed-wire fence removed, but the barracks were simply renamed "dormitories" and everybody stayed. The city jail, which never stopped functioning, sat up on a hill, a major landmark and the center of the switchblade-making industry. Every Makhachkala-born male past the age of puberty had to own a switchblade that had been smuggled out of the jail and sold on the black market.

Not that there was much of a legal economy: centrally distributed consumer goods rarely reached Russia's southern edge. Makhachkalinians wore clothes and shoes made by local tailors and cobblers—there was one of each on nearly every block—and ate fish caught in the Caspian Sea by local poachers, who went door-to-door every day hawking sturgeon and black-backed herring so fatty it could be tossed into a skillet with no oil. Yet the Caspian itself seemed to have no place in the city, or in any story about it. A gentle, light blue sea that is actually the world's largest lake, the Caspian was cut off from Makhachkala by a railroad constructed at the turn of the twentieth century. Only a thin strip of sand, barely a hundred yards at its narrowest, separated the water from the rails. The sounds of the railroad drowned out the murmur of the sea, and the bitter smell of tar, the metallic smell of hot rails, and the smoke of the engines overwhelmed the Caspian's softly salty air.

Whether people lived in nineteenth-century stone buildings or twentieth-century wooden barracks, they dwelled a family to a room if they were lucky, and used the courtyards for all their daily needs: wood-burning stoves for cooking, wooden outhouses never far away. At night young men went yard to yard, scooping human waste into large barrels mounted on their horse-driven carts, nicknamed "stinkies." Household waste flowed in open trenches along city streets until the 1960s, when, legend has it, old gravestones were used to enclose the trenches in the city center—there are still residents who claim to have seen Arabic writing beneath their feet.

Dwellings with indoor conveniences came in the 1960s, too, but in 1970 an earthquake measuring 6.7 on the Richter scale shook Dagestan. The epicenter was less than twenty miles west of Makhachkala. Thirty-one people died and half the city's population was left homeless. Twenty-two villages outside the city were completely destroyed, and their residents, too, flooded into Makhachkala even as more than a thousand aftershocks, some of them nearly as strong as the original quake, shook the city over the following six weeks. Makhachkala returned to the premodern state to which it seemed doomed.

A year later, the newly underequipped and overcrowded city was hit by a cholera epidemic. Moscow shut Makhachkala down:

anyone who wanted to leave the city had to be tested for the germ and was not allowed to travel until cleared. The city's population swelled further with those waiting to travel out of Dagestan.

ZUBEIDAT WAS BORN in Makhachkala three years before the earthquake. By the time she was a teenager, she was acutely and painfully aware of living in a backwater. Even the Chechens, who lived right next door and had been decimated by forced exile, had a real city: Grozny had fashion and music. It was from Grozny that young men would bring records and reel-to-reel tapes for Makhachkala's first *diskoteka*s—a fancy word for dances—in the early 1980s. To create disco lighting, the young men stole colored glass from traffic lights and, at great peril to themselves, flashing lights off police cars. In Grozny, young men were not too timid to wear pointy cowboy boots, which had roared into fashion; Makhachkalinians, who did not dare wear them, called them *nokhchi*-boots, or Chechen-boots. Men in Makhachkala still wore visored hats nicknamed "airport caps" for the exceedingly large flat surface they created on the wearer's head. Elsewhere in the Soviet Union these caps marked men as hailing from the remote Caucasian provinces, but in Dagestan they were privileged as city wear: country folk wore fluffy white sheepskin hats. The possession most coveted by any young person who wanted to escape Makhachkala's provincial uniformity was a white plastic bag printed with a full-color photograph of a man's behind in Wrangler jeans. These cost up to five rubles on the black market; a loaf of bread ran sixteen kopecks, or just over three percent of the price of the plastic bag.

Everyone in Makhachkala knew everything about everyone else. There was one Russian Orthodox church in the city and, directly across the street, one abortion clinic. Being seen entering either could ruin one's reputation for life—the church because of Party prohibitions on religion, and the clinic because, while most Soviet women strove to control their fertility and had few means of doing that aside from abortion, Dagestani women were having more babies than women almost anywhere else in the USSR were having, and staying home to raise them. The home was ruled by the men in accordance with Adat, a set of rules that were said to derive from Islam but were largely local customs. Most of the local populations were Muslim; the Russian colonizers had imported Russian Orthodoxy, and migrants had brought Greek Orthodoxy, Catholicism, and Judaism. The Communists had banned the open organized practice of all religions, and in Muslim groups over the course of decades the family and community practices of Adat came to reign supreme—and to be conflated with Islam in the popular understanding.

Customs differed somewhat even between closely related Muslim ethnic groups such as Chechens and Avars, the largest ethnic group in Dagestan. In both traditions, though, the eldest brother ruled over all siblings. Zubeidat was Avar, so if she wanted to go live with her brother in Moscow, she first had to ask her eldest brother, who lived in Novosibirsk, in southwestern Siberia. That was where she had gone, then, to ask his permission.

While the eldest brother was thinking it over, August, the month of entrance exams to Soviet colleges, came and went. At least Zubeidat was now out of Makhachkala, though at some point in the not-too-distant future she would be expected to travel back to Dagestan and marry a young man from an Avar family with whom preliminary arrangements had been made. The Avars did not practice arranged marriages, strictly speaking, or practice them strictly—dating and romance were allowed by some families some of the time—but marriage agreements were always made between the men of the families, and no one ever married outside the ethnic group. Premarital sex, for the women, was punishable by death: the Soviets had done nothing to end honor killings.

Novosibirsk was not Moscow, of course, but much more important, it was not Makhachkala. In fact, a city could not be less like Makhachkala: it was vast, uncrowded, its central squares and avenues a vision in Stalinist grandeur that looked better from the air than they did at street level, where all that scale made a person feel bug-tiny. Zubeidat's brother lived in a neighborhood of two-story stone buildings constructed by German prisoners of war in the 1940s, and gray-brick five-story buildings from Khrushchev's socialist-construction boom of the 1950s, a few taller apartment blocks from the 1970s, and even a few wooden barracks-like structures left over from when some group or other had been warehoused there. Still, even this haphazard collection of unattractive architecture was assembled with so much space between buildings that Zubeidat never forgot she was in the big city—and this was why she had kept stretching out the months until she returned to Dagestan.

The neighborhood abutted a trade school on one end and a jail on the other. The trade school, which trained retail-store managers, had mostly young women for students, and Zubeidat had become friendly with a few who lived in the dormitories there. Still, the proximity of the jail always made her slightly nervous about walking home to her brother's place alone, even on a May evening when the light was a soft gray and would stay that way until midnight. When she sensed someone walking behind her, she jerked around.

The man was not scary at all. In her mind she immediately marked him as *parnishka*, a Russian diminutive for "guy." He was slight, even skinny, and he was wearing a green military shirt and green slacks without the jacket or the hat that would complete the uniform; this was the way a man who had recently left the service or would soon be leaving it would dress. Zubeidat turned back around and continued walking, so relieved as to feel almost joyful. The stranger must have sensed this, because he caught up with her and fell in step.

"*Devushka*," he said—"girl"—using the standard form of address for an unfamiliar young woman, "do you happen to know Tanya, who lives in room twenty-seven in the trade-school dorm?"

"I do," said Zubeidat, and decided she was walking to the dorm. "I can fetch her for you, if you want."

"And you are her . . . ?" he asked. He seemed a little confused about what he wanted, or what he wanted to know.

"I'm just an acquaintance," said Zubeidat.

"Where are you from yourself?"

"Dagestan," said Zubeidat.

"And I'm from Chechnya," said Anzor Tsarnaev. This was not true: he was Chechen, but he had grown up in Kyrgyzstan, in Central Asia, fifteen hundred miles from Chechnya. Nor did he want anything with that girl named Tanya: she was just someone going out with a friend of his, and he asked about her because he needed something to say before he could ask this girl's name.

Now she said, "That makes us brother and sister."

"I'm so happy right now," said Anzor. "I've met a kindred spirit. You know, I was just taking a walk, I wasn't going anywhere in particular."

Which meant they could talk. Zubeidat told him that she was from Makhachkala and she was staying with her brother and that another brother was an important man in Moscow. Anzor told her he was finishing up his military service. He was a boxer and had won some competitions, and his job was coaching.

"I have to go because I have a curfew," she finally said. "My brother is strict. But if you want to know, I'll tell you that this is the building where I live, my brother's building. We come from the same land, you and I."

THEY DID LOOK like brother and sister, thin, sharp-featured, and constantly animated. They both hail from ethnic groups that come by girth naturally and cultivate it: the men wrestle, box, and engage in other martial arts that favor bulk; the women bear many children; and heavy, grainy home-baked bread is the traditional basis of all meals. Anzor and Zubeidat liked their own skinniness and worked to protect it, and friends sometimes mocked them for this. Zubeidat thought they looked as beautiful and exotic as two swans, and a quarter-century later, when they had moved halfway across the world, she took to telling people that "the Swans" had been their nickname back home. Anzor's love for Zubeidat, which he said befell him at first sight, was anything but brotherly. It was romantic in a way most unusual for men from these parts and especially for men from his culture, in which to this day the wedding ritual involves "stealing" the bride from her father's home, which in many cases indeed involves force.

"Can we see each other tomorrow?" Anzor asked. He had a way of projecting resolve and shyness at the same time, a combination Zubeidat thought was lovely. Her younger son would inherit it from Anzor, this disarming quality of being at once confident and openly vulnerable.

"I don't know," Zubeidat said. "I think we are going to the

countryside tomorrow. Maybe we can see each other in a couple of days. You can come here if you want, just make sure my brother doesn't see you." She knew he knew that without her having to say it.

Anzor came back the following day.

"We didn't end up going," said Zubeidat.

"It's like I had a feeling you'd be here," said Anzor.

The day after that they had a date, and he brought flowers. Young men around here typically always brought girls roses—in fact, Zubeidat had already rebuffed a couple of them, though it hadn't been because of the roses—but Anzor brought a mixed bouquet of wildflowers.

"It's so beautiful," she said.

"I've been walking past this flower shop every day," he said. "I've been thinking, *Someday I'll meet a girl and then I'll get her that bouquet.*"

ZUBEIDAT PANICKED EARLY, possibly as early as that first date. "They'll never let us marry," she said. "Not even my brother. Even though he left Dagestan so long ago that he lives like a Russian— he'll never let me marry someone who is not Avar."

"You know, I don't care," Anzor said. "If our families say no, we'll just run away. I'll be your mother, your father, your brother, and your sister."

But first he was going to take her to his family's home in Kyrgyzstan. By this time Zubeidat knew that, though they both claimed to hail from the Caucasus and in a way they both did, Anzor was a man born in exile. And Zubeidat was perhaps starting to sense that she was born *for* exile.

. . .

ON MARCH 7, 1944, the Supreme Soviet of the USSR passed a resolution that began:

> Whereas in the course of the Patriotic War, especially while the German fascist armies were active in the Caucasus, many Chechens and Ingush betrayed the Motherland, switched over to the side of the fascist occupiers, joined the ranks of saboteurs and intelligence-gatherers dispatched by the Germans to the rear of the Red Army, created, at the Germans' direction, armed groups to fight against the Soviet authorities, and in light of the fact that many Chechens and Ingush over the course of many years took part in armed attacks on the Soviet authorities and over the course of a long time, rather than engage in honest labor, committed armed robberies on the collective farms in neighboring regions, robbing and killing Soviet people, the Presidium of the Supreme Soviet of the USSR has resolved:
>
> 1. All Chechens and Ingush residing on the territory of the Chechen Ingush Autonomous Soviet Socialist Republic and neighboring areas shall be moved to other areas of the USSR and the Chechen Ingush Autonomous Soviet Socialist Republic shall be liquidated.

This resolution, which was unclassified but also unpublished, had been preceded by a series of secret meetings, resolutions, and decrees convened and issued over the course of about six months. As the Red Army pushed the Germans out of the Caucasus and began to advance in Belarus and Ukraine as well, Stalin had become obsessed with the Soviet citizens living in the parts of the country the Germans had occupied starting in 1941. Throughout the war he had believed that soldiers who had allowed themselves to be taken prisoner were traitors. Those lucky enough to have been freed were immediately re-incarcerated in the Gulag, for treason. What about those who lived in their own homes under German rule for years? Were they similarly contaminated? Had they welcomed the Germans? Had they cooperated willingly, cooking and cleaning for them and enforcing German rule in their own land? Had they over time come to like the Germans? Had they come to love them? Did they remain loyal to them after the occupation ended? What was the Soviet regime to do with the millions of its own citizens who were now suspect? Stalin might have liked to exterminate or exile the entire populations of Ukraine and Belarus, but they were too large to be isolated or removed effectively—and in any case, at the time he was confronted with the problem of the Caucasus, the Red Army had not yet advanced far into Ukraine and Belarus.

Stalin, who was half Ossetian—a North Caucasian ethnic group that is majority Christian—was perhaps most suspicious of the Muslims in the region. The largest Muslim group in the Russian North Caucasus were the Chechens, traditionally cattle farmers in the mountains and grain farmers in the valleys. Among them, an anti-Soviet insurgency had indeed existed, and it had welcomed the Germans, though most of Chechnya was in fact never occupied and the majority of Chechens were, by all accounts, loyal Soviet citizens. The Chechens were the largest group to face deportation, though not the only one. In all, seven ethnic groups with a total population of over 1.5 million would be removed from lands on which they had lived, and which they had defended for centuries in many wars. They would be moved to what, on the map, looked like vast empty space in Soviet Central Asia: over a million people would go to Kazakhstan and the rest to Kyrgyzstan.

Smaller numbers of other exiles had already been shipped there—the Kalmyks, a Buddhist people who had lived on the western shore of the Caspian Sea, and ethnic Germans, who had once settled along the Volga River.

On February 23, 1944, all Chechens living in Chechnya and neighboring republics were ordered to report to designated assembly points in their towns and villages. They were loaded onto trucks or marched the distance—sometimes dozens of miles over snowy forested mountains—to the trains that would take them to Central Asia. In at least one location about seven hundred elderly, disabled, and people too young or too weak to make the trek from their high-altitude villages were herded into a barn and burned alive. Resisters, protesters, and sometimes the merely confused and slow were shot on the spot. Over half a million Chechens and Ingush—a closely related smaller ethnic group—were loaded onto cattle cars, which began the nearly two-thousand-mile journey to Central Asia. About 85,000 of them would end up in Kyrgyzstan: the trains began arriving March 4, a week after they left Chechnya and three days before the Supreme Soviet issued its resolution. This was less than half a year before the first Nazi concentration camp was liberated and the Western world began a decades-long inquiry into the fates of other exiles and the trains that had carried them. The fate of the deported peoples of the Caucasus would never be similarly examined.

Over the years frightful estimates of the number of people who died en route to Central Asia have circulated, but in fact the journey was essentially undocumented: the sealed trains passed through the country anonymously, never stopping for food supplies or bathroom breaks. The exiles fashioned holes in the floors of their overcrowded cars to relieve themselves; they tried to ration such supplies of bread and water as some of them had carried;

washing was out of the question. The typhus epidemic began on the trains. When the first trains pulled into Kyrgyzstan on March 4, they carried twenty-five corpses—the exiles had thrown off the rest of the bodies along the way, in the vain hope of avoiding contagion. Eight hundred people were diagnosed with typhus on arrival.

Before the exiles arrived, local authorities had reported to Moscow that they had set aside enough supplies to feed the newcomers for four months. The rations were set at 116 grams of flour and 56 grams of grain a day per person—significantly less than the starvation rations of Auschwitz-Birkenau. By April 1, some 125,000 people had arrived from the Caucasus, members of seven distinct ethnic groups. Of them, 52,876 were judged fit for work upon arrival. Four months later, the number of those fit for work was 43,713: most of the nine thousand people who had lost their ability to work were, in the language of the corresponding reports, "extremely emaciated." In those first four months 5,128 people died, including 770 from typhus and 1,778 from starvation. The malaria epidemic began in midsummer.

If the meager supplies ostensibly prepared for the deportation ever really existed, they were not getting to the exiles. A secret report on the inspection of a collective farm in June 1944 stated that the "special settlers," as the authorities euphemistically called them, were not working, or working sufficiently well, "mostly due to the absence of food supplies, as a consequence of which the absolute majority of the special settlers are extremely emaciated. . . . Thirteen people have died as a result of typhus and starvation. Ill people in a state of extreme emaciation, essentially at death's door, as of June 8 this year number 40, including 20 children. . . . Special settlers are eating mostly grass. . . . No one is keeping track of special-settler deaths." The report described the mother of four children aged two to ten, the three youngest of whom could no longer move; she was making them soup out of grass. Reports from other collective farms painted a similar picture, but introduced a new category beyond "extremely emaciated." This category was "bloated."

Some of the exiles were placed in collective-farm housing, never spacious to begin with. Usually this meant that a local family who occupied a two-room house had to cede one of the rooms to a family of newcomers. The local families resisted, perceiving the arrival of the exiles, rightly, as a threat not only to their space but to their health: typhus soon spread to the local population. Still, for the exiles, being forced into someone's house was infinitely preferable to the alternatives: being warehoused in unfinished or vacant, usually unheated apartments, generally three families to a room; being warehoused in common village spaces such as a collective-farm cafeteria or meeting hall; or being shoved into unheated tents or mud huts. Authorities directed the collective farms to construct housing for "special settlers," but the most construction materials any of the collective farms appear to have been issued was thirty-two logs to put up barracks, the roof to be made of locally collected reeds. No construction appears to have commenced by the fall, when the weather started turning cold again.

Exiles were to be issued plots of land and seeds for planting, but most could not bring themselves to bury even a single grain seed in the ground; they ate them. The few who did manage to plant did not know how to work the local land—and the plots they had been issued were by definition the undesirable, difficult ones. No one had a harvest that year.

The "special settlers" were more than an imposition on the locals: they were, it was well established, the enemies of the people. They lacked even the limited civil rights accorded ordinary

Soviet citizens. They had to check in regularly with local secret-police representatives, as one might check in with a parole officer. Secret-police clearance was required for the most quotidian of actions, such as seeking help at a medical clinic. The secret-police officers had a range of disciplinary measures at their disposal, including fines and up to ten days' administrative arrest.

Other locals also treated the exiles as one would treat the enemy. One collective-farm chairman loaded seven families on three horse-driven carts and instructed the drivers to take them to another town and dump them at the side of the road. This was to serve as a lesson not only for these families but also for the "special settlers" remaining in his village: they too would be expelled if they did not work hard enough. In this case, law enforcement investigated the incident and concluded that none of the members of the seven families was actually physically fit to work. Other collective-farm chairmen claimed that they did not need any additional hands and simply refused to acknowledge the "special settlers," in the hope of driving them away. They not only withheld rations but also instructed the village store not to sell to the new arrivals. Inspection reports describe numerous instances of local authority figures beating the children of the exiles, sometimes to death. The beatings of adults are not mentioned, probably because they were not seen as warranting notice.

Zayndy Tsarnaev, Anzor's father, was brought to Kyrgyzstan at the age of thirteen. The family was placed about forty miles east of the Kyrgyz capital, Frunze, in Tokmok, a settlement wedged in a narrow valley between the Kyrgyz Range and the Trans-Ili Alatau mountains. Local legend has it that the Soviets once considered making Tokmok the capital, but the Chu, a furious mountain river that took over the entire valley every spring, rendered the location unsuitable. When the exiles arrived in Kyrgyzstan, an effort to harness the Chu was under way. The men were immediately rounded up and loaded onto horse-driven carts, which took them to the construction site for the future hydroelectric plant. Delivered late at night, the men escaped early the next morning to look for the railroad station so that they could go back to help their families. Secret-police files overflow with reports and complaints filed by construction supervisors, who demanded a police cordon at the site to keep the men from leaving. The paperwork details living conditions at the site. There was no shelter. There were no bathing facilities, which meant the men were flea-ridden. They received two meals a day, at six in the morning and at five in the evening. The rations consisted solely of grain and water. As the men died off, secret police conducted raids to round up new workers from among the special settlers and deliver them to the site. Construction supervisors complained the new arrivals were unfit for work because they were not only extremely emaciated but also naked and barefoot.

The death rate among the exiles remained steady through the freezing spring and the scorching summer; they entered the winter of 1944–1945 with no suitable shelter or reliable source of sustenance, and the dying continued. The following year decimated the survivors, and the year after that killed many of those who remained. And yet, after three or four years—after the death of half or more of the Chechen population, after the pain and humiliation and dread of living in an open-air prison and, incongruously, in a constant state of uncertainty—the life of the "special settlers" appeared to stabilize. They were still, in essence, prisoners, with their movement and activities severely restricted and violence a daily threat, but they gradually secured housing and, to some extent, succeeded in assimilating. Some families continued to hold

their children back from Russian- and Kyrgyz-language schools—
Chechen-language education had effectively been outlawed—but
after a few years this was a small, albeit constant, minority. Access
to the legal local economy, accorded only to fully vested Soviet
citizens, never really opened up to the exiles, but the Chechens
compensated by creating gray-market trading systems, so that
after a few years they were not only able to move out of cramped
barracks and freezing mud huts but also became providers of coveted goods for the locals—and since virtually all goods were in
short supply, most goods were indeed coveted. While most families submitted to having their children educated at Russian- and
Kyrgyz-language schools, virtually everyone still spoke Chechen
at home, considered intermarriage impossible, and continued to
live in accordance with Adat, which, in exile, gradually became
both more important and less detailed.

STALIN DIED IN 1953, nine years and one day after the Chechens began arriving in Kyrgyzstan. In another three years the
new Soviet leader, Nikita Khrushchev, began gingerly to lift restrictions on the deported ethnic groups. The Party now admitted
that the exiles had been wronged—in a meeting with a group of
them, Khrushchev even said the dictator had been paranoid and
out of control—but the bureaucracy did not know how to handle
hundreds of thousands of people who had been displaced. Their
houses and lands had long since been occupied by others, in the
concerted campaign of colonization that the state had conducted
for years after the deportation. Ethnic Russians had been moved
into Chechnya by the orphanageful, in conditions scarcely less
punishing than the Chechens were facing in Central Asia, and

those who survived had by now put down roots. What kind of violence would break out if the Chechens—or the Kabardians, or the Balkars—returned to claim their homes?

Representatives of the displaced peoples begged that they be allowed to return, in exchange for promising to not challenge the current residents and to settle on empty land, as long as it was in the Caucasus. The Khrushchev government did not believe them and, after much hemming and hawing, settled on a particularly cruel way of sawing the baby in half: the exiles would be effectively freed, which is to say, they would be given standard-issue Soviet documents and released from all limitations on freedom of movement, allowing them to settle anywhere in the USSR—except in their lands of origin. The first few groups of exiles who were offered this deal accepted it, but in the fall of 1956 the Kyrgyzstan Chechens balked en masse and refused to sign the agreements that would have entitled them to regular identity documents. At the end of that year, the Central Committee finally approved a plan for returning Chechens to Chechnya, gradually, over the course of three years, in a highly controlled manner. The process was hellish and hellishly corrupt. It also took much longer than planned. But by the mid-1960s everyone who wanted to move to the Caucasus had left. Soviet statistics make it all but impossible to determine what proportion of the exiled population went back, but thousands of families stayed in Kyrgyzstan. Those who stayed also wanted to go home—but to them, home had become an abstraction, or at least a distant goal. Some lacked the money to move. Others could not face the hardship. "No one is kicking us out of here, and no one is waiting for us there," a Chechen man in Tokmok told me in 2014.

Sixty years to the week earlier, a man named Medzhit Baiev said in the presence of a secret-police informant: "I am an old man and don't need to go anywhere, but my children will now have the same rights as all the other peoples of the Soviet Union. I am deeply grateful to the government." He was right: his descendant Khassan would grow up in Chechnya. In the 1990s he would face the war there, work as a surgeon operating on the wounded, then escape to the United States and settle in Boston, where he would eventually help another Chechen family, the Tsarnaevs, to settle as well.

But in the 1960s, the Tsarnaevs also stayed in Kyrgyzstan. Zayndy had made it by then—he ran the dumping ground that had formed in an old quarry in Tokmok. Between his official salary and a sideline of collecting scrap metal, paper, and clothing that he fished out of the refuse and turned in to the relevant recycling plants, he was making a good living. His wife was having one child after another. He ran the house like a homegrown tyrant; his wife would stay home and raise their kids to be educated and ambitious, but she would never be seen outside the home. Zayndy would invest in some land in Chechnya and build a house, so that eventually his children's children would grow up there. This was the thinking of most of those who stayed behind: they were not putting down roots in Kyrgyzstan—they were just extending their stay before their families returned home at last.

In 1985, Anzor Tsarnaev returned from his military service in Novosibirsk to his father's home in Kyrgyzstan, bringing his young wife with him. The neighborhood was Sakhzavod, so named for the nearby sugarcane-processing plant. There was also a cannery and a wool-processing plant—it was the industrial outskirts of Tokmok, which itself had come to feel like the remote outskirts of Frunze, the capital. Frunze was like a flattened version of Novosibirsk—the same vast squares and broad avenues and Soviet neoclassical buildings, only much lower. And Tokmok was like nothing in particular.

The Chu had been harnessed in 1982. It was now a tame little stream flowing through a concrete enclosure, but Tokmok itself still had a makeshift, insecure sense about it, as though every structure could be washed away any minute. With the exception of a couple of school buildings, nothing here looked like it was meant to last.

A conglomeration of settlers had nested their homes near the factories: cinder-block first stories with wooden attics and sharply pitched asbestos-board roofs. One of these roofs had given way under the feet of Anzor's older brother in 1979 as he was replacing a worn red Soviet flag on top of a trade school with a newer one, and he had fallen to his death. In 1985, when Anzor and Zubeidat came, most of the other five Tsarnaev children were still in or around their parents' house. The street on which they lived was split about equally between Chechens and ethnic Germans. The latter called their children by Russian diminutives but continued to speak German to them: "*Yasha, herkommen,*" they called out into the street at suppertime, and the children disappeared behind the cinder-block fences. The street had a blind feel to it—a single block long, lined with solid gray fences, it ran perpendicular to the mountain ranges, so neither of them could be seen from a house window. Immediately upon arriving, Zubeidat commenced dreaming of living by the sea again someday. Everyone on this street dreamed of someday going home to someplace beautiful and far away.

Two

WANDERING

The idea that they were like brother and sister because they were both from the Caucasus really held only as long as Anzor and Zubeidat stayed far away from both the Caucasus itself and their families. According to both Avar and Chechen traditions, now that Anzor and Zubeidat were married, she was to enter his parents' house as a member of his family. Had she married an Avar, she would have had the support and coaching of the women of her own family in this endeavor; as it was, she was now alone. And to her new family, she was immediately suspect. Neither Anzor nor his parents, who had grown up in Kyrgyzstan with only a mythical, vague story of the Caucasus, had ever even heard of the Avars, although they speak a language closely related to Chechen and have historically been viewed by their Russian rulers as a subset of the Chechens. To the Tokmok Chechens, Zubeidat was just not-Chechen. She worked conscientiously to fit in, quickly and easily learning to speak Chechen—though she and Anzor always spoke Russian to each other—but in other ways she was as different as a woman could be from her new mother-in-law. Liza was what Americans might call a victim of domestic abuse; her Chechen neighbors from Tokmok just say that Zayndy was "very strict" and never let his wife go out in public by herself or, for that matter, with him. Few of their former neighbors can even recall her name, so quiet and invisible was she. Zubeidat and Anzor, on the other hand, appeared inseparable; more than that, they appeared to be equal partners. Not for Zubeidat the Chechen—or Avar—custom of serving the men and never sitting down at the table with them, or with the guests. Nor did she hold back in conversation. She could be charming, she had a loud, unabashed laugh, she invited and accepted compliments, and unlike her gentle husband, she could occasionally be cutting. If anything, these rebellious ways had to do with Zubeidat's having grown up in a city, and with having made a break with her own family, but Liza had only one word for all of it: Avar.

Anzor had promised Zubeidat back in Novosibirsk that he would take her as far as they needed to go to be happy together. It is not clear how they chose Kalmykia as their destination after Tokmok. Most of Anzor's uncles and cousins had moved to Chechnya, and Zayndy was, according to his plan, slowly building a house there as well, in the village of Chiry-Yurt. But Zubeidat may have feared she would not be accepted in Chechnya, or perhaps none of Anzor's uncles had extended an invitation. An older cousin on Liza's side, though, invited them to Kalmykia, Dagestan's northern neighbor—and perhaps the idea of living on the Caspian again appealed to Zubeidat. But Kalmykia turned out to be the opposite of Makhachkala, a desert—just sand and steppes and emptiness that made even what sea it touched seem desolate. And Anzor's relative turned out to be a cattle farmer. Anzor's family, like all the Chechens in Tokmok, had always kept cows, sheep, and goats in numbers the Soviet government deemed excessive. (Most of their livestock was part of the shadow economy and had to be hidden when inspectors or snoops came around.) So Anzor easily fell into the farmwork: he was generally willing to do any kind of labor, and this he was good at. But Zubeidat, although she had family who lived in a village back in Dagestan, was herself a city girl, and she had not imagined that a cattle farm in the middle of nowhere would be the place where she would find happiness.

Happiness came in the form of their first child. Zubeidat gave birth to a boy in October 1986. They named him Tamerlan, for the Central Asian conqueror with refined tastes—Tima, Russian style, for short. He was perfect and, Zubeidat knew, always would be. And she would be a perfect mother. He was decked out in bow ties from the time he was a toddler; in grade school, he would stand out among his classmates for his clean clothes; in middle school, for his near-perfect grades. But none of this could happen on a cattle farm in the steppes of Kalmykia. For the boy's sake, Anzor and Zubeidat moved again.

THEY RETURNED to Tokmok after just six months in Kalmykia. Zubeidat was nineteen now, Anzor was twenty, and they were parents. Now that Zubeidat had given birth to a male child, Anzor's family might treat her more kindly. The move back to the Tsarnaevs' house, though, was a gamble. In the Chechen tradition, the child belongs to the father's family, and his mother is treated as merely an appendage; if there is conflict, she can leave or be kicked out, but the child stays in his paternal grandparents' home. It might have helped that the Tsarnaev home was rapidly emptying out: the eldest daughter, Malkan, had married and moved to Chechnya; the next daughter, Maret, always Tokmok's star student, was in nearby Frunze, studying law and supporting herself as a janitor; and now the youngest, Ruslan, had also been accepted to

the law college in Frunze. Alvi, an older brother, was still in Tokmok, but unmarried. Tamerlan would be the first grandchild in
the family home.

In 1988, when the baby was not yet two, the Tsarnaev family
was changed irrevocably. A quarter-century later, *The Boston Globe*
would report that Anzor's father had "died in an explosion," as
though in a blast that foreshadowed the blasts at the finish line
of the Boston Marathon. The Tokmok tragedy was more mundane
than that account implies. Working at the city dump, Zayndy
found a large metal canister of the kind usually used for natural
gas. This object could be useful not just as scrap metal but also for
parts. Canisters like these were used in retrofitting cars to run on
natural gas, and like everything that went into cars, they were in
short supply. Zayndy placed it in his own car in order to move it
from the dump. The container must have been leaking gas: when
Zayndy started the car, it blew up. It was later impossible to determine, from the scraps of the car, whether the container had been
in the trunk or on the backseat.

Liza moved to Frunze to live with Maret, who had graduated
with her law degree and was starting what would be a brilliant career. Alvi took over the dump but had little use for the family
home. Anzor and Zubeidat were now in charge of the two-story
house in Tokmok.

MEANWHILE, the Soviet Union was imploding. Far away, in Moscow, Mikhail Gorbachev declared perestroika and glasnost. All
over the vast empire, movements for independence and ethnic
self-determination were taking shape. Some struggles were beginning to lead to bloodshed. In Tokmok, glasnost—the gradual soft-
ening of censorship—meant that video-screening salons started

opening. They were not glamorous affairs, just plain rooms with a videocassette player and a screen no larger than those found in many American living rooms, but the movies they showed were more colorful, brighter, and faster than anything Tokmok had ever seen. Zubeidat and her friends liked the Bollywood films that were flooding Soviet television and the newly minted salons. Anzor and the other men might secretly have liked them as well; openly they acknowledged loving only *Police Academy*. In any case, whether or not they were ever dubbed "the Swans," as Zubeidat would claim, the couple continued to be so dramatically affectionate with each other that once their friends were exposed to Bollywood sappiness, they started calling them "the Indians." And whatever the men's taste in movies, certainly they liked that they now had a place to gather outside their homes and backyards: they loitered outside the video salons before and in between the irregularly scheduled screenings, smoking and talking about their plans for the future, which was starting noticeably to change.

The Soviet Union was gradually opening its borders, and this meant that the Germans of Sakhzavod left. Kyrgyz families moved into their houses, cutting down their neat little orchards and making the Chechens nostalgic for their old neighbors' fastidiousness. More of the Chechens were leaving, too. Anzor's last remaining relative in Tokmok, Zayndy's first cousin Jamal, who in accordance with custom had become the male authority figure for Alvi and Anzor after their father's death, sold his house in Sakhzavod and moved to Grozny. He was becoming an entrepreneur, which was the thing to be now.

There was suddenly no limit to what you could do. One Chechen man, Ruslan Zakriev, bought a city park in the center of Tokmok. For about a year he thought about what to do with it. Then he bought some equipment from an unfinished amusement park and turned Tokmok's city park into an amusement park with old-fashioned carousels and a creaky roller coaster. He took to wearing a white cowboy hat, belted jeans, and brown pointy-toed boots. Later, after the word "diaspora" had seeped into the Russian spoken here, he declared himself the head of the Chechen diaspora.

Public land was no longer public, it seemed, but was a source of private money. Alvi managed to convince somebody that the old quarry beneath the town dump was still full of copper or aluminum or both. Excavators came and found nothing, but by that time Alvi was gone with the money.

Two of Anzor's closest friends, Semyon and Alladin Abaev, became long-haul truck drivers: now that the borders were open to imported goods and private businesses were allowed to buy and sell them, truckers were in high demand. Eventually each would buy his own German-made MAN truck, and a house with a yard large enough to park it.

Some people could not figure out what to do. Anzor's other closest friend, Badrudi Tsokaev, had worked all sorts of manual-labor jobs in the Soviet era and had done well enough to support his wife, Zina, and their four children. Peculiarly, the new capitalist system seemed to have little use for a jack-of-all-trades who lacked ambition, or a way of selling himself. Still, for Anzor and Zubeidat, Badrudi and Zina, who lived at the end of their block, remained authority figures. They were about a decade older, more experienced in the ways of the world and, both being Chechen, in the way that Chechens did things. Zubeidat went to Zina with questions on practice and ritual: How do you get the kids to sleep? How do you handle bedtime with two and then three toddlers? Zubeidat had given birth to two daughters after Tamerlan. Zina gave her practical advice rooted in custom; she told her, for example, that a Chechen boy past the age of seven would have to have his own bed—and extensive praise. Zubeidat's children, especially the boy, continued to be perfect: always impeccably dressed, polite, quick to get out of the way whenever guests came to the house. Tamerlan, even at the age of five or six, had an obvious understanding of his role as older brother; he was responsible for keeping his sisters quiet when there were guests, and safe when his parents were out. Zina also encouraged Zubeidat to make sure the children prayed five times a day. Neither of their husbands had any interest in what little Muslim ritual had been passed on to their generation, but the women wanted to bring their children up right.

Anzor responded to Zina's praise for his son by saying he would have Tamerlan marry her daughter. Zina would say, "No way am I letting her marry your son! Your wife is not Chechen." Everybody would laugh.

Some people were perhaps too well suited for the new era. The brothers Alaudin and Aziz Batukaev, two other Sakhzavod Chechens, were on their way to becoming the organized-crime bosses of this part of Kyrgyzstan. They had many trades, but drug trafficking was the most important of them. Central Asian–grown marijuana had been moving into other former Soviet republics for decades, and Chechen crime groups were instrumental in setting up and maintaining those routes. Now they were also moving much more profitable drugs such as opiates from Afghanistan.

The Batukaevs' backyard abutted the Tsarnaevs', and another of the Batukaev brothers set up a car-repair shop there. Anzor became his apprentice: cars would be his business. He would buy cars driven over from Germany, fix them up, and sell them at an outdoor market on the outskirts of Bishkek, as the capital of Kyrgyzstan was now called. Mercedes-Benzes were especially popular, but Audis and even some Volkswagens also had their buyers. If you asked Anzor, he would certainly tell you that this business, unlike some others, was perfectly legal. All the cars had papers of some sort, and customs tax had been paid. Whatever money had to be slipped to customs officers to expedite the process was just part of the system. Chechens always had to pay—if you took the train from Bishkek to Grozny, say, you would be shaken down by customs and border officials half a dozen times along the way, and traveling by train surely was not illegal. In fact, many of the cars making their way from Germany to the former Soviet Union were stolen, or had been reported stolen for tax-evasion or insurance purposes, or were salvaged "sinkers"—cars with severe water damage that could not be sold in Germany and had been written off. The profit margin of Anzor's business was the product of flaws that made the cars undesirable in Germany and his ability to rectify or mask those flaws.

Anzor was making a living, but, as long as his business was conducted one car at a time, the family would never be rich. In 1992, they moved again.

BY THIS TIME, Chechnya seemed as close to a promised land as it had ever been. It now had its own president, the wildly popular Dzhokhar Dudaev, a pilot, the only Chechen ever to have reached the rank of general in the Soviet military. He was assimilated and worldly, married to a Russian woman and serving in Estonia when the Soviet Union began to break apart. He resigned from the air force and returned to Chechnya to take the helm. The new Russian president, Boris Yeltsin, was a vocal believer in ethnic self-determination who had once famously told minorities to "take as much sovereignty as you can carry." Once Gorbachev was toppled,

Yeltsin facilitated the peaceful divorce of the republics that had constituted the Soviet Union: Kyrgyzstan and Kazakhstan, where most Chechens, including Dudaev, had spent at least a part of their childhoods, were now independent countries. Chechnya remained among the eighty-nine republics and regions that made up the newly constituted Russian Federation (a number that would shrink as a few of them combined over the coming years). Of these, Chechnya would be the only one to have the courage of its convictions and claim independence.

Anzor, Zubeidat, and their three children moved to Chechnya, to the house Zayndy had been building in Chiry-Yurt. There were cars to be fixed here, too, so Anzor was busy. Zubeidat was pregnant with their fourth child. When the boy was born in July 1993, they named him Dzhokhar, for the republic's heroic president.

Chechnya had everything it needed to succeed on its own: international borders and easy trading routes with such potential partners as Turkey and Azerbaijan; oil, which it now planned to keep instead of shipping for processing to other parts of Russia; and the will to prosper once it was finally free, after nearly two centuries of the Russian yoke. The only thing it lacked was Moscow's consent to let it go. When Yeltsin talked about sovereignty, he had apparently meant other Soviet republics, like Kyrgyzstan or Ukraine, not the ones inside Russia. The prospect of one of the eighty-nine regions breaking off and starting a chain reaction was unacceptable. Indeed, Moscow needed to nip such independence movements to prevent further ones. Cracking down on Chechnya would be a popular move—most Russian citizens remained deeply prejudiced against Chechens—and would send a strong message to other regions with pro-independence movements.

Moscow imposed an economic blockade of Chechnya. When that failed to bring it back into the Russian fold, Yeltsin's government reached for other measures. In the summer of 1994, un-marked planes began flying low over Chechen towns and villages, firing at random and dropping a few bombs. Kremlin spokespeople blamed those attacks on Azerbaijan, without bothering to explain why Chechnya's southern neighbor would suddenly take to bomb-ing it. These were Moscow's warning shots, which, unsurprisingly, served only to mobilize the Chechens in support of independence.

In December 1994, Russian troops amassed on the border with Chechnya. On New Year's Eve, Russian planes bombed Grozny so hard an international expert soon compared it to Dresden. By this time, Anzor, Zubeidat, and their four children were in a battered Škoda, driving to Kyrgyzstan. They might not have learned to pick their destinations, but, with moving as their solution to everything, they did know when it was time to get out.

Three

DREAMING OF AMERICA

Tamerlan's grade-school teacher Natalya Kurochkina told me that the boy was afraid of fireworks, presumably because he had been terrified by the bombing of Chechnya. Badrudi Tsokaev, Anzor's Tokmok friend and neighbor, told me that the rear right door of the Škoda in which Anzor brought his family back from Chechnya at the end of 1994 resembled a sieve from having been shot up by a machine gun—though it is not clear whether this had been Anzor's car at the time of the shooting or someone else's vehicle that he acquired later, since he had the skills required to repair it. Years later, in America, Anzor appears to have blamed the pains and worries that plagued him on the trauma wrought by war. On the other hand, his cousin Jamal, the one who had stepped into the father role after Zayndy died, told me with some resentment that, unlike him, neither Anzor nor Tamerlan had lived in Chechnya during the war. This was true: they left at the very beginning, and things got so very much worse after that. The Tsarnaevs never had to zigzag on foot along a road for miles, trying to avoid stepping on dead bodies. None of them ever saw a drunk Russian soldier stumble through the doorway of their house and shoot someone they loved. None of them had a friend or relative die in their arms, the warm smell of his blood sticking to their clothes, their hair, their skin forevermore. As a family, they never endured the ordeal to which virtually every family in Chechnya was subjected: that of searching and waiting for a male relative who had disappeared.

Of all the experiences of war, the Tsarnaevs were fully exposed only to one—fear. Unlike the people who stayed in Chechnya, they never learned to normalize war. Reporting on the war in 1994–1996 and in 2000, I saw women in Chechnya who for months cooked family meals on open fires on city sidewalks. I saw children who did not remember ever having set foot outside their apartments and who could not sleep without the sound of artillery fire. I saw young women who had mastered the care and handling of Russian soldiers and knew that if they ever failed, their family members would pay with their lives. The Tsarnaevs simply ran for their lives. Who is to say this leaves a lesser scar?

Over the next two years, as the Russian army continued to pummel Chechnya, refugees from the war streamed into Kazakh and Kyrgyz towns where they had family. Some said they needed protection from the rebels; others said they were the rebels and needed protection all the more. They brought fear, and they brought guns, and they were not always welcome. "We are practically natives here," Ruslan Zakriev, the cowboy-hat-wearing self-appointed leader of the Tokmok Chechens, told me. "We didn't want any trouble." And when trouble came—as when shoot-outs began on the Chechen streets of Tokmok and Bishkek—they blamed it on the new Chechnya. Anzor and Zubeidat confirmed: The new Chechnya was not a place for living. Anzor said he had sold the house his father had been building in the village of Chiry-Yurt. They would not be going back.

Anzor and Zubeidat together took Tamerlan to Tokmok's

School Number Two to sign him up for first grade. It was the middle of the school year, but the other children accepted him quickly and uncritically because Natalya Kurochkina told them that this boy was running from the war. "We talked a lot about the war then," she remembered almost twenty years later. "There were kids coming to the school who had lost fathers there." Aside from a conspicuous fear of fireworks, which may be too handy a foreshadowing to be fully believed, Tamerlan stood out only for the best of all possible reasons. He was an exemplary child, polite to a fault and often speaking caringly about his younger sisters and brother.

Zubeidat's project of rearing perfect children remained on track. She was an overachieving stay-at-home mother while Anzor continued to fix cars. When he came to school, however, he wore a suit; the teachers perceived them as a white-collar couple who were seeking the best possible education for their children. Tokmok's best, however, was not nearly as rigorous, challenging, or ambitious as Zubeidat wanted it to be. At the end of second grade Zubeidat withdrew Tamerlan from the school. Here the trail goes cold for two years, but in 1999 Tamerlan was enrolled in fifth grade at Tokmok's Pushkin Gymnasium School Number One. "We got prestigious that year," the principal explained to me.

School Number One was a school for families like the Tsarnaevs, those whose plans for their children extended far beyond the boundaries of their own universe. In 1999 the state educational authority granted the town's oldest school the status of "gymnasium"—no one could be quite sure what that meant except that now it was officially the best school in Tokmok. Anzor and Zubeidat sold the old Tsarnaev family home in Sakhzavod and moved to the center of town to live near the best school. From the second-floor window of their apartment they could see the white two-story building with its Greek portico and decorative Doric columns, and a red flag protruding from the middle of the facade as though it had been stuck between the school's eyes. There was a skimpy garden in front of the school, and this was where I found the principal, Lubov Shulzhenko, sitting on a bench beneath a dry little maple tree on a scorching morning in July 2014. She was a bleached-blond woman in her early sixties, very short and very overweight, and she had been running the school for twenty-five years. She wanted me to know what a good school it was. She wanted everyone to know. In her office, the walls were literally covered with citations. She made sure her students entered every competition, big and small, in everything from Russian spelling to rope-skipping, and she maintained a carefully curated rotating exposition of the citations, because even her impressively sized office walls could not hold them all.

She bragged about the graduates who had fulfilled their parents' dreams, like a young man named Sergei who had won a mathematics scholarship and was now writing software for a German company. Inside the school, Sergei's picture was one of a dozen in a display featuring the distinguished graduates of Pushkin Gymnasium School Number One. His accomplishment appeared more impressive than any of the others', but the caption indicated he had graduated more than a decade earlier. Miracles do not happen very often. Most of the other graduates, including the distinguished ones, had stayed in Tokmok, doing what their parents did—working as clerks in the bloated town government or one of the other outposts of state power. And for the majority of graduates, the most useful skill they acquired at Pushkin Gymnasium School Number One was so-called professional training: woodworking for the boys and sewing for the girls.

ANZOR'S SIBLINGS who had left Tokmok were living an entirely different life. Bishkek, where Maret, Ruslan, and Alvi were living, was less than an hour's drive away, but it seemed a century closer to the Technicolor world of the video-screening salons. Bishkek has its own Chechen neighborhood on its own outskirts, called Lebedinovka, or Swan Village. It is as flat and dusty as Sakhzavod, though the houses and gardens, hidden from view by tall concrete fences, are often larger and better tended than those in Tokmok. Many of the families who live here have relatives in Tokmok, including the Tsarnaevs and the Tsokaevs; some grew up in Tokmok. As Muslims, they pray five times a day and hold the fast during Ramadan; as Chechens, they acknowledge that children are the property of the father's side of the family, and some of the women do not sit at the table with the men; and yet, life in the capital has a perceptibly different quality from life in the provinces, however close they may be.

Ruslan was studying law at the university. Almost every night he stopped at the house of Badrudi Tsokaev's niece Madina—rather, the house of her husband's parents—and stayed until three in the morning. Incredibly, Madina's mother-in-law, the head of that household, had no objections to a mixed-gender young crowd that talked endlessly and finished just about every night by dancing the Lezghinka, a fast, even frantic dance traditional to many of the cultures of the Caucasus.

Then something truly incredible happened. Maret, who was now a judge, came to see an old classmate, Badrudi Tsokaev's sister Yakha, at work. Yakha was a saleswoman at a small grocery store, and one could always stop by for a chat. Maret said she wanted to get married to a man who was "mixed." Yakha thought this meant he was only half Chechen and assured her friend that if he was Chechen on his father's side, the marriage would be accepted. But Maret was simply easing her friend into the news. There was nothing "mixed," and nothing Chechen, about her fiancé: he was a Canadian. When she left for Canada with him, she did not even go to say good-bye to her old friends.

Ruslan graduated and got a job with PricewaterhouseCoopers, the giant American consultancy, which was running a large-scale privatization program funded by the U.S. State Department. Then he started dating a young woman who worked there with him—an American woman, not a Chechen-American but a real, blond American named Samantha, who wore trousers, collected swords, was thoroughly used to getting her way, and had a father who had worked for the CIA. Then Ruslan moved in with her. Among the Chechens of Lebedinovka, a rumor began to spread that Ruslan was setting things up for a fake marriage so he could move to the United States. But the rumor did not stick: the impending marriage was in fact scandalously real. Ruslan and Samantha married in a Muslim ceremony and in 1996 moved to the United States, where Ruslan planned to go to law school—word at Lebedinovka was that he would be going to Harvard, though in fact he would eventually be accepted at Duke University Law School.

And then Alvi went to the United States. He did not have a law degree or an American spouse—he was making money as a handyman and his wife was very much Chechen, and living in Kyrgyzstan—but he got a tourist visa and took off. By this time the entire Tsarnaev clan agreed: the future was in the United States—and the United States was within reach. Anzor and Zubeidat told all their friends that they were moving to America. They said it was the only place their children could get the education they deserved. In preparation, both Anzor and Zubeidat would obtain college degrees in law, as Ruslan and Maret had done.

MEDIA ACCOUNTS of the Tsarnaev story generally state as fact that Anzor worked at the prosecutor's office in Kyrgyzstan—this was apparently what he consistently said after the family moved to the United States. Even the FBI investigators seem never to have questioned this claim. Some accounts add that at a certain point, as the political situation in Kyrgyzstan deteriorated, Anzor, as a Chechen, could no longer work in law enforcement. In fact, while it is true that Kyrgyzstan has seen extreme ethnic tensions and violence in the past twenty years, most of it has been directed at the large ethnic Uzbek minority; the tiny Chechen minority has not been affected—that is, it has not been marginalized further than it was before the collapse of the Soviet Union. Friends do recall that a few years after Anzor and Zubeidat began studying law, Anzor started showing off an employee ID issued by the Pervomaysky District Prosecutor's Office in Bishkek. There is, however, no record of anyone named Anzor Tsarnaev ever having worked for the Pervomaysky or any other prosecutor's office in Bishkek.

"He had a friend who worked at the Pervomaysky Prosecutor's Office," explained Badrudi. "He fixed Anzor up with an ID. It made talking to the cops a lot easier." In other words, it was a fake ID. There was a fake uniform that went with it; no one remembers seeing Anzor actually wearing it, but he was photographed in it at least once. It is true, though, that Anzor got a new job in the late 1990s: he went to work for his older cousin Jamal.

My first meeting with Jamal Tsarnaev was set to take place at Grozny airport, a crowded and disorienting place. "How will I recognize you?" I asked him over the phone. "Oh, you'll recognize me," he responded. Then he paused and added, "You'll know me by my hairdo." Jamal turned out to have a perfectly naked, blindingly shiny skull. On the right side of his head there was a depressed patch about an inch and a half square—and it was almost perfectly square, with four round marks at the corners, where screws had been removed. As we settled in at a café for the interview, I asked Jamal what he did for work.

"Does that have anything to do with the story?" he asked tersely.

"No," I said. "I'm just making small talk." Asking him about his head injury or brain surgery was clearly out of the question.

He relaxed a bit and after a moment's reflection said, "I pick up things that are not in their proper place."

Translated, this meant something like: *I am a crook. I don't have a specialty—I am more of an opportunistic, general-interest criminal.*

In the late 1990s, Jamal told me, he started a business transporting tobacco from Kyrgyzstan to Russia. By "tobacco" he could have meant just about anything, including tobacco—or drugs. Jamal was based in Grozny, and Anzor was his man in Kyrgyzstan. A prosecutor's ID and a uniform would have been handy in this line of work.

Anzor and Zubeidat were not lying about going to America, though, or about studying law. They had both signed up to be correspondence students, a system that dated back to Soviet times, when it allowed full-time workers to obtain college degrees without taking time off—but also, in most cases, without learning much. They would travel to their colleges for one or two weeks each semester, to take exams. Anzor and Zubeidat always liked studying—Zubeidat generally grasped any new information as quickly and easily as she had learned Chechen, and Anzor had had the love of learning beaten into him by Zayndy, even if Anzor never was as good a student as his lawyer sister and brother. They were raising Tamerlan to be a good and versatile student, too. Not only was he getting near-perfect grades at Pushkin Gymnasium School Number One, he was also enrolled in extracurricular sports, advanced study of school subjects, and piano lessons.

In 2000, the Tsarnaevs left Tokmok. No one there saw any of them again until the summer of 2012, when Anzor showed up in the Sakhzavod neighborhood one afternoon. He knocked on the metal gate of the house of Badrudi's brother, on the street where they all had grown up. To his delight, he found the old crew there, Badrudi and his brother and the brothers Abaev, sitting around a table in the garden, eating lamb kebab and drinking brandy. They filled him in on the neighborhood news of the last dozen years: a few marriages, a couple of divorces, some kids, a number of deaths, and the brothers Batukaev—Alaudin had been gunned down right here in Sakhzavod, and Aziz had been in prison for over five years and kept racking up more sentences for inciting unrest there. To his old friends, Anzor looked thinner and older than they had expected, but he sounded as good as ever. His eldest, Tamerlan, he said, was "the hope of the U.S. Olympic team" in boxing. The girls were both married with children. And little Dzhokhar was attending the best university in America on a scholarship. The story made sense to the men: everything had gone pretty much as Anzor and Zubeidat had planned.

WHEN ANZOR AND ZUBEIDAT disappeared from Tokmok in 2000, those who did not know them very well assumed that, after four years of talk and preparation, they had finally gone to America. Those who did know them knew that Zubeidat was "a dragon-fly, never able to stay in one place," as their Tokmok next-door neighbor Raisa Batukaeva put it. "She was always dragging him off." This time they went to Dagestan. Why? It is possible that Zubeidat's longing for the sea temporarily overpowered her American dream. It is possible that they could not conjure a way to move to America—studying law was not going to magically make it happen—and had the idea, however vague, that the troubled Russian Caucasus might make a better launching pad. It is possible that Anzor's work for Jamal and his habit of impersonating a law enforcement official were starting to get him in trouble. Most likely, it was a combination of all these factors. They sold the apartment in Tokmok, which would have been worth about three thousand dollars at the time, and moved to Makhachkala.

Nothing—not even observing the radical changes in Tokmok after the collapse of the Soviet Union—could have prepared Zubeidat for what she found where the city of her childhood used to stand. It was as though every single building in Makhachkala had been impregnated by an architectural alien that caused it to sprout tentacles and grow other random organs. Everywhere something was being sold: cheap garish clothing imported from Turkey, counterfeit everything—cosmetics, underwear, electronics, footwear. Dagestan was still cobbling its own shoes, an estimated million pairs a year on which no one paid any taxes or extended any guarantees, but now these shoes looked like they had been made in China. The new trading outposts were kiosks assembled from plastic panels, panes of mismatched siding, metal sheeting, acrylic, and whatever else was handy. They would spring up overnight, sometimes blocking the sidewalk, and then change hands, begin to disintegrate, and disappear just as quickly, only to rematerialize as someone else's shop that sold something else but looked and felt exactly the same as the one that was there before.

There were plenty of places for the residents of Makhachkala now to buy, sell, and haggle, but there was no place for them to conduct the business of being urban dwellers. No cafés or restaurants—only a very few larger stores provided the public space essential to the fabric of any city. Public transport, such as there had been, had fallen into disrepair, replaced by privately owned small vans that followed routes of their own choosing. At the same time, the city was ballooning: its population had gone from 300,000 to 800,000 in less than ten years, but only 100,000 of those who had lived there a decade earlier remained. Everyone was a newcomer, and almost no one had ever lived in a city before. Villages began to sprout at the outskirts of Makhachkala, unregulated construction that used much the same material as the kiosks; rural Dagestanis were trying to make a place for themselves in the capital. Virtually nothing and nobody remained of the city Zubeidat had loved and hated when she was growing up there.

While Makhachkala was swelling, Dagestan itself was starting to fracture in an unprecedented way. A generational religious chasm had opened up. Throughout the seventy years of Soviet rule, most formal study and practice of Islam had lived underground. The dangers inherent in practicing and teaching the religion varied with time—being an observant Muslim could land one in prison in the 1940s or bring reprimand from the local authorities in the 1970s—but the isolated state of Soviet Muslims remained a constant. Sheikhs—elders and teachers in the Sufi tradition—passed their knowledge from generation to generation, and with each iteration something changed. By the end of the twentieth century, Dagestani Muslims practiced local traditions, such as worshipping at the grave of a sheikh, that would strike a Muslim from a place like Saudi Arabia as nothing short of sacrilegious. And the Dagestani Muslims' knowledge and understanding of the Koran would seem woefully superficial.

It was to Saudi Arabia and, to a lesser extent, the United Arab Emirates that young men from Dagestan began to travel in the 1990s, once the borders opened. There they discovered an Islam based on the rigorous study and discussion of the Koran, as practiced by the Salafis. Many of them stayed and studied for several years. Then they returned and confronted their village elders. Some of the young Salafi neophytes were driven from their villages; others left of their own accord; virtually none lived in peace with local elders, or with their families. Makhachkala's uneasy boom was at least in part the result of an influx of these newly urban, newly religious disenfranchised young men. Those who continued to practice Sufi Islam, and the secular authorities who increasingly relied on the Sufi hierarchy, called these young men Wahhabis—a dangerous misnomer.

WAHHABISM is a modern fundamentalist movement in Islam, and in the late 1990s its presence was beginning to be felt in the Caucasus. The war in Chechnya, which began with Moscow's crackdown on a secular ethnic self-determination movement, had changed Chechen society profoundly. Hundreds of thousands of Chechens had been killed or had left during the armed conflict from 1994 to 1996. When a peace treaty was finally signed in August 1996, giving Chechnya essentially the autonomy it had been seeking but without the official status of an independent state, its population had been depleted, its earth had been scorched, and its economy had been destroyed. Its leader, Dzhokhar Dudaev, had been killed by a targeted Russian missile in April of that year. He was replaced with Aslan Maskhadov, who had been his right hand. Maskhadov was very much in the Dudaev mold, also a former officer in the Soviet army, also entirely secular and assimilated, but he lacked Dudaev's ruthless charisma, and by the time he signed the peace treaty with Moscow he lacked full authority over Chechen rebel fighters.

In the desperate years that followed, radicalism of every sort flourished. A small number of proselytizers from Saudi Arabia and other countries found a large number of young men willing to listen to them, and to begin proudly calling themselves Wahhabis. They believed another war was in the offing; Russia remained the enemy, but the soldiers' new fervor was religious rather than ethnic. For several years they fought a guerrilla war that looked more like a number of gangs preying on vulnerable people under the guise of a holy war: they kidnapped journalists, foreign humanitarian workers, and even Chechens; some of the hostages were killed and others released for ransom. Then another war really did begin.

In the summer of 1999, armed Chechen fighters began crossing over into neighboring Dagestan. In August and September 1999, Russia was terrorized by a series of apartment-building explosions that killed more than three hundred people. Russia's newly appointed prime minister and Yeltsin's anointed successor, the former KGB colonel Vladimir Putin, blamed these bombings on Chechens, linked the acts of terror to the new Chechen armed presence in Dagestan, and unleashed the Russian military on Chechens in both Chechnya and Dagestan. The new war, which would drag on for years, catapulted the previously unknown Putin to national popularity, ensuring he would indeed become Russia's next president. In the years after the start of the second war, a wealth of evidence emerged pointing to Russian secret-police involvement in both the apartment-building bombings and the Dagestan incursions, but with Putin quickly turning Russia into an authoritarian state, this evidence never became the object of official investigation. Journalists, politicians, and activists who tried to conduct their own investigations were assassinated.

Dagestan, meanwhile, found itself in the middle of a war. In response, local authorities did something that essentially ensured the war would go on for years to come and the supply of soldiers would be limitless: they outlawed Wahhabism, by which they also understood Salafism. The urban young men whose conflict had been with their own fathers and their village elders were now, dangerously and romantically, outlaws. Their everyday religious practices were forced underground: even the imams of Makhachkala's two large Salafite mosques took to pretending they were Sufis.

The local police and the federal troops now stationed in Dagestan soon settled on a singular, and singularly ineffective, tactic for fighting the enemy they had conjured—a witch hunt. Local authorities compiled lists of suspected Wahhabis. A young man could land on the list for wearing a beard, for attending the wrong mosque, or for no reason at all. Men whose names were on the list were detained, interrogated—in a couple of years some would report being asked, "Where were you on September 11, 2001?"—and, in the best-case scenario, released only to face further harassment. In the worst case, they disappeared.

In response, some of the young men took up grenades, mines, and bombs. These were most often used to blow up police vehicles. Makhachkala and much of the rest of Dagestan became a battleground, with explosions and gunfights erupting daily. This was the Dagestan to which Anzor and Zubeidat brought their four children, including Tamerlan, who at fourteen was on the verge of becoming that most endangered and most dangerous of humans: a young Dagestani man. Anzor and Zubeidat had to move again, to save their children—again.

They would go to America after all.

PART TWO

BECOMING
THE BOMBERS

THE FAILED ESCAPE

A reconstructed route of the hijacked SUV shows that the brothers haphazardly hit every spot they knew, as though looking for somewhere to hide.

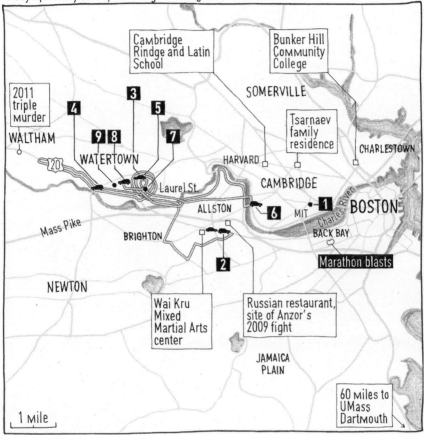

1. MIT security officer shot
2. SUV hijacked
3. Luggage moved from Dzhokhar's Honda to SUV
4. ATM withdrawal
5. Returned to parked Honda
6. Escape of SUV driver
7. Tamerlan fatally injured
8. SUV abandoned
9. Dzhokhar found

Four

COMING TO AMERICA

M any media accounts of the Tsarnaev story have hinted or simply stated that they lied to get into the United States, that they never should have been granted asylum—indeed, that had the asylum process worked as it should, weeding the worthy victims from the dangerous ones, a tragedy could have been averted. In fact, the Tsarnaevs typified asylum seekers in America, and the process in their case worked as well, or as poorly, as it does the vast majority of the time. Future asylum seekers usually come to the United States on visitors' visas and then, relying on a network of family and friends, try to make ends meet, not quite legally, while they apply for asylum. And yes, they usually lie, or at least embellish.

Making your case to the immigration authorities is different from making a case in court: rather than tell a coherent story, you, the asylum seeker, tell of everything that has gone wrong in your life—at least the things that went wrong that the asylum officer might find worthy of notice. You exaggerate, you mold your story to fit the requirements. It probably would not work to tell the officer that you were born in a country where you could never be a full citizen, a country that then broke apart into several others, which you crisscrossed trying to find a home and could not, and so you came to America. Instead, you have to say that you have been subjected to persecution based on your ethnic origin and you are fleeing a war. The Tsarnaevs did just that: they relied on the war in Chechnya and the ethnic discrimination in Kyrgyzstan to establish their credentials. Anzor appears to have claimed that he was briefly jailed and tortured in Kyrgyzstan as part of a broad anti-Chechen crackdown. He may indeed have been detained in Kyrgyzstan toward the end of his time there, though this was most likely to have been connected to his work for Jamal's business. It would have been much too complicated to try to explain to an asylum officer that the Chechens' very existence on the permanent wrong side of the law in Kyrgyzstan and elsewhere was a function of generations of disenfranchisement. Anzor could be said to have used shorthand.

THE TWO CHECHEN WARS, the one in the mid-1990s and the one that began in 1999, displaced hundreds of thousands of people. Many of them stayed in the former Soviet Union, joining relatives in Central Asia or Russia. Tens of thousands sought refuge in countries of the European Union, where they often spent years in refugee camps. Very few made it all the way to the United States. The people who came were not always the ones who most needed to escape: they were the ones most capable of escaping. "With any country early on in a conflict, the people who claim asylum first are usually the elites or people who don't actually live there," says Almut Rochowanski, a Columbia University legal scholar who in the early 2000s started an organization that helped new Chechen refugees find legal representation, although she herself was born in Austria and had no personal connection to Chechnya until research and human rights work took her there. The first Chechen refugees to arrive in the United States were members of the Dudaev pro-independence government and Chechens from Central Asia. Later came the people whose family members had been disappeared by the Russian authorities or the Chechen fighters. In refugee camps and in tiny Chechen communities that formed abroad, they often mixed with people who had actually been fighters—making for messy alliances at best and open conflict at worst.

The Chechen community in and around Boston numbers only a handful of families. This was the community that Anzor and Zubeidat joined when they came. It also happens to come close to representing the entire range of the Chechen immigrant experience in the United States. Makhmud Mazaev was probably the first to arrive—in 1994, just as the war was about to break out. He had been a urologist in Grozny, but learned upon arrival in the United States that he was too old to requalify as a doctor. He got a nursing certificate and worked as a visiting nurse. Later he created a thriving business, a day center for elderly Russian speakers. It is called Zdorovye, the Russian word for "health." In the morning a half-dozen Zdorovye vans make the rounds of several Boston neighborhoods, collecting elderly people who are well enough to live on their own but not to care for themselves during the day. Zdorovye attends to their meals, tracks their medical appointments, and celebrates their birthdays with them. Mazaev is the classic—and rare—example of a successfully assimilated Chechen refugee. He goes by the name Max; his American-born son, Baudy, who is about Dzhokhar Tsarnaev's age, is a student at competitive Boston University; and he has friends in Boston's large community of Russian-speaking Jews, from which he draws most of his clientele. One friend is a younger Russian Jewish doctor who often joins Mazaev on trips to New Hampshire, just an hour's drive north, where Mazaev likes to go for target practice: even an assimilated

Chechen man wants to get his shooting done, and the range in New Hampshire is the only open-air one in the area.

Not far from the shooting range, in a ground-floor apartment in a complex in Manchester, New Hampshire, lives Mazaev's cousin Musa Khadzhimuratov, an entirely different kind of Chechen refugee. Khadzhimuratov joined the war effort in Chechnya as a teenager and in a few years became the head of security for Akhmed Zakayev, a former actor who served as foreign minister in the separatist government. At the beginning of the second war, a wounded Zakayev fled Chechnya—he would later be granted political asylum in the United Kingdom—and Khadzhimuratov went into hiding. Russian troops found him, shot him, and left him for dead. He survived. His family moved him to Azerbaijan, where he underwent a series of operations. He is paralyzed from the waist down, he lacks sensation in eighty percent of his body, he has frequent petit mal seizures, and he requires around-the-clock care, but he is alive. Khadzhimuratov, his wife, Madina, and their two small children were brought to the United States by a refugee foundation, on a plane with one other family from Chechnya and a score of families fleeing Afghanistan. The Khadzhimuratovs landed in New Hampshire by accident—they had been told they were going to the Boston suburb of Chelsea, where one Chechen family already lived, but were rerouted at the last minute to what they thought was Manhattan but turned out to be Manchester. They were placed in a second-floor apartment that had a hallway with a step in it, which meant that Khadzhimuratov could not make it from the bedroom to the bathroom. The entire family stayed in the living room, with Khadzhimuratov and his son sleeping on a mattress on the floor and Madina and their daughter sleeping in armchairs. By the time they found a ground-floor, wheelchair-accessible apartment a few weeks later, they did not want to think of changing cities. The Khadzhimuratovs live on public assistance, but perhaps because the relative isolation of New Hampshire requires this, they have also assimilated to a significant extent. Their spotless two-bedroom apartment is as open as any traditional Chechen home: the kids of the Sudanese family from upstairs come here after school with the Khadzhimuratov children and never leave; a retired American named Jim, who lost all ties to his family after a bitter divorce, has adopted the Khadzhimuratovs, or has been adopted by them—he is here every afternoon. Madina, on whom Khadzhimuratov is dependent for constant care, shows none of the deference traditional for a Chechen woman. She sits at the table with everyone else and interrupts with laughter and even with the occasional correction.

That other family from the Khadzhimuratovs' plane made it to Chelsea, making a total of two Chechen families in that suburb. They were a middle-aged woman, her son, his wife, and their toddler daughter: the woman's husband and her other son had been taken away by Russian security services and never returned. The other Chelsea family was that of Hamzat Umarov, his wife, Raisa, and their seven small children, who had come by way of a refugee camp in Turkey—and before that, they had crossed the border from Chechnya on foot, at the height of the fighting. An equally dramatic escape story belongs to the Boston Chechen community's celebrity, Khassan Baiev. Before the first war, Baiev was an up-and-coming plastic surgeon with a profitable practice in Grozny and a side business not unlike Jamal Tsarnaev's. During the war he ran a field hospital where, he says, he treated the wounded from all sides. At the start of the second war he was targeted, ostensibly for having aided the rebels. A human rights organization virtually smuggled him out of Russia and helped him apply for asylum in the United States; eventually he was able to bring his wife and three children over. Like Mazaev, Baiev concluded he would be unable to be recertified as a doctor in the United States. He tried to volunteer at a hospital. He wrote a memoir with the help of a Boston journalism professor who had once been posted to Moscow. Eventually, after the war ended, he drifted back to Russia, where he now once again has a lucrative plastic surgery practice, which keeps him in ostentatiously expensive clothes and his family living in the middle-class Boston suburb of Needham, in a cul-de-sac with a playground in the middle.

When the Tsarnaevs arrived in Boston, the two doctors' families—the Mazaevs and the Baievs—were already there, as was Hamzat Umarov's large family in Chelsea. The others had not yet arrived. The Tsarnaevs' timing was as bad as it had ever been: they landed in America precisely at the moment when they and their kind were seen as most suspect.

AMERICAN SOCIETY, perhaps more than some others, goes through distinct cycles, separated by shifts in the national psyche. But to a new immigrant, nothing was here before—and there is no inkling that things will be different after. There is only the mood of the present moment, and this mood becomes what America feels like. The Tsarnaevs arrived a few months after the September 11, 2001, attacks on New York and Washington had united Americans in fear.

The family had plenty of experience with the power of tragedy to bring a nation together. They had seen this most recently in Russia, in August and September 1999. On three nights bombs had gone off in apartment buildings, burying people under the rubble in their sleep. More than three hundred people died, and

Russia, gripped by terror, quickly turned against the Chechens, who were blamed for the attacks. Chechen men throughout Russia were rounded up, Chechen children were hounded out of school, Chechen families were chased out of their homes. The war in Dagestan started. What was now happening in the United States did not look very different: there were the witch hunts, and there was the punitive war in a faraway abstraction of a land. It was called, tellingly and absurdly, the War on Terror, an emotion all nations would like to declare war against if only that were possible. Instead, they waged war on the Muslims. It was always the Muslims.

The Tsarnaevs came to this land, terrorized by the specter of terrorism, from a land and a moment where terrorism looked markedly different. For Americans, terrorism seemed to come from nowhere and to attack them for no reason. In Russia, the first terrorist act that shook the country in the 1990s had been a direct consequence of the war in Chechnya. In June 1995 rebel field commander Shamil Basayev led his troops across the Chechen border into the predominantly ethnic-Russian Stavropol' region and seized over six hundred hostages in a civilian hospital and in the surrounding area. This hostage-taking is almost certainly unique in modern terrorist history: first, because most of the hostages survived but were not freed by force; second, and most incredible, because this act of terrorism accomplished its avowed goal.

Russian prime minister Viktor Chernomyrdin negotiated with Basayev over the phone, and some of the negotiations were caught on tape by Russian television reporters. Chernomyrdin sounded desperate. In the end he negotiated the release of most of the hostages—except for a busload of volunteers, most of them journalists and human rights activists, whom Basayev would take to Chechnya. They were to be released once Russia pulled back its troops and sat down to negotiate with the rebels. This happened.

The second major act of terrorism that originated in Chechnya (not counting the apartment bombings in 1999 that had almost certainly been falsely blamed on the Chechens) occurred less than a year after the Tsarnaevs arrived in Boston. On October 23, 2002, a group of men and women led by a twenty-three-year-old Chechen commander named Movsar Barayev seized a large Moscow theater during a musical performance, taking about eight hundred hostages. The standoff lasted three days. On Day Two, Khassan Baiev, the plastic surgeon now living in Boston, was called upon to negotiate with the hostage-takers over the phone, to try to secure the release of some of the hostages. He tried and failed. Earlier, a number of other people, including several journalists, had also talked with the hostage-takers, and some even managed to enter the theater; young children and non-Russian citizens had been released as a result.

The standoff ended on Day Three with a military operation that was as well conceived as it was spectacularly botched in execution. First, sleeping gas was pumped into the building through its plumbing system, knocking out everyone inside. Russian armed personnel rushed in. They shot dead all the sleeping hostage-takers, making a subsequent investigation impossible. Then they carried the unconscious hostages out and laid them on the porch of the theater, where none of them received prompt medical help. One hundred twenty-nine people died, most of them choking on their own vomit or asphyxiating because they were placed in a way that blocked their breathing.

The tragedy, so clearly created through negligence and, on a more basic level, so clearly a result of the continuing war in Chechnya, drew comparatively little media coverage and virtually no political attention in the United States. After September 11, America had stopped criticizing Russia for waging war in Chechnya. In the post-9/11 era, Russia got to reframe Chechnya, and the continuing bloodshed in Dagestan, as part of a war it was now fighting alongside the United States—the war against radical Islamist terrorists. The United States and Russia agreed to share information on the Islamist threat. Tokmok appeared on the map of the world, and of American–Russian relations: for eight years starting in December 2001, United States military planes would be taking off from Manas Air Base just outside Tokmok—by agreement with Kyrgyzstan and with Moscow's acquiescence.

In this new era, when the United States stopped viewing Chechen rebels as freedom fighters and started seeing them through Russian optics, as likely Islamic terrorists, a new regulation blocked anyone who had provided "material support" to any of the extralegal fighters from receiving refugee status and a green card.

Musa Khadzhimuratov, though he came over as a refugee, would never be issued his green card. Had this regulation been in effect earlier, it could also have applied to Ruslan Tsarnaev, who at one point after moving to the United States started a group of Chechen exiles who may or may not have had ties to the pro-independence forces. Fortunately for Ruslan, by the time the new regulation went into effect, he was a full United States citizen.

RUSLAN'S AMERICANNESS had cost him a great deal. When he first moved to the United States with his wife, they lived in her parents' house in Washington state. Graham Fuller, a former high-level CIA official, was a onetime Russia scholar, an expert on

Islam, and a charming, enthusiastic talker. He and Ruslan spoke Russian with each other. But other than talking with his father-in-law while Samantha worked on her business-school applications, Ruslan did one of two things: he tried to master English by memorizing his way through a Russian–English dictionary, ignoring Graham Fuller's counsel that this was no way to learn a language, and he sat on a couch in the basement, watching, over and over again, the same videotape of a Chechen celebration with Lezghinka, which they used to dance every night back in Bishkek. Eventually he began making contact with other Chechens in America, and he even registered his new organization at Fuller's address. This activity brought him back to life, but by this time his marriage had collapsed.

His sister Maret's marriage also ended, though once she arrived in Canada it began to appear that she had planned this all along, that her husband had been merely a means of transporting her across the Atlantic. All is fair in immigration. Except one thing: You never talk about the pain of dislocation. You do not describe the way color drains out of everyday life when nothing is familiar, how the texture of living seems to disappear. You breathe not a word of no longer knowing who you are, where you are going, with whom, and why—and the unique existential dread of that condition. Most important, you never question your decision: from the moment you cross the border, there is only ever the future.

Most immigrants eventually come out the other side, as Ruslan did. He completed his studies at Duke, married a Chechen woman he met in the United States, and eventually took a job in Kazakhstan, as an American, intending to return to the United States. He was now in a position to help his siblings. When his elder sister, Malkan, divorced as well, he took in her children, and he also offered to temporarily take Anzor and Zubeidat's children while they engineered their move to America. Going to the United States, Ruslan was more certain than ever, was what they should do—if they wanted their children to have a future.

Tamerlan and the girls, Bella and Ailina, went to Kazakhstan to stay with Ruslan. In the Chechen tradition, it is the older brother who is the boss and caretaker of the family, but a big part of becoming a successful immigrant is knowing when to choose pragmatism over tradition: both Anzor and Ruslan would have to accept the reversal of family roles. Anzor, Zubeidat, and eight-year-old Dzhokhar traveled to the United States on tourist visas. They chose Boston because Maret and Alvi were both there at the moment. Neither had a stable living arrangement, however, so at first the newcomers stayed with Khassan Baiev, with whom Maret had become very close when he first came to the United States.

Dzhokhar started attending second grade at the public school where two of the Baiev children, Islam and Maryam, went. Max Mazaev helped Anzor get a few odd jobs. The family applied for asylum—once it was granted, it would extend to their other children, who would then be able to move to the United States. In April 2002, Anzor and Zubeidat found an inexpensive apartment in Cambridge, Massachusetts. Over the next ten years, it would witness the slow and catastrophic demise of a whole set of immigrant dreams.

Five

A DECADE OF
BROKEN DREAMS

For a new immigrant, the simplest and smallest of life's obstacles can be insurmountable. Take, for example, this scenario: You are an asylum seeker looking to rent an apartment over the months it takes to assemble your case. You are in the United States on a visitor's visa. You have no credit history, no pay stubs, no tax returns to show to a potential landlord. You also have no way to tell the good from the bad, the normal from the crooked. You get swindled by brokers, pay out a fortune in application fees, get your hopes up, get your hopes dashed, lower your standards, and ultimately understand you just have to hope for a miracle.

Joanna Herlihy was the Tsarnaevs' miracle. She was sixty-eight when they met—the youngest of her four children was roughly the same age as Anzor and Zubeidat—and for most of her adult life she had been trying to save the world. With a first marriage behind her, and once her children did not need her at home, she had joined the Peace Corps. She was a fixture of city politics in Cambridge, where she now lived. At the time Anzor and Zubeidat met her, she was taking care of one aging ex-husband (her second), and her grown children continued to drift in and out of her house.

She had bought the house in 1994 for the very low price of $45,000, at a foreclosure auction. It was what Bostonians call a three-family, a wooden three-story house with one long apartment on each floor. Three-families are common to the working-class neighborhoods—Dorchester, Jamaica Plain, Somerville. With postage-stamp-sized yards and on-street parking only, they used to represent cheap and unambitious city living. The house sat right on the Cambridge–Somerville city line, on the Cambridge side. It was modest even by three-family standards: it was built in the back of a shared lot and lacked the porches and small balconies typical of such buildings. When Joanna bought it, it was uninhabitable: it had not been heated, and the pipes had burst all over the house, causing extensive water damage. But it was also a three-apartment building in a city where property values were about to skyrocket: Cambridge would soon make every list of America's overpriced cities. Over the next few years, Norfolk Street, which was an orphaned corner of Cambridge when Joanna bought the building, would shed its many junkyards and acquire more condominium complexes than a street so small could be expected to fit. She gradually replaced the plumbing and rectified the worst of the damage. She lived on the first floor, and eventually rented out the top two floors at below-market prices, ensuring that at least two units of Cambridge housing remained affordable.

Maret heard about the apartment from Khassan Baiev, who had probably heard about it from the journalist with whom he had written his memoir, a member of Cambridge's loose network of Russophile intellectuals. Joanna had studied Russian at the University of Chicago, where she had earned her bachelor's degree while still in her teens, like another precocious coed there, Susan Sontag. Joanna's first husband was Alexander Lipson, a brilliant linguist and an inventive teacher of Russian who had taught out of their Cambridge home and taken his students, and his wife, by Volkswagen bus on tours of the entire Soviet Union, including Central Asia.

The third-floor apartment was not, strictly speaking, available for rent: the walls, which Joanna had repositioned, were unfinished. Maret, who was in charge of the negotiations, said the Tsarnaevs would happily finish the improvements themselves—they were just desperate for a place to live, now. They could have the apartment for eight hundred dollars, easily a third below the market rate. There were three bedrooms, all of them small, but Anzor and Zubeidat could move right in along with Maret and Alvi, even though they were likely soon to be joined by their children. Indeed, from the moment Joanna met the Tsarnaevs, she passionately wanted them to live in her home. She seemed—as they surely sensed—uniquely positioned to help them. She got them: she spoke Russian, she had seen where they came from, she had even studied Sufism. And she was primed to see the Tsarnaevs exactly as they wanted to be seen.

They presented themselves as having studied law. Anzor said he had worked in the prosecutor's office. They were fleeing ethnic strife. They were clearly modern people, Zubeidat with her low-cut dresses and elaborate makeup, Anzor with his clean-shaven face and athlete's body. That they were separated from their children—even Dzhokhar, whom they left at the Baievs' for the moment, so as not to interrupt his schooling midyear—was a measure of the gravity of their situation. And they manifested an anger about the injustices of the world that was not unlike Joanna's own. They were, as she was, at once profoundly disappointed by the world and stubbornly looking for a way to live on their own terms. Anzor and Zubeidat also saw a kindred spirit: a beautiful, odd bird. Joanna had the body and the physical energy of a woman half her age. She wore skirts and leather sandals, and her long hair was undyed—it still had some natural blond streaks in it. To the Tsarnaevs, who were always finely attuned to the aesthetics of their situation, to encounter in Joanna's manner and appearance some of their own distinctiveness seemed fateful.

FOR ALL of Joanna's commitment to community, when the Tsarnaevs arrived, the house was a collection of single, separate people. Two or three unmarried men from Tanzania lived on the second floor. Friends and acquaintances of Joanna and her children set up camp, often semipermanently, in this building and in another property she owned. Joanna kept power tools in the kitchen. Taking in all of that, and the coming and going of Joanna's children, Zubeidat saw a woman who had a clan, much as the Chechens had clans, but who lacked the skills to manage it. Zubeidat started inviting the landlady up for tea. Gradually they started having communal meals. Zubeidat and Anzor told their stories. Joanna reacted with compassion and appropriate outrage and, often, proposed solutions.

Reinventing your own story is one of the benefits and requirements of immigration. It was natural and even right that Anzor and Zubeidat would skew and embellish their narrative to make it more intelligible and compelling to an American, and to gain a foothold at a higher station in their new life. Zubeidat said that she might apply to Harvard Law School. Joanna took her, along with Max Mazaev's wife, Anna, to an Amnesty International event at which the Russian human-rights group Memorial presented its findings on Chechnya. Afterward, Zubeidat volunteered to translate some of the documents—a gesture that got her a Harvard Law School ID, though no pay. This affiliation did not last long: Zubei-

dat's remarkable aptitude for languages made her an able inter-
preter, but she lacked the formal education that would have been
required to translate human-rights documentation accurately. Joanna suggested a Harvard Extension School course on negotiation,
and most likely paid for it. Zubeidat dropped the course after the
unit on the Israeli–Palestinian conflict.

For Anzor, Zubeidat, Maret, and Alvi, it was a strange period of
living as a family of adults, with all their children farmed out.
Maret ran the household, taking charge even of her brothers' work
negotiations: she was a woman, yes, but she was the eldest—and
then, this was not Chechnya. Dzhokhar was still staying at the
Baievs' and spent only the weekends at Norfolk Street, and the
rest of Anzor and Zubeidat's children, along with Alvi's, were in
Central Asia, waiting to be brought over. Most of Joanna's conversations with the family focused on the mechanics of getting everyone to the United States. She tried to help Alvi's wife, Zhanar, and
their two children, Aindy and Luiza, get visas. The attempt failed,
and soon after, Alvi divorced Zhanar and moved out of the house,
starting a journey around the United States in search of a place
where he would want to live; he eventually settled in Maryland.
Back in Almaty, Ruslan, who was still taking care of Anzor and
Zubeidat's three older children, adopted Aindy. Ruslan's own children were in Brighton, a Boston neighborhood, with their mother,
who was about to give birth to a third child. Maret went to stay
across the Charles River with them.

When the school year was over, Dzhokhar came to live with his
parents on Norfolk Street. He was already a different kid. The
Baievs were strict about speaking only Chechen in the house, and
Dzhokhar had barely understood a word. The Baiev children—
Maryam, who was Dzhokhar's age, and Islam, who was a year
younger—understood Dzhokhar when he spoke Russian but

tended to switch into English whenever their parents were out of earshot. Before he left the Baiev house, Dzhokhar was already speaking English with the other kids—an extraordinarily fast accomplishment, even for an eight-year-old. He had also already become part of the community of Chechen seven-to-nine-year-olds in Boston: the Baiev kids, the Umarov kids, and the Mazaev kids, with whom he spent much of the summer of 2002, before entering third grade at a Cambridge public school. He would be bumped up to fourth grade before the school year was over.

For roughly the first year in the United States, an asylum applicant has no right to seek employment or to ask for public assistance. Anzor and Zubeidat were probably making rent with Ruslan's help. Little by little, Anzor started getting under-the-table work fixing cars. He charged ten dollars an hour, and part of that went to one or another of the neighborhood garages in return for temporary work space. Zubeidat focused on her English: she made fast progress, unlike her husband, who would never really learn to speak this new language. Once she received her work authorization, in 2003, she followed Max Mazaev's recommendation to look for work as a personal-care attendant. He connected her with the people who would become her first clients, and she would work for some of them for many years. It was unattractive but honorable work, the work Max Mazaev himself did for years before launching his adult-care center.

By mid-2003, the Tsarnaevs were granted asylum in the United States. Bella, Ailina, and Tamerlan were now entitled to visas. Maret traveled to Kazakhstan to collect the children and travel with them to Istanbul, where they stayed with friends while their U.S. papers were processed. She then brought them to Boston and left for Toronto, where she would finalize her divorce and embark on a career as an immigration lawyer.

. . .

A YEAR AND A HALF after Zubeidat and Anzor arrived in the
United States with Dzhokhar, the family was reunited and looked,
finally, like it was on solid ground. The Tsarnaevs' housing was
guaranteed, thanks to their landlady and the federal government.
Official asylee status meant that they could apply for public assistance, and they qualified for Section 8, a federal housing subsidy
program for low-income families. Anzor and Zubeidat were both
working—hard, low-paying, typical recent-immigrant work. The
additional adults were gone from the house, and the kids were all
in one place—Dzhokhar, who was now practically an American
child, and the three disoriented newly arrived Chechen teenagers
from Almaty.

Immigrant families often suffer from a sort of inversion: kids
stop being kids, because the adults have lost their bearings. The
kids do not turn into competent adults overnight; they go through
a period of intense suffering and dislocation made all the more
painful for being forced and unexpected. But at the other end of
the pain, they locate their roles and settle into them, claiming their
places in the new world.

Dzhokhar's role was that of the sweet kid, the kid everyone
loves. All the descriptions of him that have emerged from conversations with people who knew him, including people who cared
for him deeply, are spectacular in their flatness. Those who
watched him from a distance describe him as a social superstar. To
those who thought they got closer, he was charming. Indeed,
charm appears to be his sole distinguishing personality trait.
Teachers thought he was bright but uninterested in thinking for
himself. Dzhokhar was the kid who said the things that made others like him. Many of the articles that have been published since

the Boston Marathon bombing have noted that Anzor and Zubeidat did not attend Dzhokhar's wrestling matches, or his graduation
from middle school—as though those absences signified notably
grievous parental neglect. But Dzhokhar did not need his parents
there and he probably did not want them there. Anzor and Zubeidat's presence had a lot of weight and texture, entirely unsuitable for a boy making his way in the world as a sweet, weightless
cloud. Joanna—American, sociable, quintessentially Cambridge—
attended Dzhokhar's graduation from middle school.

In 2003, Dzhokhar entered fifth grade, which was appropriate
for his age. Ailina, at thirteen, and Bella, at fifteen, were older than
most of their new seventh- and ninth-grade classmates. Tamerlan,
entering tenth grade as he neared his seventeenth birthday, was a
giant among sophomores—but this was his chance to prepare for
college. Tamerlan and Bella started at the city's only public high
school, Cambridge Rindge and Latin. The school has an odd hy-
brid identity: it is a large urban high school with a pervading hip-
pie ethos—the legacy of the many progressive teachers who have
shaped it over the years. It maintains a distinct cult of itself. Its
students seem, with a few exceptions, to hew to a powerful collective identity as residents of the special brilliant society of Cambridge and as students of an outstandingly diverse school. At the
same time, Harvard and MIT professors, on whose presence so
much of Cambridge pride is predicated, send their children to private schools. Cambridge Rindge and Latin's genuine diversity
comes courtesy of immigrant and poor populations: a third of the
students come from low-income families, a third speak English as
their second language, and only a third are white. For test scores,
the school ranks at 213 out of the state's 347 public high schools.

Joanna took the family to performances and movies and loaned them DVDs. Zubeidat suggested that *The Chronicles of Narnia* was an allegory about Chechnya. The landlady tutored all three teenagers in English; Ailina picked up the language as fast as she learned the habit of riding her bicycle to school, but Bella and Tamerlan, who would never shed their accents, were placed in English-as-a-second-language classes at Rindge. Tamerlan was also trying to teach himself English by reading Sherlock Holmes stories, which had been popularized in the former Soviet Union by excellent translations and a series of inspired short films. It may not have been as masochistic as Uncle Ruslan's dictionary-based approach, but it was just as transparently self-defeating. Consider this single sentence from "The Adventure of the Speckled Band," arguably the most famous of Conan Doyle's stories among Russians: "'Alas!' replied our visitor, 'the very horror of my situation lies in the fact that my fears are so vague, and my suspicions depend so entirely upon small points, which might seem trivial to another, that even he to whom of all others I have a right to look for help and advice looks upon all that I tell him about it as the fancies of a nervous woman.'"

THE BIG QUESTION facing the family was how to make Tamerlan succeed. One look at him and you knew he was destined for greatness—an impression confirmed by people outside the family. The physical grace of his large body, and his sharp features and large dark eyes, turned heads and messed with them. But he had lived in seven cities and attended an even greater number of schools. True, he could play keyboard and aspired to good grades, but with his late start in America, how was he to assert his potential? Anzor and Zubeidat did what immigrants do: they asked others for advice. They were lectured on the relative merits of different colleges, and learned that even the public ones carried a frightening price tag. They sorted through lists of possible professions. Would their golden boy be an engineer, a performer, an entrepreneur?

Khassan Baiev suggested martial arts. It was a terrible suggestion. If Almut Rochowanski, the legal scholar who founded the group for Chechen refugees, were to classify immigrants from the Caucasus, she just might divide them into two groups: those who push their male children into martial arts and those who do not. It is the second group that will succeed; the first group's assumptions come from the old country. Back in the Caucasus, if you took at least one national title in wrestling, boxing, or any other fighting sport, you were set for life. In return for the honor you brought your region, you would get a gym of your own to run and, more often than not, a seat on one of the so-called legislative bodies. In the United States, a martial-arts career was generally a dead end, one that would leave a man cocky, injured, unemployed, and unassimilated by his late twenties.

Khassan Baiev's own experience was exceptional, but neither he nor Anzor and Zubeidat knew this. He had been a man with a career in Russia, then a man with money, then, in Chechnya, a man with a mission. In the United States, he was a man with a tragic and glorious past and too much time on his hands. He tried volunteering at a Boston-area hospital and quickly despaired of ever building a medical career in the United States; he also grew profoundly disillusioned with the American medical system. Then a friend suggested he try competing in sambo again—the sport had once helped him overcome discriminatory Soviet university admissions policies and set him on his way to becoming a doctor. Again it worked a miracle. Baiev became a champion in his early forties. It did not exactly lead to making a good life in the United

States—he ended up starting a practice in Russia and supporting his family's neat middle-class Boston life from there—but for him martial arts were a proven magic bullet. What is more, this was the one thing Anzor could do for his son in the new country: he started training Tamerlan in boxing.

Tamerlan was a naturally gifted fighter, if an unconventional one—though it is impossible to tell whether his unusual stance came naturally or was the result of Anzor's training. Rather than defend his body and face while he boxed, he let his long arms hang down. He could look overconfident if he was winning, which he often was, or vulnerable, literally unguarded, if he was beaten, which happened rarely. After training with Anzor at home, he worked his way through a series of Boston-area gyms to the Wai Kru Mixed Martial Arts center in the neighborhood of Allston, just across the river from Cambridge. When he first showed up, he had no mouthpiece, helmet, or other standard protective gear and insisted that he did not need them. This suggested to the owner that Tamerlan was either a buffoon or a boxing genius; with time, it seems, he concluded that the boy was a bit of each.

One of the few documents of Tamerlan's life to have become public before his crime and his death is a photo essay shot by a young man named Johannes Hirn in 2009 and published in a Boston University graduate student magazine the next year. Titled "Will Box for Passport," it offers a tellingly inaccurate narrative: Tamerlan says his goal is to make the U.S. Olympic team and become a naturalized citizen that way—though as an asylee, he should have qualified for citizenship anyway. He also says, "I don't have a single American friend. I don't understand them," though his best friend at the time, former classmate Brendan Mess, was an American. He also claims to be from Chechnya and to have fled it with his family in the early nineties, when the fighting broke out.

None of this is gravely untrue, but all of it is a sort of shorthand for a story he had come to tell about himself, one in which he was a stranger in a strange land and boxing his only hope. The photographer seems to have had an inkling that Tamerlan's self-presentation was not entirely accurate. One large black-and-white picture in the spread shows him wearing high-tops, chinos, and no shirt, smiling while sparring with a young woman. The caption reads: "Tsarnaev says he doesn't usually remove his shirt when among women at the gym."

The strange thing about Anzor and Tamerlan's outsize ambition for Tamerlan's boxing career—the plans for stardom and for a spot on the Olympic team, if not the expectation of Hollywood-style prosperity to follow—was that it was not entirely unreasonable. With his ability, training, and drive, Tamerlan could have had an Olympic career. But he did not.

His first victory came in January 2004, just six months after coming to the United States: he won in the 178-pound novice class in the Golden Gloves amateur competition in Lowell, Massachusetts. He got a trophy and gave an interview to the Lowell *Sun.* "I like the USA," he said. "You have a chance to make a lot of money here if you are willing to work." He had not yet seen anyone who had actually made money in the United States, but this was what he had been told. He started climbing quickly but dropped boxing abruptly during his senior year of high school—he needed to concentrate on academics in order to graduate.

In 2006 he started at Bunker Hill Community College, a lonely sixties building perched at the intersection of two highways in Charlestown, near the boundary with Cambridge. This two-year college, which he attended part-time, was not what anyone had imagined in Tamerlan's brilliant future. He did not return to competing until 2008—but when he did, his boxing prospects again began to shine. In 2009 he made it to the national amateur boxing competition in Salt Lake City. The next year, he got the Rocky Marciano Trophy for winning the New England Golden Gloves competition. He did not, however, go on to the nationals that year: the federation had changed its rules, and noncitizens were now excluded. After that, he let his amateur boxing registration lapse.

There is a footnote to Tamerlan's boxing career. More than a year after it was over, he called Musa Khadzhimuratov, the paraplegic former bodyguard living in New Hampshire, and said he was traveling to a competition, flying out of Manchester, New Hampshire, and wanted to leave his car with Khadzhimuratov. "He had a cold," Khadzhimuratov told me later. "I noticed on the way to the airport how bad it was. I said, 'They are not going to let you compete in that condition, there is no point in getting on the airplane.'" They stopped at a drugstore and loaded up on antihistamines and decongestants. When Tamerlan returned a few days later, he said he had come very close to beating his first opponent but then the judge had noticed he was ill and disqualified him.

TAMERLAN had long since dropped out of Bunker Hill. He still planned to be a star, though. He played keyboard. He talked of becoming a performer, a musician and dancer. He often, though not always, dressed ostentatiously: flowing shirts unbuttoned all the way down to his navel, huge scarves, and pointy shiny shoes that accentuated his swagger. He looked like an Italian gigolo, and he told the graduate student photographer that he dressed "European style." He had two girlfriends, a pretty, white American-born woman named Katherine Russell and an aspiring model named

Nadine Ascencao. Tamerlan had gone to Rindge and Latin with Nadine, except there she had been one of the least popular girls in the ESL crowd. Sometime after graduation, she transformed herself: she got the clothes, the hair, and the makeup that she had lacked in high school, and she dropped her Cape Verdean identity, claiming instead to be Italian. She also started dating Tamerlan, who had been the object of desire of so many Rindge girls—while he claimed that boxing was his only "babe." At some point in 2009, both Nadine and Katherine may have been living at 410 Norfolk Street.

By this time, taking multiple wives had become if not common then at least accepted back in Chechnya, which was in the process of inventing its own form of fundamentalist religious rule. So his parents might not have objected to such an arrangement. Anzor did object strenuously to Tamerlan's plan to marry Katherine. Boston Chechens gossiped that Anzor told his son, "Look how marrying a non-Chechen woman got me nothing but trouble. Don't make the same mistake." The fact that Katherine, who had grown up in Rhode Island, the daughter of a surgeon and a nurse, converted to Islam in order to marry Tamerlan did not convince Anzor. If anything, it irritated him—his wife and son had slowly, in spurts, begun exploring religion, but in Anzor's mind Islam had nothing to do with being Chechen; it merely obscured the real issue, which was that Katherine was not and could not be one of them.

Like Zubeidat before her, Katherine, who after converting called herself Karima, had to leave the family's home to have her baby; unlike his father before him, Tamerlan did not accompany her. Karima was staying with her own parents in Rhode Island when she gave birth to a daughter, Zahira, in October 2010. About four months later, Tamerlan moved them to Norfolk Street. Zahira did what babies do: she created family. Soon Zubeidat was spending all her free time with her, and both Anzor and Dzhokhar appeared smitten with the baby and her mother.

By 2011, Tamerlan was neither a boxing champion nor a music star nor even a college student, but a twenty-four-year-old father living with his parents, his siblings, and his own family in a three-bedroom apartment. What was he doing for work? Since his first year at Bunker Hill, he had made some change delivering pizza. He had done some van driving for Max Mazaev, who had started his senior-care center and was rapidly expanding it. In 2009, Tamerlan got an arrest record when Nadine called the police to Norfolk Street after he slapped her. Though she eventually dropped the charges, this may be why he did not have his U.S. citizenship, for which he should have been able to apply in 2009 or 2010—and this helps explain both the unexpected discovery, on the part of the Golden Gloves association, that he was not a citizen, and the almost magical thinking evident in what he told the photographer about "boxing for a passport." At some point, Tamerlan had also started dealing pot. He was small-time, a runner—an occupation that often goes hand in hand with delivering pizza, so it is not clear which came first.

Pot was the scourge of Cambridge Rindge and Latin. Some kids would just start fading out, and by the time they graduated they seemed to have no presence. Brendan Mess, Tamerlan's best friend, had been like that. His grades had tanked and his college ambitions had evaporated. But a few years later, he seemed to get his act together. He had been accepted to college, he was boxing— his friend Tamerlan had been taking him to the gym—and he looked more pulled together than he had since junior year in high school. Then he was dead: on September 12, 2011, Mess, thirty-one-year-old Erik Weissman, also a Rindge graduate, and thirty-seven-year-old Raphael Teken were found in Mess's apartment in

Waltham, a western suburb of Boston. Their throats had been slit. Their bodies were strewn with loose cash and loose marijuana—thousands of dollars' worth. When Mess and Weissman were buried in a joint ceremony, Tamerlan did not show up. A whisper kept shuffling through the crowd: "Where is Tam?" or "Where is Timmy?" depending on who was asking.

Tamerlan might in fact have been at his mysterious boxing tournament—the one from which he claimed to have been disqualified because of a cold—or, with his registration as a fighter expired for more than a year, the entire exercise might have been a ruse invented for the purpose of getting himself and his car out of town for a few days. After the murders, he stopped going to the gym where he had been training with Mess.

The murders were never solved or, really, investigated. The police appeared to write them off as just more drug-related crime, even though Boston's drug dealers had not been known to settle scores in ways so gruesome and so bizarre. It was in the course of talking to people who had known Tamerlan or Mess, however, that I discovered that Tamerlan had also been dealing.

How was it possible for the adults not to notice that Tamerlan was not so much delivering pizzas or senior citizens as making money selling marijuana, which is what kept him in his flashy clothes? The answer is, there was no one around to notice. The household's relationship with money had created a mess of debts. The family's federal benefits were revoked and reinstated at irregular intervals. Unanticipated, sometimes catastrophic medical expenses became a regular occurrence, creating more debts covered by impossible promises. No one was thinking straight about money—or about anything else. Each member of the Tsarnaev family was descending into a separate personal hell.

AILINA'S TROUBLES started out small. In eighth grade she began
getting into fights, especially with one girl. The school required
counseling, and the Tsarnaevs complied. Joanna suggested that
instead of going on to Cambridge Rindge and Latin, where the
social dynamics might follow her, Ailina apply to a newly formed
charter school. She did, as did Dzhokhar, and both were admitted.
(Dzhokhar was two grades behind Ailina, but there was no division between middle and high school levels at this school; after he
finished middle school, though, he enrolled at Rindge and Latin.)
The girl with whom Ailina had been fighting also entered the
school, but, much to the relief of everyone at 410 Norfolk Street,
she was expelled within a month.

The summer before ninth grade, Ailina joined Bella on a trip
to Washington state to stay with Uncle Ruslan, who had returned
from Almaty, and his family. Ruslan's wife had a younger brother,
Elmirza Khozhugov, who was studying at a nearby college. It
seemed like a good idea for him to marry one of the Tsarnaev girls.
Bella would not hear of it, so this left Ailina. To most Americans,
the looming arrangement would have looked disturbing. Ailina
was a rising high school freshman, a slight girl with typical American teenage speech and a gaggle of friends from her hip-hop class;
she liked to lead people to believe she was Latin American. Joanna probably saw more of the nuance: Ailina was slightly older
than her classmates, and by the time of the wedding, she would be
around the age her own mother had been when she married Anzor.
And unlike their own mother, Ailina and Bella did not have parents trying to force marriage matches on them. Anzor, for example, accepted Bella's refusal to marry Elmirza—as long as she

accepted the fact that she would be allowed to marry only another Chechen.

As soon as Ailina finished ninth grade, she and Bella traveled to Almaty. Ailina and Elmirza had a big wedding. It is not customary for the bride's parents to be present at a Chechen wedding, so there was nothing conspicuous in Anzor and Zubeidat's absence.

Elmirza and Ailina returned to Washington state at the end of the summer, in time for him to resume college and for her to enroll in a high school program for pregnant teenagers, which by that point she was. In the spring of what would have been her sophomore year of high school, Ailina moved back to Cambridge to give birth to a little boy, Ziaudy; then she returned to Washington. It is not clear when everyone at Norfolk Street became aware that Elmirza was beating Ailina, but by 2008—less than two years after the wedding and barely a year after Ziaudy's birth—Elmirza was taken into custody after repeated reports of domestic violence, and Ailina and the baby were back in Cambridge. Tamerlan was dispatched to Washington with bail money so Elmirza could leave the country before he had to face trial—and prison time. Ailina destroyed her green card and other documents in fear that Anzor would try to force her to follow her husband.

In the wake of the Boston Marathon bombing, Ruslan would publicly condemn his nephews and reveal that he had not communicated with Anzor's family in several years. The media generally assumed the estrangement had resulted from a difference of views on Islam and on what it meant to be Muslim and Chechen in America. Far more likely, the rift was caused by Ailina's split with Elmirza. Chechen men beat their wives. When they do not, other men often suspect them of weakness and subservience to their women. When they do, the wife's family usually tries to mitigate the effects without interfering—sheltering the wife in times of crisis and sending her back after a few weeks. No one ever calls the police. No one lets the men be jailed, disgraced, and effectively deported. Ailina ruined Elmirza's American dream and broke Chechen tradition by keeping Ziaudy, who rightfully belonged to his father's family. However Americanized Ruslan had become, he would have had a very difficult time justifying the situation to his wife's family back home.

BELLA'S TROUBLES began in 2006. Anzor took her out of school after learning that she had been seen holding hands with a boy, and a non-Muslim boy to boot. Back home—and by now Anzor imagined that place to be the Caucasus, where he had spent all of a couple of years—Bella's behavior would have warranted an honor killing; all Anzor did was deny her the opportunity to complete eleventh grade. Tamerlan sought out the boy and knocked him out with a well-placed punch. It is not clear that he had been dispatched to do so, but when the school counselor called, Anzor said that his son had done the right thing. He probably lacked the English to explain, but it is the older brother's duty to protect his sisters' honor. Tamerlan had been vigilant for two years, always lurking around the group of ESL girls Bella had quickly joined, and ensuring that she did no socializing after school, when the rest of the group may have wanted to go to the mall or to hang out at Harvard Square. Tamerlan, then a senior, got a week's suspension.

Anzor let Bella return to school eventually, after placing severe restrictions on both girls' movements, but it was too late for her to get credit for junior year. Her schooling was effectively over, so it was time for her to marry. She stayed on in Kazakhstan after Ailina's wedding that summer, working as a translator at a law firm and circulating in the local Chechen community, where an eligible man was sure to materialize. Within months she was engaged to Rizvan, a young man from Chechnya who had been visiting relatives in Kazakhstan.

Bella and Rizvan went to live with Rizvan's widowed mother in Chechnya, then still one of the most dangerous and damaged places on the planet (just three years earlier, a United Nations report had called Grozny "the most destroyed city on earth"). Bella became ill with cytomegalovirus, developed complications, and had to be hospitalized in Dagestan, where Anzor and Zubeidat, taking their first trip home—visiting Kazakhstan and Dagestan, that is—found her. It was probably they who persuaded her to return to the United States to give birth to the baby she was carrying. She flew back in the fall of 2007 and became, briefly, the woman doing most of the cooking and cleaning at 410 Norfolk, before giving birth to a boy, named Ramzan, in 2008. Rizvan, who tried to follow his wife, was denied a U.S. visa. When Bella returned to Kazakhstan and Chechnya the next year, she developed an even more serious infection and was hospitalized in life-threatening condition. It is likely to have cost a great deal of money to get her well enough to travel, and to get her on a plane back to the United States; this could only have added to the family's financial woes.

Bella returned to Cambridge in the winter of 2009. Baby Ramzan was back in Kazakhstan with his father and the father's relatives. Bella had applied for Russian papers for him, and until they came, he was temporarily unable to travel. Zubeidat flew to Kazakhstan in the spring on a dual mission: to fetch Ramzan and to raise money to repay debts by selling something she claimed was worth a fortune back in the old country. She returned with Ramzan but without the money.

. . .

ANZOR did not maintain the pretense of being a lawyer, or aspiring to be one, for long. He was a working man, and Russian speakers who met him at any point during his decade in the United States describe him as such: *rabotyaga*, a word that suggests a man who works with his hands, a hardworking man, a dependable man, but one who probably drinks when he is not working. He did. Both Kyrgyzstan and Dagestan are proud of their brandy, and so was Anzor proud of the bottle he invariably placed on the table when he went to visit or when someone visited him.

Anzor's American acquaintances recall that he had health problems—something people who knew him just before he left Russia do not mention. He may have developed them around the time of the move, or they simply may not have seemed like much to his friends back home. What man doesn't have health problems as he nears forty? All those cigarettes smoked, all that brandy consumed, all those fights—the things that tend to kill a post-Soviet man of Anzor's generation before he reaches sixty—are bound to start making themselves known. Anzor had persistent abdominal pain, debilitating headaches, and, evidently, night terrors.

But he was a *rabotyaga*.

In 2004, he became friendly with the owner of a rug shop who let him use his driveway to work on cars. It was old-fashioned Soviet-style work: rather than place a car over a pit or hoist it up on lifts as one would in a garage, Anzor hitched cars up on simple jacks and slid under them, lying on his back for hours, his hands raised to reach the underside of the car. He worked most often on vehicles that would have seemed at home in such a rudimentary care setting—old carburetor clunkers suffering from knocks, whistles, shortness of breath, and other mysterious afflictions. Among Boston-area Russian-speaking owners of cars long past their prime, he developed a reputation as a friendly, inexpensive, and inventive mechanic.

Even being a *rabotyaga* got him into trouble in America. When the Tsarnaevs moved to Norfolk Street, a condo complex was going up across the street, replacing an old junkyard. It was part of the new Cambridge: cedar-lined structures separated by ersatz-cobblestone paths, with units as small as 230 square feet. The condo complex had something else that 410 Norfolk lacked: a driveway. It was actually a temporary parking lot for up to three cars, for condo residents only, to park for no more than fifteen minutes at a time. This was a perfect place for Anzor to do repairs: enough room to place the car and spread out all his tools, out of the way of traffic. One day Rinat Harel, an Israeli-American art teacher who had bought one of the tiny units, told Anzor that he shouldn't be doing his work on the association's property. "His reaction—wow! He puffed up—I saw how tall he was now. And he was screaming in Russian, then there were some English words, the point was, he was telling me I can't tell him what to do." Harel, not a small woman and not one to scare easily—this was a point of pride for her as an Israeli—walked away shaken and, after that incident, stopped going through the Norfolk Street entrance, using the back gate to the property instead. Most of the time, the job of shooing Anzor off the premises fell to Chris LaRoche, a hulking software engineer who shared a condo with his husband. His conversations with Anzor generally followed the same script as Harel's. The consensus at the condo association was that this was one of those typical conflicts that gentrification engenders.

When Anzor and Zubeidat traveled to Kazakhstan in 2007, one of their goals was to seek traditional healing help for Anzor. His health problems had become pronounced enough for even the Russian speakers, at least in Boston, to acknowledge them. The wisdom in the Chechen community was that he had ruined his health by working on cars outside, in all weather, wearing nothing but a sweater.

In the summer of 2009, Anzor managed to rent a garage for a month while the owner traveled home to Ethiopia. He used the time to teach Tamerlan the basics of auto repair. Dzhokhar looked in on some of the lessons too, though he was working at a day camp that summer. In the fall, Anzor got into a fight at a Russian restaurant in Allston. His skull was fractured, landing him in the hospital. Tamerlan got the police involved and they apparently found Anzor not at fault; he even received some financial compensation. But his health suffered further. At the age of forty-three, he had begun to look like an old Chechen man: emaciated rather than slender, gray, and, it seemed, perpetually exhausted.

ZUBEIDAT TRIED perhaps harder than anyone else in the family—for herself and for her children. Her efforts at translating documents or attending classes on negotiation were not just an unreasonable reach given her education and background: they were also unreasonably brave. To help her children succeed, she pursued whatever seemed like a good idea at the moment. In 2004 she asked Joanna to help the girls join a church choir. Joanna enrolled them in the Handel and Haydn Society youth chorus, where they would sing for a year and a half. Joanna did much of the driving for the girls. She also introduced Bella to several folk-dancing groups until the girl joined one she liked in Concord, Massachusetts, fifteen miles away.

In 2006, Zubeidat enrolled in the Catherine Hinds Institute to study to be a beautician—not exactly Harvard Law, but more glamorous than home care. The institute was a good fit. Beautiful herself, chatty, and attentive, Zubeidat was a natural at what was, in effect, her first occupation, acquired at the age of forty. She supplemented her education by taking private lessons in cosmetic tattooing. A Russian woman studying alongside her was planning to open her own salon as soon as they graduated in the spring of 2007. She offered Zubeidat a job, and soon Zubeidat was commuting to Belmont, four miles west of Cambridge. Things at the salon began well but slowed in the aftermath of the 2008 financial crisis. As time went on, Zubeidat got less and less business there. Some of the post-bombing reporting has suggested that her new religiosity was to blame, but this does not appear to have been the sole or possibly even the main reason. Business was slow, and by the end of 2008 the salon shut down.

SOMETIME IN 2010, or maybe 2009, it would have become clear: it was as though the Tsarnaevs had never come to America. They had struggled with the language and with the people, and with buying furniture on credit. The living room now had a large plush sectional sofa, oriental rugs, and a mirrored credenza housing plates and thin-walled cups chosen to look as though they had been in the family for at least a generation. They had achieved the look every Chechen living room had, from Grozny to Tokmok to Boston, but then, their own living rooms in those places had boasted that look as well.

Tamerlan was dealing drugs.

Anzor was fixing clunkers in the street.

The neighbors hated them.

Bella and Ailina had neither graduated from high school nor succeeded in their marriages; their children were with them rather than with the fathers' families, so their chances of finding new Chechen husbands were vanishingly small. No one had gotten an education, if you did not count Zubeidat's aesthetician certificate.

Ziaudy, Ailina's son, had a learning disability.

The apartment was bursting with people. In the second half of 2009, the small three-bedroom was home to: Anzor, Zubeidat, Tamerlan, Dzhokhar, Bella, Ailina, the toddlers Ramzan and Ziaudy, and Malkan's teenage son Husein, whom Ruslan had brought to the United States but placed with Anzor's family. In the summer, the teenagers took possession of the barbecue area at the condo association across the street, drinking, smoking, and playing music until all hours; the residents seem to have been too timid to confront them. The apartment was clean, but crowded and cluttered beyond reason: it no longer felt like community—it resembled a refugee camp. Anzor and Zubeidat had stymied Joanna's efforts to help. Instead of easing the immigrants into her reality, Joanna had fallen into theirs, with its imaginary family heirlooms capable of covering debts that had grown hopeless. At some point the smell of defeat became so thick that everyone had to run away.

At the end of 2008, Zubeidat managed to place Ailina in an independent living arrangement under the auspices of a battered women's shelter. Ailina stayed a few months and then took off for New York, where she had somehow acquired friends. After her own trip to Kazakhstan to fetch Ramzan, Zubeidat went to New York and brought Ailina and Ziaudy home, too. Bella started attending the Catherine Hinds Institute. Ailina was admitted to a school where she would study to become an X-ray technician, but she could not borrow money for tuition because she had destroyed her American papers. Then Bella's green card disappeared as well.

At the end of 2009, after two years at Cambridge Rindge and Latin, Husein moved to Maryland to stay with Uncle Alvi.

At the start of the summer of 2010, Zubeidat went to Russia, alone, and stayed for six months.

Soon after she left, Bella and Ailina and their children disappeared—presumably, to New York again. No one at Norfolk Street would hear from them until Zubeidat returned in December. She reported that they were doing all right: Ailina was home with the children and Bella was working as a waitress. Later there was some conflicting information about that. Ailina was apparently back in town in the fall of 2010, at least long enough to get arrested for trying to use counterfeit money to pay a restaurant bill. She was arraigned in Boston in January 2011 but failed to show up for her hearings—when she finally appeared in court two and a half years later, she would tell the judge she had been indigent.

Zubeidat went back to home health aide work, which now seemed to involve more overnights. By mid-2011 she was rarely staying at Norfolk Street.

Dzhokhar graduated from Rindge and in September moved to live on campus at the University of Massachusetts Dartmouth, just outside New Bedford, about an hour's drive south of Boston.

In the fall of 2011, Anzor and Zubeidat filed for divorce.

At the start of 2012, the apartment was home to Tamerlan; his wife, Karima; their daughter, Zahira; Zubeidat, who was not really there; and her now ex-husband, Anzor. Zubeidat had also arranged for Ziaudy to attend kindergarten in Cambridge, so he was there, too, primarily in Karima's care.

In January, Tamerlan went to Dagestan, ostensibly to renew his Russian passport—something that could have been done at the Russian consulate in New York, which would have charged him a lot for it, but still less than the cost of a round-trip ticket to Russia.

In February, Anzor moved out of the apartment to stay with a friend. Once he received his U.S. passport, in May, he left the country. Zubeidat, who was now visiting the apartment only occasionally, said that Anzor was traveling to Germany for diagnosis—a tumor had developed at the site of his skull injury and American doctors wanted to operate, but the Germans might be able to spare him the surgery. In fact, he went straight to Dagestan.

In June, his kindergarten year over, Ziaudy returned to Ailina.

Tamerlan came back from Dagestan in July. Two weeks later, Zubeidat left for Dagestan: she said she had to care for her brother there—he had cancer. When I met Zubeidat a year later, she was indeed caring for him as he died. At the time she left the United States, she was facing criminal charges for shoplifting at a Lord & Taylor in the Boston suburb of Natick—she knew that leaving meant she would be unable to come back, unless she was willing to face jail.

Karima took over Zubeidat's home health aide work. Tamerlan stayed home with Zahira. He was good at it: responsible and caring and sure to take her for a walk or a tricycle ride at the same time every day. Most days now, he wore loose sweats rather than his flashy "European style" clothes.

WHAT DID AMERICA look like from the third floor of 410 Norfolk Street ten years after Anzor and Zubeidat first crossed the Atlantic Ocean? It made scarcely more sense now than it had back then. Television news combined with their landlady's conversation and Cambridge's progressive civics and history lessons never formed a coherent picture, much less the kind of flow of information that allows immigrants—at least those who successfully integrate into their new society—to inhabit the same story as the people among whom they now live. Instead, information continued to come in scraps, as it does to newcomers. Each scrap is tried on for size as a theory of everything. The more crudely it simplifies reality, the better it is suited for that purpose.

Starting in 2009, both Zubeidat and Tamerlan began studying the Koran. Neither of them spent much time in any mosque—though Salafism can allow room for women to study. They both relied on the Internet and on occasional intense conversations with better-informed acquaintances. The Koran did not get in the way of Tamerlan's lifestyle, at least not in the first few years: he carried a small prayer rug in the trunk of his car and could take it out and spread it anywhere in between smoking a couple of joints. The Muslim Internet did help explain the world, though. Tamerlan, for example, found a compelling video called *Zeitgeist: The Movie*, one of a series of three two-hour extravaganzas of conspiracy theories purporting to debunk every historical construction, starting with Jesus Christ and ending with the September 11 attacks. The latter, as it explained with high-quality graphics and an articulate narration, was the product of a plot in which the U.S. government had been complicit.

Approaching the Koran also helped Tamerlan and Zubeidat place themselves in the Chechen community even as their family began disintegrating. Everyone here and back home had a relationship to Islam now. Some families split, like Badrudi Tsokaev's back in Tokmok: his wife and children became observant, holding the fast at Ramadan, while Badrudi insisted that he had not needed religion in Soviet times and did not need it now. Over in Cambridge, his old friend Anzor assumed the same line of argument, even though the two had not spoken in years. Islam provided a new connection to home, too. It seemed the later someone came over, the more likely he or she was to be observant. Musa Khadzhimuratov, who left Chechnya in 2000, prayed five times a day—his prayer rug was also always with him—but his wife Madina wore bright clingy low-cut dresses. Women from a family who came later than the Tsarnaevs were covering themselves—and now so was Zubeidat, abandoning her own collection of revealing dresses. Around 2009, Bella and Ailina began covering as well.

A couple of years into his relationship with the Koran, Tamerlan disposed of some ring binders, but one of them was retrieved. It contained clippings a younger Tamerlan had hoped would help him master the world: instructions on how to seduce women and hypnotize people, articles exposing the dominance of Jewish actors in Russian entertainment, and an article in Russian with references to *The Protocols of the Elders of Zion*. The *Protocols* themselves, a tsarist-era forgery purporting to expose a Jewish plot for world domination, had supernatural staying power in Russian culture, where it reentered circulation every few decades, and it had supernatural staying power with Tamerlan as well. In the fall of 2012, while going through his books stored in the basement of the house, he called Joanna's attention to the *Protocols*. She took it to read so she could later try to argue Tamerlan out of believing it: Joanna was not one to give up on the power of persuasion. She had not finished the *Protocols* by the time her tenant died.

Some information about the world outside came courtesy of Donald Larking, a longtime home-care client of Zubeidat's who was among those she handed over to Karima. In the forty years since Larking had been rendered disabled by a gunshot wound to the face, he had developed an affinity for a variety of conspiracy theories and the media that broadcast them. Larking took to giving the Tsarnaevs copies of newspapers to which he subscribed— *The Sovereign*, which calls itself "Newspaper of the Resistance!" and on its home page showcases the "9-11 Truth Proclamation," purporting to prove the Twin Towers in New York were blown up by the U.S. military; and *The First Freedom*, an Alabama-based tabloid with the tagline "Inviting the Zionist-controlled media'cracy to meet a rising free South."

Larking read the papers and underlined some passages before gifting them. He also gave Tamerlan and Karima a subscription to the *American Free Press*, a Washington, D.C.–based weekly full of libertarian, commie-baiting, and anti-Semitic rants with a few conspiracy theories thrown in. It was a lot more accessible than the sort of media Joanna had been recommending, such as Bill Moyers's television program, with its nuanced approach to complex issues, or the critique of globalization she had given a nineteen-year-old Tamerlan when she found him reading a book by Thomas Friedman. Anti-Semitism and conspiracy theories aside, libertarianism is as good a theory of everything as politics has produced, and as late as 2012 Tamerlan was saying he agreed with Ron Paul, the perennial libertarian presidential candidate, and his analysis of American politics.

That fall Joanna approached Karima to ask her to register to vote so she could support senatorial candidate Elizabeth Warren. Karima demurred. She and Tamerlan had different values—not in the sense that they opposed the Harvard Law professor's campaign to rein in the banks, but in the sense that they did not vote at all. This did not, however, keep them from continuing to accept public assistance—and it was this contradiction that, after ten years, finally compelled their landlady to ask the three remaining Tsarnaevs to move out.

ONLY DZHOKHAR was still in his cloud of sweetness and light. As his older sisters tumbled into disaster, as his nephews got bounced between cities and continents like a couple of precious but useless objects being regifted, as his brother sank into conspiracies, and as his parents peeled away, Dzhokhar had continued to make good grades and good friends and make everyone happy. He joined the wrestling team and charmed the coach by doing what teenage boys never do: asking what he had done wrong and what he could do better. Soon he was captain.

He was also both smoking and dealing weed, but he was such a perfect mirror of everyone's best expectations that even the most experienced Rindge teachers saw none of the usual signs: his clothes were purposefully messy, not stoner-messy; his big brown eyes appeared focused, if only ever for the minute or two it took to have a meaningful interaction with any of them in the high school's vast hallway. Dzhokhar became friendly with one of the school's most experienced teachers, retired history instructor Larry Aaronson, who was now working as Cambridge Rindge and Latin's official photographer and unofficial cheerleader. Aaronson first took pictures of Dzhokhar at wrestling practice and then asked him to spell his name for him. It emerged that the boy was Chechen, and from Russia. Aaronson was instantly heartbroken for him, but Dzhokhar insisted: "I am lucky!"

"You are lucky? You were born in Russia, and you are Chechen—and you are lucky?"

"Larry, I got asylum. My whole family got asylum. I live in Cambridge! And I go to Rindge and Latin!"

Aaronson decided that the boy would be his poster child "for these kids from war zones who go to Rindge." Together they devised a new, easier spelling of the boy's name: Jahar. This was far more elegant than the solution Tamerlan had found when he was at Rindge; he just started telling people to call him "Timberland, like the shoe." Tired of explaining what Chechnya was, he had also started saying he was from Russia. At some point Jahar discovered his new friend was also a neighbor. Aaronson lived just a few houses up the street, on the Somerville side of Norfolk. Jahar's reaction: "I am so lucky!"

Aaronson was the teacher who was still trying to talk sense into his old stoner students Brendan Mess and Erik Weissman, years after they had graduated, yet he missed the signs of chronic pot use in Jahar. Still, he was stymied in his efforts to get to know the boy better. "Whenever I tried to talk to him about being Chechen, it meant nothing to him."

HAVING YOUR ETHNIC IDENTITY mean nothing to you, however, is unusual for American high school students, especially those attending a progressive, aware school like Cambridge Rindge and Latin. Everyone is somebody, and it always means something. Over at Needham High School, Islam Baiev was struggling: "No one has heard of Chechnya," he told me. "It gets tiring to explain every time. Normally I say we used to be independent and now we are part of the Russian Federation. And then it gets into this whole debate about whether I'm Russian or not. People have tried to convince me that I'm Russian, and I say, 'No, we have a completely different language and culture.'" And if Chechens were Russian, perhaps Moscow would not have tried to bomb them out of existence throughout the nineties and the aughts.

That sort of discussion was much too convoluted for Jahar. Perhaps because he felt he needed a smoother narrative, or perhaps because a paper on one's identity is always a good thing to show an American college, during his senior year at Rindge, Jahar set out to write a paper on being Chechen. It was his second year taking an English class with a young teacher named Steve Matteo, who had on first meeting him made fun of his name, then still spelled Dzhokhar: "Don't they have vowels in Chechnya?" At least he had heard of Chechnya. In fact, Matteo could claim a connection to Chechnya, through a handshake or two. His wife was Muslim, from Turkey, as was the wife of one of his best friends, Brian Williams, a man who claimed to teach "the world's only course on Chechnya." Williams taught at the University of Massachusetts Dartmouth.

Matteo suggested Jahar contact Williams for help with the paper. He did—as Williams recalled a couple of years later, "His questions were totally uninformed, very general"—and Williams sent him the lengthy syllabus for his course, with advice to pay special attention to two books. One was Khassan Baiev's *Grief of My Heart*, with the story line that was intimately familiar to Jahar; the other was *Allah's Mountains: The Battle for Chechnya* by British journalist Sebastian Smith, a lucid, if rather romanticized, history of Chechnya and the North Caucasus under Russian domination, including the two post-Soviet wars. From what Matteo could tell when Jahar submitted the paper, he had not read the book.

Williams complains about the myths and misconceptions that abound about Chechens—including the myth of a "Chechen Jihad" and of Chechen involvement in al-Qaida, which, he says, has never been documented but has often been described by those who make generalizations in the absence of evidence. Google "Chechens" and the Chechen Jihad will come up. Williams claims he is "on a one-man mission to debunk the myths" spread by the Internet. In Jahar's case, he apparently failed. Tamerlan, though, put *Allah's Mountains* on his online book list around the time his younger brother would have been considering reading it; with all the time on his hands in 2010–2011, Tamerlan may even have done so.

Around the same time, Jahar took another step toward reconnecting with his Chechen and Russian identities. It was an unusual move, though only in retrospect would it appear disturbing. He started an account on VK.com, a Facebook clone site on which most Russians his age maintained their social media lives. In his profile he indicated that he spoke Russian and Vainakh, the language of the Chechens. The inclusion of his ancestral language was a fib, since he did not really speak it, while the omission of English from the list appears conspicuous. He proceeded to post on the page in Russian—a bit of a linguistic feat for a kid whose Russian-language schooling was interrupted in second grade.

Jahar graduated from Rindge with honors in May 2011. He had been accepted to several colleges. He had not set his sights all that high, ruling out from the start the most competitive Boston-area schools, such as Tufts and Boston University, where Hamzat Umarov's children were studying. He told friends these schools were too expensive. He would have to finance his education through loans. Of the schools to which he was admitted, Jahar chose the least academically challenging, the University of Massachusetts Dartmouth. On the plus side, one of his best friends from Rindge, Robel Phillipos, was also going to go there.

LOOKED AT from a very particular angle, and from a great remove, by the time Anzor and Zubeidat moved back to Dagestan, their children were settled. The girls were in the great city of New York. The baby of the family was attending college on a scholarship: the City of Cambridge had granted Jahar $2,500 upon graduation. Anzor would not tell his friends he had divorced his wife, and her absence from his side would not make anyone suspect a thing, because, as one of their friends in Tokmok told me, if those two ever split up, red snow would fall from the sky. And Zubeidat would tell everyone that her beautiful firstborn son was taking care of the entire family, just as the eldest boy should.

Six

HIS PLACE
IN THE WORLD

Tamerlan flew to Dagestan in January 2012. Anzor and Zubeidat claimed he needed to renew his Russian passport. This had been the reason for one of their own trips back, but in Tamerlan's case this was a pretext and almost certainly a lie. Tamerlan was doing what the Tsarnaevs always did: going from one place to another, looking for the one where he belonged. This time, he found it.

Tamerlan had spent less than two years in Dagestan, but at a crucial moment in his life. He had been a young teenager, the age when the world comes into relief. And compared with either the Kyrgyz or the Chechen countryside—the two places he had known before—Makhachkala was spectacular: bursting with life, saturated with people, bordered by the sea. Plus, Zubeidat, who had once run away from Makhachkala, now seemed to think Dagestan was the promised land. It certainly felt like it. When you return after a decade, especially to a place the love of which has been impressed upon you, but even more important, a place where you were a teenager, everything feels right. The air itself is familiar, the light, the sky, the smells; even your own posture seems more comfortable, as though you have returned to the place for which your body was molded.

Makhachkala had changed over the decade: it had, after its own fashion, turned into a city. The most outrageous of the haphazard construction had ceased; kiosks no longer sprouted overnight, blocking sidewalks. Instead, orderly-looking apartment towers went up, even if they were often shoddily built and fated to stay half empty. The city cleaned up its act, polished old monuments and erected a couple of new ones. A new road into the city was paved, smooth enough within city limits to inspire drag racing, rough enough on the outskirts to cause shame. The city's population sorted itself into groups, classes, and neighborhoods again, and businesses mastered the science of appealing to distinct audiences. There were cafés that served halal food and provided prayer rooms, and clothing shops that sold only to women, and only appropriately concealing dresses; and there were sushi restaurants where waitresses wore short skirts and the sushi tasted as bland as in any such place throughout Russia and most of Eastern Europe.

What made Makhachkala palpably different from every other hub of post-Soviet conspicuous consumption was the distinct and dangerous undercurrent of tension: between the women with exposed long, tan arms and the women in hijabs; between the clean-shaven men and the men with beards; between the local police and the young men suspected of having ties to radical Islam, often on the basis simply of being young and male; between all the locals and the Russian federal law enforcement, which had been policing Dagestan with unwavering brutality for more than a dozen years.

. . .

SINCE 1999, when Dagestan outlawed the people it called Wahhabis, life here had settled into a bloody pattern. The federal law enforcement, sometimes acting with or through the local police, hunted down suspected radicals. The bust went down in one of two ways: a young man was detained and disappeared or, far less frequently, tried and convicted of terrorist activity; or a SWAT team surrounded his house and laid siege to it for hours, until at the end of the day the suspected radical died in a blaze of gunfire. Roughly once a month law enforcement reported that a leader of the radical Muslim underground had been "annihilated"—the Russian term of choice, which conveyed much better than simply "killed" a sense that a less-than-human being had been fully destroyed. "Are we supposed to think that the insurgency breeds a new leader every month?" one Dagestani journalist grumbled. For every supposed terrorist who had been "annihilated," one or two or three of his male relatives joined the resistance, sometimes going so far as to "go into the forest," meaning to join the guerrilla fighters who lurked in the woods of Dagestan.

The actual size of the guerrilla force at any given time was probably closer to one hundred than to several, but in the imaginations of both sides the might of the forest fighters swelled, as did the fear of escalating violence. The damage "the forest" did was inescapably real: for years, an explosion would kill one or several law enforcement officers every few weeks. Each of these attacks invariably brought another round of retribution from the federal troops, ensuring that the cycle of slow-burning warfare was never broken.

Retribution was not, however, the only or even the most significant motivating factor in this war. Alexei Levinson, a leading Russian sociologist who was studying Dagestan around the time Tamerlan was there, concluded that what he was observing was war for war's sake. "All this barbarity and brutality stem not from human qualities—it's not that the federal troops have assembled a collection of lowlifes there, though that's also the case," he told me. "What this is, if we are to be exact, is terror." To a Russian intellectual, the word is more evocative of Stalin's Great Terror than of the many uses and misuses of it since September 11. Levinson was talking about a system designed for the random application of extreme brutality. And very much like the Great Terror, this system was ineffective and inefficient; if intimidation and control had been the goal, they could have been exercised far less expensively and more consistently. Instead, the machine's primary function was the reproduction of violence. "If the federal troops succeed in conquering, in suppressing the underground, they have to pack up and go home," he said. "What they need is a conflict on low heat." Even the federal troops' compensation structure reflected this: they were paid extra for the hours spent in combat— hence the long, elaborate siege operations that were, in the end, assassinations by extreme firepower.

The economy of a region locked in a state of permanent war cannot function normally, not just because the constant presence of danger changes preferences and priorities—people invest in nothing, spending their money and themselves fully every day— but also because there can be no consensus on what the law of the land is. Conflicts in Dagestan were decided in accordance with Russian civilian law, Sharia law, or Adat—the set of local customs that mixed reliance on the Koran with tradition passed on through generations. The choice of laws depended on the parties' preferences, interests, and relative influence. At the same time, the government of Dagestan, which in the Putin era began to be appointed by Moscow rather than elected locally, was forging an ever closer allegiance with the imams representing the Sufi Islam traditional to Dagestan. The government was taking its cues from the Kremlin, which was relying more and more heavily on the Russian Orthodox Church. In Dagestan, as Sufi mosques allied themselves with officialdom and through it with Moscow and the federal troops, nontraditional Salafite mosques began looking increasingly appealing to a growing number of young men.

Men of Tamerlan's age had grown up in Dagestan's slow-burning war, and this distinguished them from the previous generation of local Salafites. The new Muslims of the nineties had often studied abroad; their religious evolution represented an investment in their own and their children's urban, worldly future. The men who came of age in the aughts had, like all children of war, no investments and no future. They also usually had no education past high school and no jobs in any institutional setting: they were overwhelmingly engaged in financial scams. Caught in its own cycle of war, corruption, and blackmail with Dagestan, Moscow kept pouring into the troubled region money from a federal budget swollen with oil revenue. The money failed to ensure peace, but it did provide for the relative economic well-being of a large number of young men. The federal money was recycled into bogus, or at least partly bogus, housing construction, credits and mortgages that would never be repaid, and subsidies that did not always go to persons and institutions that actually existed but always, without exception, involved kickbacks. The combined effect of Dagestan's shifting religious–political axis and its crooked economy was to turn all of its young men into outlaws and to link them all through an intricate web of money, blood, and what might or might not have been properly considered crime.

WHEN TAMERLAN LANDED in Dagestan, it was not only the physical environment that would have seemed made for him, as if his body had been plugged into its place in a puzzle: there was a social space ready for him as well. Dagestan was full of men in their twenties and early thirties who spent their days talking about themselves, their religion, and the injustices of the world. They sat around at cafés all over Makhachkala, sipping coffee at small round lacquered tables or eating lamb at long wooden ones; they went to one another's family homes on special occasions and talked there; but most important, they went to the mosque on Kotrov Street.

The mosque is built like so much of Makhachkala: outsize, at once grand and shoddy, whether because of lack of money or lack of skill. Each of its four levels provides a large space for prayer. In its sizable front yard sits a four-foot-high stack of rugs that will be laid out on the concrete come Friday. Even with all that room inside, there is always an overflow crowd of men praying, most of them young men with neatly trimmed beards. Inside is a large light-filled airy space, but the walls in many places are unfinished sheetrock. A rounded wooden stairway that looks like it was airlifted from the private mansion of an aspiring oligarch leads to the imam's top-floor office, furnished like a Soviet bureaucrat's. (But perhaps the stairway was here all along: one of Dagestan's wealthiest men was building a house for his son on this site when he died suddenly in 1998 and someone decided to build a mosque here in his honor.) There is an unmanned security post in the corner of the office, six screens streaming the views from six surveillance cameras and, in front of them, an empty office chair with one missing armrest.

I found the imam himself sitting behind a very large desk in the office. His name was Gasan Gasanaliyev, he was seventy-three, tiny with an unevenly trimmed gray beard, and he had been an imam since he was twenty-five. "Back then, if you studied the Koran, you got five years in jail." I asked him if he had studied underground. "You could say that," he answered cautiously. For his first quarter-century as imam, Gasanaliyev was employed as a construction worker: without an official job, he would have been arrested and charged with the crime of parasitism. The imam is a lifelong keeper of secrets. I asked him about Tamerlan Tsarnaev. "I have no idea who comes here and who doesn't," he snapped. "But I asked every single person who comes here and none of them ever met him." He also told me his mosque is Sufi, not Salafite, an assertion that made more than a few Dagestani Salafites laugh when I told them about it.

TAMERLAN REMET HIS RELATIVES, most of them near-mythical figures he had seen only a few times as a child. Jamal, Anzor's organized-crime uncle, was around; nothing about him was ever clear, but he appeared to be based mostly in Grozny now: the capital of Chechnya is less than a three-hour drive from Makhachkala. Zubeidat's side of the family hovered over the boy in Dagestan. Although the clan had once been concentrated in Makhachkala, the relatives who remained in Dagestan lived elsewhere now. Her brother, a law enforcement officer, was struggling with cancer up in a mountain village; her cousin lived in Kizlyar, a town of about fifty thousand that had once been part of Chechnya and had been gifted by Stalin to Dagestan in 1944, after the Chechens were deported. That and the town's proximity to the Chechen border were enough to make it a presumed hotspot of insurgent activity in the eyes of the Russian authorities. Founded as a fortress more than two centuries earlier, Kizlyar felt very much under siege every day.

The drive from Makhachkala to Kizlyar takes two hours through a valley that seems nearly deserted, a jarring impression in this region where land is at a premium. The emptiness is the effect of a war all its own. Dagestan's nomadic and settled ethnic groups, who had for centuries existed in a state that could reasonably be called peace, were now battling over these lands. The nomads were not only expanding their pastures but also increasingly settling down, especially in the parts of the valley where ethnic Russians now lived. This was the other war the indigenous peoples of Dagestan were waging against Russia, and this one would evidently be won. The Russians were dying out in these parts, and this, too, served to underscore the nature of their presence: it was occupation. For now, you could see Dagestan's past and future standing side by side along the road from Makhachkala to Kizlyar— abandoned collective-farm structures, long and low barracks-like buildings, and cinder-block private houses, barely half of them inhabited and the rest incomplete, their windows gaping with the dashed hopes of generations. As one got closer to Kizlyar, the Russian-made Lada Prioras increasingly ceded the road to ancient motorcycles with sidecars, and cows—yellow and reddish and brown cows that seemed to wander unattached. A massive federal checkpoint, a hundred-fifty-yard labyrinth of brick half-walls, greeted visitors to Kizlyar. The name of the checkpoint was Lesnoy, or the Forest One.

Kizlyar is low and feels like the valley itself. The center is full of long gray-brick five-story apartment buildings; the outskirts are private houses, hidden behind concrete walls and covered front yards. Small shops sell identical local-fashion T-shirts and trousers with Ferre and Ice labels sloppily appended to them. For young men, the meeting place of choice—not that there is much choice— is Café Nostalgy, a cavernous space with large private booths that have low carpeted platforms for reclining.

Nostalgy was where Tamerlan's second cousin Magomed Kartashov liked to schedule meetings. The son of Zubeidat's first cousin, Kartashov would have been considered a close relative by Dagestan standards: ordinarily, he and Tamerlan would have met as small children—Kartashov was less than a decade older—and seen each other at numerous family events throughout their lives. But at the point when Tamerlan was, briefly, a resident of Dagestan in the early aughts, the difference in their ages had been prohibitive. Tamerlan was still a boy, and Kartashov was a young man who had joined the police force in Kizlyar. He resigned a year later, and by the time Tamerlan met him properly in 2012, he was the leader of a group that some people perceived as nebulous and others as menacing; it was probably both.

The Union of the Just, as it was called, was commonly known to be allied with Hizb ut-Tahrir, one of the largest Islamic organizations in the world. Hizb ut-Tahrir proclaims the goal of creating a caliphate that would unite the Muslim lands of the world. This pan-Islamic state should be created by peaceful means, through political and philosophical struggle only. Hizb ut-Tahrir has consistently condemned acts of terror, including the September 11 attacks and the July 2005 bombings in London, but some analysts in both the United States and the United Kingdom have cast doubt on the sincerity of these statements. More to the point, Hizb ut-Tahrir is often viewed as a gateway organization that facilitates young Muslims' passage from peaceful civilians to jihadis. In Russia, as in a number of other countries, Hizb ut-Tahrir is banned, which is why the Union of the Just kept its affiliation with the group quiet.

Kartashov had launched the Union of the Just a few months before Tamerlan arrived back in Dagestan. In August 2011, Kartashov was one of the organizers of a protest against detentions carried out by law enforcement in and around Kizlyar. By the time he organized his second such protest, in November, his organization had a name and, apparently, a structure: Kartashov was chairman. In addition to protesting detentions, the Union of the Just claimed to address issues of social inequality and injustice in Dagestan—and, depending on whom I talked to, seemed either to have the financial resources to undertake a project of that magnitude or to be financially strapped and full of hot air. One impression local journalists consistently had of the group was that it had a complicated relationship with law enforcement. The head of the Kizlyar police, on one hand, expressed undisguised hatred for his former officer Kartashov; on the other hand, the Union of the Just had a way of learning about detentions before they became public knowledge—suggesting that it had a mole in law enforcement. Then again, as one of Kartashov's defense lawyers would tell me later, long after his client had been sent to serve time in a prison colony thousands of miles away, "Law enforcement and the insurgents are all equally dumb, uneducated, and all affected by the same virus," meaning the infectious desire to engage in permanent warfare. He then told me what he thought should be done to solve this conundrum, but he asked me not to print it; his solution was bitter and brutal and desperate.

In all, the Union of the Just, to which Tamerlan discovered he belonged virtually by birthright, was a quintessential Dagestan organization: a group of self-important young men who trafficked mostly in words and yet balanced unmistakably at the edge of constant and extreme danger.

The man with whom Tamerlan connected most closely was not his cousin Magomed Kartashov but Kartashov's Union of the Just deputy Mohammed Gadzhiev (the two men had the same first name, but Gadzhiev preferred the less Russian-sounding, more Arabic pronunciation). Gadzhiev lived in Makhachkala, where Tamerlan felt much more comfortable than in dangerous, backwater Kizlyar. Gadzhiev was Tamerlan's age; he was a snappy dresser, though not as flashy as Tamerlan; he had about him the confidence of an extremely good-looking and remarkably well-spoken man: he and Tamerlan were of a kind, and they hit it off instantly when Kartashov introduced them at a friend's wedding in the spring of 2012. "Meet my American relative," he said to Gadzhiev, and from that point on the two men saw each other several times a week.

They talked. Tamerlan had things to tell Mohammed about America. He said it was a racist country and a deeply divided one: there was a giant gap between rich and poor. Foreign policy was as xenophobic and as shortsighted as Mohammed had suspected—as bad, in fact, as what he had heard on Russian television, which could be presumed to lie about everything except this. Morally, too, America was in decline. Mohammed had suspected as much, but he was pleased to have his general impressions confirmed and elaborated—and Tamerlan turned out to be a good storyteller, capable of supporting his passionate generalizations with carefully drawn detail. He described his friends, their struggles, the crooked cops of Watertown—he talked so much about this town that Gadzhiev was sure that was where he lived—

and, for the first time in his life, Tamerlan got to feel like an expert. Gadzhiev could ask questions for hours, and his interest and trust in Tamerlan's knowledge never wavered. He even accepted the positive things Tamerlan had to say about America. Tamerlan said there was freedom of speech, it really was a country open to all sorts of people—and it would even give them an education, such as the one Tamerlan's beloved younger brother was now obtaining, thanks to a city scholarship.

They talked about Russia as well, and concluded that its racism, religious persecution, and propensity for manufacturing criminal charges against undesirables made the two countries substantially similar. Russia's foreign policy was better—at least it did not support either Israel or the secular forces in the Arab world—but the deep-rooted corruption inside the country more than made up for this comparative advantage over the United States. "I refuse to choose between two kinds of fecal matter," Gadzhiev concluded. "Both taste like shit." Tamerlan concurred.

On topics other than the United States, Tamerlan got little credit. Gadzhiev found his knowledge of the Koran cursory at best. He appreciated that Tamerlan claimed being a Muslim as his primary identity, but criticized him for vague statements and uncertain ideas. "If your goal is to fight injustice and promote God's law in the world, then you have to achieve clarity," Gadzhiev would say. "As long as your ideas are hard to comprehend, your actions, too, will be dispersed. You have to be specific." Gadzhiev introduced Tamerlan to the concept of intention, essential to the interpretation of the Koran. "You must know that your actions are right even if you will never see the results of your actions—then you must trust that one of your descendants will see them in the future." Tamerlan listened.

Gadzhiev saw his friend as a bit of a baby. Tamerlan stood out in Makhachkala. Some days he wore a long Arabic-style shirt of the sort rarely seen in Dagestan, slicked his hair back with peanut oil, and lined his eyes with kohl. Other days, he put on regular trousers with brightly colored sneakers, and this looked as foreign as his ersatz Middle Eastern getup. Gadzhiev himself dressed stylishly, but in keeping with the understated ways of local men: he wore dark-colored T-shirts and trousers over neutral flip-flops. When Gadzhiev reprimanded Tamerlan for sticking out too conspicuously, his American friend seemed to take it as a compliment. Indeed, he regarded all expressions of interest as both complimentary and wondrous. One time a girl at a party slipped him a scrap of paper with her phone number written on it and he showed it around to his friends, asking aloud what it was they thought she wanted. Gadzhiev and others found this indiscretion both regrettable and endearing: Tamerlan's cockiness had a way of coming off as innocent, and in his friends it produced a feeling of benign condescension.

AFTER THE BOSTON MARATHON BOMBING, there would be much speculation about whether Tamerlan had been "radicalized" in Dagestan. The question was not unreasonable. Dagestan presented many opportunities for a young man in search of a radical future. He could have joined the struggle in Syria; dozens and possibly hundreds of men were recruited in Dagestan around the time he was there. If he was a budding jihadist opposed to U.S. foreign policy, the Syrian opportunity would have seemed perfect—but Tamerlan did not take it. Even more obvious, he could have joined the guerrillas in the forest. He did not, though Kartashov later told the secret police he had talked about it—and Kartashov felt he had talked him down. There were rumors, later, of Tamerlan's making contact with William Plotnikov, who had emigrated from Russia to Canada at the age of fifteen, become a boxer, and gone to Dagestan to join the Islamic insurgency. There does not, however, appear to have been any connection between the two, aside from the eerie coincidence of superficial details of biography. Plotnikov died in the typical blaze of gunfire in a Russian security operation in July 2012; ultimately the only people who linked him to Tamerlan were unnamed Russian secret-police operatives who leaked the information to an enterprising but notoriously unreliable Russian newspaper. The same unnamed sources claimed Tamerlan was connected to another insurgency fighter, Mahmud Nidal, who, by the time this unsubstantiated leak appeared, had been killed in another firestorm, in May 2012.

In the end it seems that most of what Tamerlan did during his six months in Dagestan was talk. Talking—and having someone not only listen to what he had to say but also take it seriously enough to question and criticize and try to guide him—was a radically new experience for him. Feeling, for the first time in his life, like he belonged most certainly entailed a kind of radicalization, a fundamental shift in the way he perceived the world and himself in it—but that is just as certainly not what anyone has meant by suggesting that Tamerlan might have been radicalized in Dagestan.

IN MID-JULY 2012, Tamerlan told his friends he had an issue with his documents that required him to return to the United States at once. Like the claim that he went to Dagestan to have a new Russian passport made because his old one had expired, this documents story is murky. Given that at the time the Tsarnaevs left Russia the country was issuing only five-year passports, Tamerlan's Russian passport actually would have expired years earlier. Unless the Tsarnaevs had a passport made for Tamerlan at the Russian consulate in New York—which appears exceedingly unlikely, because Anzor and Zubeidat went back to Russia to get their own documents in 2007—he would have had no Russian document to renew and would have had to travel to Dagestan on his United States documents. Another clue suggesting that Tamerlan was likely traveling as an American is that about halfway through his stay in Dagestan he went to Azerbaijan for a few minutes. Jamal told me about the trip: he drove Tamerlan to the border, and Tamerlan crossed it and came right back. It had something to do with his documents. But if Tamerlan had indeed been in the process of renewing his Russian passport, he would have been unable to leave the country just then. It would appear that he was in Dagestan as an American, with a Russian visa that allowed a maximum three-month stay—and he had to leave and reenter to restart the countdown.

He had no desire to leave Dagestan for even a few minutes. He told Jamal he wanted to stay, and the older man berated him. "What are you going to do here?" he shouted. "Herd sheep? Go back to America and get an education!" Tamerlan told Gadzhiev he wanted to stay, and Gadzhiev understood and welcomed his desire. And when Tamerlan had to leave, he said he would return soon. Whatever was calling him back clearly had nothing to do with his Russian documents: it was an American exigency.

TWO MONTHS after Tamerlan's departure, the Union of the Just staged a protest that criticized not only the Russian regime but also

American foreign policy. Shocking onlookers in Kizlyar, the protesters burned a United States flag—a gesture that had never before been seen in Dagestan. Months later, when Gadzhiev was interviewed by men representing the FBI, he would taunt them by recalling that protest. One could say, if one were so inclined, that it was Tamerlan Tsarnaev who had radicalized the Union of the Just.

Seven

PATRIOTS' DAY

Tamerlan returned to Cambridge in July 2012. A couple of weeks later, Zubeidat left for Dagestan. There was an understanding in the family now: Dagestan was the place to live. Anzor was back there, starting a car-repair business with Jamal's help. He was not the reason Zubeidat was going back—she had her own family in Dagestan. Jahar was talking about going the following summer. Tamerlan now thought of Dagestan as his home—he just needed to get his U.S. passport and he would be on his way. Joanna asked him once why he would want an American passport, given how he had come to feel about the United States, and he seemed not to understand the question. A U.S. passport was and always would be a valuable commodity—no matter how inherently hypocritical Tamerlan might find the American electoral system or how inherently unjust the American mode of government. It was an odd exchange. Joanna was employing rhetoric that had too often been used against lefties like her: *If you hate America so much, why don't you just get out?* Tamerlan saw no contradiction in his response. There were many things he disliked about America, and he saw valor in speaking out about them—but he saw no reason to reject so prized an asset as an American passport. If his English and his political education had been better, he might even have said that dissidence is the highest form of patriotism.

Things had not been good between Tamerlan and Joanna in a while, as this uncharacteristically confrontational encounter might suggest. Norfolk Street, where the Tsarnaevs had lived longer than anywhere else since Zubeidat and Anzor met, was no longer home. In September, Jahar returned to college, leaving only Tamerlan, Karima, and Zahira. In November, Joanna asked them to move out, which she had not done even when the rent was severely in arrears. Now she served Tamerlan a formal eviction notice.

But they were a family breaking up, and the eviction notice was just one of the many steps in this jerky process. Tamerlan and Joanna went through stages when they attempted if not a reconciliation, then at least a connection. In January 2013, Tamerlan gave her a phone number for his sister Bella and suggested she call her. Bella said she had just returned to the New York area from Chechnya, where she had divorced Rizvan. Ramzan, their son, was staying in Chechnya, as the rules required. Bella said her health was worse: the problem had spread to her heart. Perhaps Tamerlan had hoped that Joanna would help Bella seek medical treatment and pay for it; perhaps Joanna tried to. But when she next checked in with Bella, the young woman said she had found medical assistance in New Jersey and was doing all right. Tamerlan said that Ailina had remarried, and her husband was Muslim. Joanna told Tamerlan she would let him stay until June 2013.

Time and again that winter she steered their conversations away from Ron Paul and conspiracy theories, and toward what Tamerlan might do with his life. He said he wanted to go into auto electrics. He mentioned a private school that offered vocational training in that field—a school on a par with the Catherine Hinds Institute. Joanna talked about ways of getting a more serious education. Once when they were standing in the front yard, she suggested he was better than what he was aspiring to. Tamerlan seemed taken aback, sheepish and confused. But what was it that he was better than, exactly? There were so many ways in which Joanna had been disappointed and so many ways in which he had given up trying—but in all likelihood this conversation, too, concerned needing to make a living. This was likely the last time they spoke.

JAHAR HAD A NEW ROOMMATE in room 7341 of Pine Dale Hall, a sophomore dorm at the University of Massachusetts Dartmouth. Andrew Dwinells was a studious engineering major, the kind of kid who would surely turn a degree from a middling state school into a stepping-stone to a decent graduate school, a respectable career, and a solid middle-class childhood for his future offspring. This was supposed to be Jahar's path—that was the story told in Kyrgyzstan, Dagestan, and even Cambridge—but Dwinells's presence served up daily reminders of how little Jahar had in common with a young man who was actually living the American ambition. They never talked. They exchanged text messages only when one of them was locked out of the room, which happened often enough. The door locked automatically when shut, leaving whoever had forgotten his key card to stare at the light-wood veneer with the colorful name tags—Andrew and Jahar—and cutout stickers that, with some difficulty and no small doubt, could be identified as a lily pad and a turkey. The residential advisor had placed these on the door, as if the boys were eight years old. Inside, the decor was just as unimaginative and inelegant. Two long, narrow strips of furnishings mirrored each other: twin beds hiked up on banks of drawers; desks pushed up against opposite walls; two narrow cupboards that blocked the window. The two sides of the room were identical, except Jahar's was always a mess and Andrew's was neat bordering on uninhabited.

Andrew rose early to go to class. Jahar was invariably asleep when he left. Andrew did most of his studying in the library or the common area in the dorm; when he returned to the room, it was always dark and Jahar was either absent or staring at his computer screen. Sometimes, the small television perched on a desk would be on. Very rarely, one of the boys would make a comment about something that was on television. Once, this was something about September 11, 2001, and Jahar said it had been a government conspiracy. A lot of people at the University of Massachusetts Dartmouth believed a lot of different things. Andrew thought Jahar was a weird one, but not in any extraordinary way.

Andrew saw students come in and out of their room. Most came because Jahar was a campus pot dealer; a small group were Jahar's friends. On occasion, one or two of them would hang with Jahar in their room; more often, their small clump moved off somewhere, in a thick cloud of marijuana smoke.

It was as tight and purposeless a group as any set of college friends ever was. At its core were Jahar and two kids from Kazakhstan who had come to Massachusetts to go to college. Dias Kadyrbayev was a skinny boy from a middle-class family in Almaty. His coming to the United States was a triumph of his and his family's will. He was the only one in the group who had anything resembling ambition, but much of it was focused on a girl named Bayan, whom he had been dating in Kazakhstan since sixth grade. Bayan came from money and planned to get a business degree in the United States, so Dias beat her to it: the year she was finishing high school back at home, he was already a freshman at the University of Massachusetts Dartmouth, and Skyping incessantly with her. His sophomore year, Bayan enrolled at Babson College, west of Boston, where she studied business with the sons of Middle Eastern sheikhs; Dias drove sixty miles north every Thursday to pick up Bayan to bring her to his off-campus apartment in New Bedford, next to Dartmouth, for the weekend.

Azamat Tazhayakov, a short boy with a face and broad-chested body that would surely, with age, become as perfectly round as his father's, was the son of an oil executive who fancied himself one of the dozen most influential men in Kazakhstan and was probably one of a hundred. All the boys in the family would be educated abroad and all would go into oil—this was preordained—but probably because Azamat went first, he landed at UMass by mistake. His father had confused the University of Massachusetts with Massachusetts Institute of Technology, and signed Azamat up for the Bachelor Pathway Program, the fancy name of a revenue-generating program for foreigners that does not guarantee admission to a degree program but does provide English instruction and a way to secure a student visa. Once Azamat arrived, it became clear not only that UMass was not MIT but also that it offered no major appropriate for a future oil magnate. His father wanted Azamat to transfer to the University of Texas, but Azamat, who disliked upheaval more than anything else, showed uncharacteristic resolve and convinced his father that all American universities were essentially the same for the first couple of years. He was allowed to stay.

Azamat and Dias met at the very beginning of freshman year, and both of them met Jahar a short time later. Both the Kazakhs spoke Russian as the second of their household languages, and this made them good and tolerant enough company for Jahar, who was re-Russifying himself. He was spending an increasing amount of time on Russian-language social networks, which provided not only virtual company but also copious amounts of pirated music and films in Russian.

Their first year, Dias and Azamat also made friends with a girl named Pamela Rolon, who introduced them, the following September, to her younger sister, Alexa Guevara, and a medical lab science major named Tiffany Evora. Robel Phillipos, Jahar's friend from Rindge and Latin, rounded out the group. The Kazakhs managed to persuade their parents to allow them to rent the off-campus apartment in New Bedford starting their sophomore year. They claimed it would be easier for them to study there. By "study," they—or at least Dias—meant "get stoned." Jahar provided the weed for free in exchange for Dias's acting as both a runner and a sort of customer liaison.

The boys furnished their apartment with a sort of 1980s panache that put one in mind of a café on the outskirts of the former Soviet empire. There was a fair amount of black lacquer, there was a plush sectional sofa, and there was a large television set. The group spent three or four evenings a week on that sofa, getting stoned, watching movies, and eating. The boys played FIFA, a soccer video game; the girls talked about which of the boys might be the hottest lovers, though it does not appear that anyone but Dias was getting much action. The group made several weekend runs to New York, though once they got it together to make the three-hour drive, they usually had just time enough to snap a picture in Times Square, or in front of the Statue of Liberty or the *New York Times* building, and post it on a Russian social network before making the drive back. On one of those trips, though, they found the time to go to New Jersey to buy a used BMW for the Kazakhs. Azamat's father was bankrolling this purchase—Azamat had explained to him that it was too hard, always having to ask Jahar for a ride to and from campus—and Jahar helped pick out the car, using what Anzor had taught him. It is not clear who picked out the vanity license plate for the front of the car (Massachusetts requires only that the back plate be state-issued) or whether it was there from the start. It read TERRORISTA#1. It was funny.

The Kazakhs and Jahar were practically family. In fact, family was exactly what they were in the eyes of T-Mobile: because Jahar was the only person in the group who had a Social Security number, required to enter into any financial contract in the United States, all four of them—he, Dias, Azamat, and Bayan—had a family cellular plan, with Jahar as the primary subscriber.

At first glance, the group Jahar assembled at college was not dissimilar to the group he had in high school. His ability to make friends with kids different from him and from one another had been one of the qualities that impressed teachers, marked him as a "good kid" in Cambridge's progressive hierarchy. But a closer look would have shown that something had changed, perhaps profoundly. He was no longer shifting effortlessly among groups. This tiny crowd was insular. And it was, essentially, a group of outcasts. Dias and Azamat were still fairly disoriented in their American life. All the Americans in the group came from difficult families except for Robel, whose mother had raised him resolutely alone. Jahar was the only member of the group who had the option of identifying as white—an option still important for fitting in at a state school in Massachusetts: UMass Dartmouth was roughly seventy percent white. Of course, Jahar was white only in the United States. In Russia his sharp features and curly black hair marked him as "black," and though he had never experienced this himself, he would have heard from Tamerlan about the ordeal of moving through Russia while being recognizably Chechen in ethnicity; one need only spend a couple of hours in Moscow changing planes in order to feel the hostility and the heightened police attention.

What Jahar did have was the experience of growing up Muslim in the United States after September 11. In his case this experience was barely mitigated by the experience of commonality and belonging that many other Muslims enjoy: he hardly ever went to mosque, and while some years he fasted (and abstained from smoking pot) for the daylight hours during Ramadan, in his family this was an individual rather than a group choice. In his life, being Muslim was purely a mark of otherness. He did not share even this experience with the Kazakhs. Though they were similarly vaguely practicing Muslims for whom Islam was code for heritage and family rather than religious practice, they had grown up in a country where the majority of the population shared their identity. They had never before encountered people who found the very idea of Islam frightening. Toward the end of the first semester of his sophomore year, Jahar tried spending a bit more time at mosque, but this too failed to give him a sense of community. Here he stood out because of his height and his pale skin, and people kept asking him when and why he had converted.

With the possible partial exception of Tiffany, no one in the group was much concerned with studying. Robel was suspended for a marijuana violation toward the end of the first semester of sophomore year and was not allowed to return in the spring. Azamat, the only nonsmoker in the group, got a letter in early January notifying him that he was suspended for failing to maintain the required grade-point average. He did not bother to do anything about this, even though the notice rendered his student visa invalid. As it turned out later, the system had made a mistake: Azamat's grade-point average was good enough. Jahar's grades, on the other hand, were slipping. At the start of his sophomore year, he changed his major to biology; this did not seem to help his grades or his morale.

In February or March, Jahar saw Larry Aaronson across Norfolk Street and called out to him.

"Are you in school?" Larry asked. He was always worried about kids staying enrolled—though he had never seen any reason to worry about Jahar.

"Yes."

"Are you wrestling?"

"No."

Larry was surprised.

"It's a lot harder than I thought, this second year," said Jahar.

Perhaps Aaronson sensed a lost quality in Jahar; perhaps he imagined it later. There was nothing in the boy's demeanor or dress that seemed to have changed. Larry suggested Jahar could come to him for help with his studies, and Jahar seemed happy at the offer—and when he seemed happy, he always seemed genuinely happy. He never called.

From Cambridge, Tamerlan stayed in touch with his friends back in Dagestan by Skype. Skype has a special place in many Chechen immigrants' homes. Those who have arrived in the United States after broadband Internet connections became widely available often maintain a semipermanent link with relatives at home, creating a close approximation of daily life still lived as a clan, with news and gossip exchanged while chores are done and meals are consumed or even virtually shared. Tamerlan now had his own connection to "back home." He showed Mohammed Gadzhiev his daughter and the long beard he had grown as though on behalf of his brothers in Dagestan: they could never wear a beard that ostentatious without being identified, arrested, and likely executed for supposedly being Wahhabis.

Tamerlan boasted of his growing outspokenness. He had twice raised his voice in mosque—in fact, he had twice either staged a walkout or been removed from mosque for objecting to the imam's acknowledgment of non-Muslim holidays. First it was Thanksgiving, and then Martin Luther King, Jr., Day in January. Gadzhiev reacted with his familiar mix of approval and condescension: Tamerlan was still acting like a big baby—speaking up against the imam in mosque is not a done thing—but on the other hand, his heart was clearly in the right place, even if his intention was still muddled.

On January 23, Tamerlan filed his petition for naturalization as a United States citizen. The form asks applicants if they want to change their name—an option many people take to Americanize their first names and to simplify spellings that have often been copied from foreign-issue documents. Tamerlan wrote that he wanted to change his first name to Muaz, presumably in honor of Emir Muaz, an insurgent killed in Dagestan in 2009. The emir's name at birth had been Umar Sheikhulaev, and he had been the anointed leader of Dagestan in an aspirational greater Chechen state called the Caucasian Emirate.

ONE EVENING in late February or early March, Azamat, Dias, and the girls were cruising for some weed. The search naturally led them to Jahar. He said he had something else in mind, and everyone got into a car—some people were in the BMW and some were in the car Jahar was driving. He had banged up his green Honda Civic a bit and had given it to Tamerlan to fix, so somehow he had a black Camaro on loan, which gave the evening a tinge of gangster glamour. He led the group to the banks of the Charles River, where he got a black backpack out of the trunk and some fireworks out of the backpack and set them off. Then everyone got back into the cars and drove back to New Bedford, where there was pot to be smoked. It had been pretty. It had also been cold. Fireworks, unless set off by professionals as part of a licensed display, are illegal in Massachusetts. But then, so is the sale of marijuana.

IN EARLY MARCH, Tamerlan was calling Musa Khadzhimuratov in New Hampshire to arrange a time to drop in: Musa's mother-in-law was visiting from Chechnya, and custom dictated that every Chechen in the area stop by to pay his respects. The matter was urgent because the old woman's stay was coming to an end. Tamerlan wanted to come on a weekday—he wanted to bring his family, and Karima worked weekends. Musa had endless medical appointments during the week, so he resisted. In the end, Tamerlan and Karima figured out a way to visit on the last weekend of March, which also happened to be the old woman's last weekend in the country.

Musa's mother-in-law thought they were a gorgeous family, and attempted to tell Karima as much in Chechen.

"Mama, she doesn't understand."

The old woman switched to Russian.

"Mama, she doesn't understand that, either."

"What's such a beautiful boy doing with a girl who doesn't understand anything?"

Everyone laughed.

Tamerlan made mistakes, as always: he picked up Zahira, in violation of a custom that prohibits Chechen men from picking up children in front of elders. Musa ribbed Tamerlan about being more Dagestani than Chechen. Tamerlan said he still thought of himself as more of a Chechen but regrettably had no family in Chechnya. (Jamal, though he was often there, maintained his home base in central Russia now.) He said his aunt Malkan had recently sold her place in Central Asia to move to Chechnya—maybe he would be able to visit there more often now.

OVER A MEAL IN MARCH, Jahar told Dias and Azamat that he knew how to make a bomb. He said he had learned it in chemistry class. He also said there were things, perhaps some things in the Koran, that were worth fighting for, using force. His friends did not think anything of it: they spent a lot of time together, and a lot of things were said. Jahar was no Muslim fanatic—Dias and Azamat had both seen a couple of those, and Azamat thought maybe Tamerlan was one when he foisted some book on him during the one night Azamat spent at Jahar's place in Cambridge. Jahar just had a way with random pronouncements. Like, on New Year's Eve he tweeted, "I meet the most amazing people, spent the day with this Jamaican Muslim convert who shared his whole story with me, my religion is the truth."

Three weeks later, he tweeted, "To be honest, I don't care for those people that wanna commit suicide, your life b, do what you think will make you happy. #selfishbastards."

And in another month he tweeted, "Share the love, the knowledge and the wealth."

On April 9, he posted several videos on his VK.com page, including one about the carnage in Syria that ended with the line "Syria is calling. We will answer," and one about a blind boy who spends all his time studying the Koran.

And on April 12 he tweeted, "Now we ain't come here to start no drama, we are just looking for future baby mamas."

And eight minutes later, "Dreams really do come true, last night I dreamt I was eating a cheeseburger and in the afternoon today, guess what I'm eating . . ."

He used his Facebook page that week to advertise some Ed Hardy clothes for sale, new with tags.

And among all that, there were hundreds of tweets and posts about girls, food, sleeping habits, the drudgery of college, and a couple of sophomoric jokes in Russian thrown in. Who knew what could come out of the guy's mouth?

ONLY THREE STATES in the union observe Patriots' Day, the anniversary of the 1775 Battles of Lexington and Concord. Massachusetts is the only one of those states that has actual celebratory practices for the holiday: the battles are reenacted; the Red Sox play their home opener at Fenway Park; schools and state offices are closed; and the Boston Marathon is run. It is like Massachusetts' own big American holiday. Though if you have never lived anywhere in America outside Massachusetts, you might just think Patriots' Day is a big American holiday, period. Kind of like a second Fourth of July.

Patriots' Day 2013 fell on April 15, tax day—an ironic coincidence for a big American holiday. At 2:49 p.m. that day, a couple of hours after the winner completed the Boston Marathon, when runners were crossing the finish line in a steady stream, two bombs went off near the end of the route, killing three people and injuring at least 264 others, including sixteen who lost limbs.

Eight

THEY ARE US

In the immediate aftermath of the bombing, police scanned the crowd for people who looked suspicious, which is to say Muslim, which is to say darker than Boston-white. A twenty-year-old man from Saudi Arabia was among the walking wounded—the dozens of people with burns, scratches, and bruises from being thrown who were making their way, with the assistance of uninjured runners, to the assembled ambulances. Abdulrahman Ali Alharbi, an English-language student who had been on his way to meet friends for lunch and decided to get a glimpse of the marathon on the way, had been thrown by the second explosion. He had burn injuries on his head, back, and legs. His jeans were torn. He was covered in blood, most of it other people's. A police officer directed Alharbi, along with other victims, toward the waiting ambulances—but when the student boarded one, several officers followed him into the vehicle. At the hospital, more than twenty police officers and FBI agents surrounded his bed. At 4:28 in the afternoon, less than two hours after the bombs went off, the *New York Post* reported that law enforcement were talking to a suspect in the bombing. By evening, the media had his name and address, and the FBI had his Facebook password. By Tuesday morning, the *Post* had published a picture taken in the street in Revere, the Boston suburb where

Alharbi lived, Fox News had reported his name, and other media had published a mistranslation of a Facebook post of his: "God is coming to the U.S." In fact, he had written, "Thank God I arrived in the U.S. after a long trip." CBS stated that a spectator at the marathon had seen Alharbi "acting suspiciously" and tackled him. Other media reported that he had had burns on his hands, pointing to the probability that he was the bomber.

Alharbi was exonerated by the FBI within twenty-four hours of the bombing, but by this time he had no home—his address was now so widely known that he felt he would be unsafe there—and no money: the FBI never returned his wallet. The Saudi embassy provided Alharbi with food and a hotel room.

After Alharbi came Sunil Tripathi, Salaheddin Barhoum, and Yassine Zaimi. The last two were Moroccan immigrants, a seventeen-year-old high school track competitor and his twenty-four-year-old coach, who had been fingered by amateur online detectives. On Thursday, April 18, the *Post* published a photograph of them on the cover, with the banner headline BAG MEN: FEDS SEEK THESE TWO PICTURED AT BOSTON MARATHON. The evidence, as analyzed by the online crowd: one of the men was wearing a black backpack—and a black backpack, or what remained of it after a bomb exploded inside, had been found at the scene. Plus, they looked dark and were indeed Muslim.

Sunil Tripathi was a brown-skinned American student at Brown University who had disappeared almost a month before the bombing. This suspect too came courtesy of Internet amateurs, but the social network Reddit gave it such traction that for a day or two those following the case were all but certain this young man was the prime suspect. In fact, he had been dead for weeks—his body was found another week later.

At five o'clock on Thursday, the FBI called a press conference at a Sheraton hotel in Boston. Within half an hour media had released pictures of another pair of young men: one older, one younger, one wearing a white baseball cap and the other a black one—oddly, all of this was also true of the two Moroccans, and in some quarters confusion persisted. The pictures were taken from surveillance tapes; the FBI believed the two men to be the bombers, and was asking the public for help in identifying them.

LARRY AARONSON is the sort of person who engages with everything that happens in his city and feels responsible for everyone he has ever known. This time his personal investment was overwhelming: he knew three of the people who lost limbs. One was the son of a fellow Rindge and Latin teacher, a special boy who had been doing relief work in war zones. Another was the daughter of a teacher. A third was a teacher who was dating a former student. Aaronson felt personally injured, and he was glued to Facebook, where friends and strangers were exchanging the latest news and rumors. His own suspicion was that the bomber was a rogue Tea Party member who had chosen the coincidence of Patriots' Day and tax day to protest the government by killing amateur athletes.

But then he saw reports on the Saudi student, the Moroccans, and the boy who looked Sri Lankan. They seemed no more and no less absurd than any other possible suspect. Then he saw the picture of the men the FBI said were suspects. One of them looked uncannily like Jahar. As Thursday evening wore on, the pictures Aaronson was seeing on his screens became more and more clear: as the resolution went up, the bombers were coming into focus.

Man, this is looking a lot like Jahar, he was thinking. *I should call him and tell him, "You better go to the police, because they are showing pictures of this kid who looks just like you."*

Ginny, a receptionist at a Cambridge hospital, recognized Tamerlan right away. She had the day off, so, like many people in the Boston area, she was home in front of her television set when the pictures were first shown. "That's the fucking guy who used to come in and talk to me!" Ginny shouted to her husband. "He delivered for Mona Lisa!" Mona Lisa was the pizza place down the street from the hospital, just across from Rindge and Latin. It was owned by two brothers—Ginny was pretty sure they were Brazilian (they were actually Egyptian)—and Tamerlan had spent a couple of months delivering for them. On one of his first deliveries, he'd asked the receptionist her name, though he never introduced himself. From then on, he would come in, always dressed in jeans and a hoodie, and say, in his strong accent, "I'm from Mona Lisa. How you doin', Ginny?" Her first thought on seeing his photo on television was, *He knows my name!* She barely considered going to the authorities: "I was scared. I didn't want to become a target."

OVER AT the University of Massachusetts Dartmouth campus, just about every television set had been on for three straight days. Sixty miles' distance from Boston made it all feel a bit like a video game. Few of the students were familiar enough with the multi-million-dollar town houses and luxury shops of Back Bay to have the sort of visceral reaction to the television footage through which the brain and the body tell each other, *This is us, it is our home that is under attack.* The kids at the UMass campus fielded calls and messages from family, affirmed that they were well and far from the scene of the attack, and commenced watching what felt like a reality TV show on the bombing. And then they saw Jahar.

Unlike Larry Aaronson, many of the UMass students saw Jahar several times a week, or even daily. They did not think that television was broadcasting the picture of a kid who looked like Jahar: there was no doubt in their minds that this *was* Jahar. And then again, there was doubt.

Very soon, many of Tamerlan's and Jahar's friends would be telling the FBI and the media that it was impossible that the brothers were the bombers—there had been no sign. Surely, the friends would say, if the two had been plotting something so huge and horrible, they would have seemed distracted. Or emotional. Or pensive. Or somehow, clearly, not themselves. But this assumption was a misconception. The psychiatrist and political scientist Jerrold Post, who has been studying terrorists for decades, writes, "Terrorists are not depressed, severely emotionally disturbed, or crazed fanatics." Political scientist Louise Richardson, an undisputed star in the tiny academic field of terrorism studies, writes of terrorists: "Their primary shared characteristic is their normalcy, insofar as we understand the term. Psychological studies of terrorism are virtually unanimous on this point."

Nor do terrorists tend to behave out of character just before committing an act that, to them, appears perfectly rational and fully justified. One of the September 11 hijackers called his wife in Germany on the morning of the attacks to tell her he loved her; she apparently heard nothing extraordinary in his voice. Having made the decision to commit an act of terrorism, the future bomber—even a suicide bomber—develops, it would appear, a sort of two-track mind. On one track, life goes on exactly as before; on the other, he is preparing for the event that will disrupt his life or even end it. It is precisely the ordinary nature of the man and the extraordinary effect of the act about to be committed that ensure the two tracks never cross.

When students at the University of Massachusetts Dartmouth saw their classmate's picture on television, their minds became the perfect mirrors of Jahar's: on one track was the full knowledge that they were looking at a picture of their friend; on the other was the certainty that Jahar could not possibly be responsible for the marathon bombing. "I knew it was him because I recognized him, but I didn't believe it was him," Tiffany Evora said in court fourteen months later. Testifying at the same trial, Alexa Guevara could not force the words out and had to be coaxed by a lawyer.

"When you saw the images, you did not believe it was him, did you?"

"No," she said, though she had acknowledged that she had recognized Jahar.

"You didn't believe he was capable of something like that, did you?"

"No," she said, and started crying.

Between the track that was telling these college kids that the person in the pictures on television was undoubtedly their friend, and the track that kept insisting this was impossible, they chose the middle road. Rather than go to the police or the FBI, as the voices on television kept imploring them to do, they went to Jahar's dorm. Why? None of them could answer that question clearly in the aftermath, but it seems that in the hope of calming their exploding minds, they wanted to ask Jahar himself if he had set off the bombs.

The door to room 7341, with perhaps a lily pad and a turkey glued to it, was locked. Befuddled students came in a steady stream, tried the door handle, exchanged concerned glances, som-

ber nods, and the occasional unconvincing reassurance, and am-
bled off, back to the screens in their own dorm rooms.

HAD ANY OF JAHAR'S college friends gone to the police, they
could have reported that they had seen Jahar in the days after the
bombing—he had been on campus and he had been himself: just
Jahar. Azamat could have said what he told the FBI later, that Jahar
had not joined his friends for spring break in Florida in mid-March,
and that when they returned he had apparently stopped smoking
weed—though not necessarily selling it. That he did not see Jahar
or text with him on Sunday, April 14—Jahar must have gone to
Cambridge for the day or the weekend, which was hardly unusual.
Monday was the holiday, another no-school day, and Azamat had
texted Jahar, asking if he was around. "I 'have' to make my passport, so 'tomorrow,'" was the response, with the emphasis quota-
tion marks around two words. Then a friend from Kazakhstan had
texted Azamat, asking him if he was all right—this was how Azamat found out about the bombing. Azamat texted Jahar, asking in
turn if he was all right—and learned that he was. At 4:19, Azamat
got another text from Jahar: "Don't go thinking it's me, you cooked
bastard." Azamat was thinking no such thing; the only odd thing
about this message was that "cooked" means "stoned," and Azamat never smoked.

On Tuesday, Azamat and Dias drove to Boston. The plan was
to do some shopping, which was really an excuse to check out the
state of Back Bay. They headed for Boylston Street, only to discover that all the stores there were closed. Dias dropped Azamat
off in Cambridge, near Jahar's house. Jahar came down and drove
Azamat back to New Bedford in his green Honda Civic while Dias
used the shared BMW with the TERRORISTA#1 license plate to go

see Bayan at Babson. Back at Azamat and Dias's apartment on Carriage Drive, Jahar and Azamat played FIFA on Xbox for hours—except for a short break Jahar took to go into the bathroom and use his phone to Skype with Tamerlan. This was all normal enough. One of the three Kazakhs on the T-Mobile family plan—most likely Dias, who had lost his T-Mobile phone—had failed to pay his share of the monthly bill, and T-Mobile had suspended their account. Now none of them could use regular phone service: they used iMessage, an Apple program, to text, and Skype to talk on the phone, but they could do those things only when they had an Internet connection. There was nothing strange about Jahar's wanting some privacy for his call with his brother—and Azamat knew whom he was talking to, so Jahar was not exactly being secretive.

That day Jahar also tweeted a bit, as usual. Among other things, he, like millions of other Americans, commented on a picture of a woman who had been injured in the bombings. The photograph had been circulating with a caption that claimed the woman's boyfriend had been planning to propose to her the day she was injured—and that she had died. "Fake story," wrote Jahar. It was.

On Wednesday, two days after the bombing, Azamat and Jahar went to the gym together in the evening. Afterward, they played FIFA until midnight. Sometime that evening Jahar also dropped by a soccer-team get-together at an Italian restaurant.

On Thursday Azamat ran into Robel on campus. They had not seen each other in over a month, while Robel was on suspension; now he was on campus for a hearing on his violation. It was around one in the afternoon and they were near the cafeteria, so they got lunch. Robel asked if he could spend the weekend at the apartment on Carriage Drive. Dias had the BMW that day, so after lunch Azamat texted Jahar, asking him for a ride home. Robel and

Azamat walked over to Pine Dale Hall. They spent about half an hour in Robel's friend Lino Rosas's room. Lino always said he liked Robel the moment he saw him, at the beginning of freshman year, because he had "finally found someone skinnier than me." Both boys were dark-skinned, well over six feet tall, and so thin they looked breakable and made Azamat seem positively roly-poly. Azamat hung around with them for about half an hour in Lino's room, then tagged along as they went down to the parking lot, and sat in the back of Lino's car as they got stoned with the windows rolled up.

It was nearly four in the afternoon when Jahar became available to give Azamat a ride to Carriage Drive. He, Azamat, and Robel spent less than ten minutes in the car on the way to the apartment, and then Robel returned to campus with Jahar. That would make Robel the last person to have seen Jahar before his picture was broadcast to the world—the boys parted ways in Pine Dale Hall less than an hour before the FBI press conference. Before leaving his dorm room, Jahar retweeted a post by a Zimbabwean mufti: "Attitude can take away your beauty no matter how good looking you are or it could enhance your beauty, making you adorable."

Andrew Dwinells, had he gone to the police, would not have been able to tell them much. His roommate had seemed the same as he'd ever been. He slept when Andrew left for class, and was out when Andrew returned.

And even if all the students who had seen Jahar in the days following the bombing had gone to the authorities with their stories, the FBI would have learned only Jahar's name. Jahar's observed behavior contained no clues to what he and Tamerlan were planning to do and where they were planning to hide once their faces were known—because the brothers had no plan. While Boston was reeling from the marathon bombing, nothing extraordinary had happened to the bombers themselves.

AFTER JAHAR dropped him off at Carriage Drive, Azamat took a nap. About an hour and a half later, Dias and Bayan walked in. Now Azamat took the car: he went to the gym, and Dias stayed at the apartment, where, prompted by a text message, he eventually turned on the television and saw the picture of his best friend wearing a white baseball cap with the visor turned back. The first person Dias texted was Jahar:

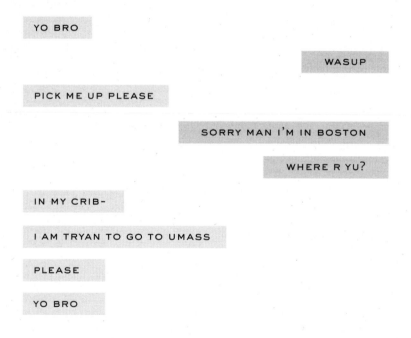

Dias's mind had not just split into two tracks: it had all but imploded. He wanted to go to campus to find out if Jahar, his best friend, was the Boston Marathon bomber—and he wanted Jahar, his buddy with the car, who was texting him right back, as usual, to drive him there. It took him a minute to grasp that Jahar was out of reach. At 8:43 in the evening he texted Jahar again.

U SAW THE NEWS?

YEA BRO I DID

FOR REAL

I SAW THE NEWS . . .

BETTER NOT TEXT ME MY FRIEND

LOL

U SAW URSELF THERE?

AHAHA

HAHAHA

IFYU WANT YU CAN GO TO MY ROOM AND TAKE WHAT'S THERE:)
BUT IGHT BRO SALAM ALEKUM

WHAT'S WRONG WITH YU?

HAHA;)

CAN'T RIGHT NOW MAN

Dias began frantically texting Azamat, who had finished his workout and gone shopping at Target. In the space of ten minutes Dias sent ten messages, all of them imploring Azamat to pick him up at once. "Azkro," they began. "What yu doing," "Will yu pick me up?" "Please," "Azik!" and so on. Azamat dropped his shopping and rushed home. Dias was waiting for him at the sliding door—this would have shaved half a minute off the time required to exit the apartment and enter the car. Dias told Azamat to drive to campus, then explained that he had seen a photo on the news and it looked like Jahar.

By the time they got to Pine Dale Hall, Jahar had been gone more than four hours and the haphazard pilgrimage to the locked door to his dorm room had lasted more than three. Robel, whom Dias had also texted, was there, as was Lino, who had been smoking weed with Robel in his dorm room. Like all the students who had come here in the last few hours, they knocked, jerked the handle, confirmed that the door was locked, and commenced a few minutes of standing around looking somber. All agreed that the picture on TV looked like Jahar. All nodded their heads. Then there was nothing left to do. The four young men went to Lino's room and started a game of Xbox. After about five minutes, Dias said he was going back to Jahar's room, and left.

For every four cramped residential double rooms in Pine Dale Hall, there is one common study area, also cramped; this makes the four rooms a "suite." Dias found Andrew working on an essay in the common room. When he said he needed Andrew to let him into the dorm room, Andrew thought nothing of it: he had accommodated such requests before, whenever Dias, the only genuinely frequent visitor to Jahar's side of the room, had forgotten his iPhone charger there. It was in the room that Dias showed Andrew the text message from Jahar: "Ifyu want yu can go to my room and take what's there:) but ight bro Salam alekum." To Andrew, who had not yet seen the news, the message read as somewhat cryptic but also unsurprising: he could imagine Jahar, who had never seemed to be quite there in the first place, picking up one day and vanishing.

Dias began a frantic search of Jahar's side of the room—the wardrobe, the dresser drawers under the bed, the desk. Azamat and Robel came, summoned by a text Dias had sent to Robel: "Come to Jahar's." They sat impassively on the bed, staring at images moving across the television screen—it was *Project X*, an unfunny 2012 comedy about three high school students trying to throw the party of a lifetime—as Dias continued his search. What was he looking for? Pot? But he knew where Jahar kept his stash, so, barring the possibility that he was too agitated to remember even that simple fact, he had no reason to be conducting a search. More likely, he was still seeking what everyone who had knocked on Jahar's door that day had sought: an answer. He thought he might have found it when he came upon a black JanSport backpack with some emptied-out fireworks in it: a larger hollow cylinder and a half-dozen long ones, barely thicker than a cigarette, which had been removed from the large one and then relieved of the gunpowder. He also found a half-empty jar of Vaseline. From something he had either watched on a screen or heard in conversation, Dias knew that gunpowder and Vaseline could be components of explosive devices. He placed the open backpack in front of Azamat and mouthed the words "I think he used these to make the bombs." Azamat nodded.

But finding the backpack could not have helped reconcile the conflicting tracks of Dias's mind. The fireworks looked so ordinary. The larger cylinder was a meek blue; the thin inner cylinders were just paper. They looked like the remnants of a long-ago New Year's, or like that March night on the bank of the Charles River when Jahar had set off the fireworks while the rest of the crew watched. And the jar of Vaseline was just a jar of Vaseline. Dias may have known that these objects could be the remnants of making a bomb, but all of them were of this reality, not of the fantastical, otherworldly, disastrous realm of the carnage on television.

When Dias, Azamat, and Robel left Jahar's room after about half an hour, they took with them: the black backpack with the fireworks and the Vaseline, a black Sony VAIO computer, a thumb drive, a brown clay ashtray, a small bag of marijuana, a pair of red Beats headphones that Azamat did not exactly remember loaning to Jahar a few months before, and a red baseball cap that Dias decided he liked.

Andrew returned to the common room and told the friend with whom he had been studying there that Dias and company had been acting "suspiciously." He texted Jahar: "Hey your friends said you left." He got no response.

AT SOME POINT he saw the news. He saw Jahar's face. He also saw, unfolding, one of the most bizarre manhunts ever to reach the small screen. FBI investigators working out of the Boston office had zeroed in on Jahar as early as Wednesday morning—he was the only person on the surveillance tapes who exhibited no reaction to the explosions. While others ran, ducked, or at least screamed in terror, he kept walking, his white baseball cap turned backward, his step bouncy. They noticed Tamerlan second—he was walking a few people away from his brother, but they appeared to be in step. The investigators called them Black Hat and White Hat: they had no names for the suspects and no idea where to look for them. Facial-recognition software evidently could not be used because of the angle at which the surveillance camera had caught the brothers' faces. So the FBI chose to show the faces to the

American public, with a warning: "We consider them to be armed and extremely dangerous." Said Richard DesLauriers, special agent in charge of the FBI's Boston division, during the press conference called to release the photographs: "No one should approach them."

Five hours later, a member of the campus police force at MIT was shot at close range while he sat in his patrol car. According to the media narrative that followed, members of Massachusetts law enforcement were immediately certain that Black Hat and White Hat were behind the murder. It is possible, though, that they reacted with similar certainty to every violent crime committed in and around the city in the days after the bombing. State Police Superintendent Timothy Alben even told the press that the bombers were responsible for the robbery of a 7-Eleven store in Cambridge on Thursday night. At the scene of the MIT murder, police and the FBI found Officer Sean Collier's body with five gunshot wounds, including two to the head, and no clues that might help them find the brothers, if they were indeed the killers. They had not even taken Collier's gun—they had been unable to work his locking holster.

It was over an hour before a 911 call came in from a Cambridge gas station. The brothers had hijacked a car driven by a young Chinese-immigrant engineer who would become known to the media as "Danny." After a meandering, harrowing ride around Watertown and Cambridge, Danny had managed to escape while the brothers were filling up the tank. They were now driving a new Mercedes SUV that belonged to Danny. The car had a GPS device that would allow the police to track the brothers in real time.

From the aimless way the brothers had driven around in his car, Danny ventured that they might return to Watertown. He was right: the Mercedes was next seen in East Watertown, where they had ditched the green Honda a short while earlier. There appeared to be no rhyme or purpose to their actions, either while they were driving around with Danny or now—most likely because they had no plan. With them they had five homemade explosive devices, a semiautomatic handgun, a machete, and a hunting knife—the arsenal of monstrous children who seemed to have packed everything they had in the apartment that was in some way a weapon, and then bought the Ruger 9mm pistol off a Rindge and Latin friend of Jahar's who had become a far more serious drug dealer than Jahar himself. They had apparently planned to travel in one car—and had transferred their eclectic armory into the Mercedes—but now they decided to reclaim the Honda. They had, it would seem, not considered the possibility of being identified, and they had no idea where and by what means they would go. This made them dangerous in a way entirely different from what those who were looking for them had imagined. Danny, who had had a conversation with Tamerlan as he drove at gunpoint, told the police that his kidnapper had boasted of having set off the bombs at the marathon and that he had mentioned possibly going to New York. He had also identified himself as a Muslim American.

Just before one in the morning, police from Watertown and a number of nearby municipalities converged on Laurel Street, two blocks of modest one- and two-family houses that on any other night or day might have been called sleepy, and began shooting haphazardly. A transit cop named Richard Donohue received the worst gunshot wounds, from one of his own. There is no indication that a negotiating team was present: the only conversation on record appears to be an officer yelling to the brothers to "give up." In response, Jahar hurled the explosive devices, which turned out to be pipe bombs and a pressure-cooker bomb—literally a pressure cooker stuffed with small metal objects such as nails and ball bearings as well as explosives. The bombs used on Monday at the marathon finish line had been pressure-cooker bombs too. But this time, the explosives going off on a narrow residential street appeared to have injured no one.

The final gun battle took place between Watertown policeman Jeff Pugliese and Tamerlan. Pugliese hit Tamerlan several times; Tamerlan hit nothing aside from the walls of a couple of houses, ran out of ammunition, and threw his gun at Pugliese, finally hitting him. Tamerlan then tried to run, but Pugliese and another officer tackled him, pinning him to the pavement. Jahar jumped behind the wheel of the SUV and charged at the three men struggling on the ground. The officers jumped out of the way, and the Mercedes ran over Tamerlan, dragging him about thirty feet down the block. In a book published a year later, two *Boston Globe* reporters, Scott Helman and Jenna Russell, wrote: "Tamerlan was left lying on his stomach, clinging to the final moments of his life. He tried to lift up his head. Blood pooled around his body, streak marks visible on the street where the SUV had dragged him. Pugliese ran over, put cuffs on him, and pressed a foot into his back. Then he called for an ambulance. At long last, Tamerlan was theirs."

Tamerlan was delivered to Beth Israel Deaconess hospital around 1:20 in the morning. He was unconscious and naked—his clothes had been cut away, exposing several gunshot wounds, a large gash on his torso, and burns from being dragged along the street by the SUV. Trauma teams dressed in protective gear first checked him for radioactivity, using a Geiger counter, and then intubated him. At 1:35 they pronounced him dead.

Meanwhile Jahar drove away from the scene of the battle. Probably because they were all still focused on the gunfight and also possibly because they were officers from many different forces acting without a clear center of command, police trailed him by almost a minute, giving him enough time to ditch the Mercedes and vanish into the suburban maze.

LULU EMMONS'S MOTHER called just before six in the morning on Friday and told her to turn on the news. She knew Lulu's boyfriend left for work at six, and she thought it might not be a good idea for him to go out. Lulu had been living away from her mother for just a short time. She had graduated from Rindge and Latin in 2011, done a year of college, found it very difficult, and was now regrouping, working as a waitress and living with her boyfriend in a neat and homey apartment on the first floor of a house in Watertown. Lulu turned on the news and saw Jahar's face. She and Jahar had shared at least one class every year of high school. Sometimes they walked over to the athletics building together: he was going to wrestling practice and she to swimming. For a while Lulu dated a boy who was on the wrestling team, and he would often mention Jahar. "The general consensus was that he was really good," she told me almost a year after the bombing. "Not the best, not like going to go on to something, but good." She also told me she knew Jahar "was from the Czech Republic, we knew he wasn't from here because of the way he spelled his name, but his English was fine." She never knew what his religion might be.

When she saw Jahar's face on television, Lulu texted a friend from high school: "Do you think it's Jahar?" They texted each other that they were shocked and crying and did not believe that it was Jahar. But then the television was saying that the surviving suspect in the marathon bombing had been positively identified as Dzhokhar Tsarnaev and that he was on the loose after the previous night's shoot-out in Watertown.

Terrorism works by striking at random. It is the understanding that anyone—including you and your loved ones—could become the victim of a terrorist attack that multiplies the fear-and-shock effect far beyond what simple killing and even carnage could engender. And the effect is multiplied exponentially if you learn that your loved ones, or at least your friends and neighbors, could become not only the victims but the terrorists themselves. "It is not Jahar," said Lulu, willing her reality to split into two. "It may be his body, but it is not Jahar."

For the next minutes or hours—they could not tell—Lulu and her boyfriend sat in front of their large-screen television, constantly switching between the news in English and in Spanish, which Lulu's boyfriend understood better. Then Lulu looked up and saw a group of men in SWAT gear entering the house through the back porch. Their boots stomped simultaneously up and down the back stairs. Lulu called the landlord, who lived upstairs. He said that he was all right: he must have left the basement door ajar and law enforcement noticed it during a sweep of the street. The men in SWAT gear stomped through the house and out of it. Lulu and her boyfriend returned to switching between coverage of the hunt for Jahar in English and coverage of the hunt for Jahar in Spanish.

AFTER LEAVING PINE DALE HALL on Thursday night, Dias, Azamat, and Robel drove to Taco Bell. They ate there and continued to Carriage Drive. Bayan was on the couch, about halfway through *The Pursuit of Happyness*, a 2006 movie about a salesman who becomes homeless. Azamat and Robel, who gravitated to any lit screen in any room, joined her. Dias filled a pipe with the pot he had taken from Jahar's room, then joined the other three on the couch. They watched the rest of the movie in the fog of the pot and the nagging anxiety about the television picture that had looked so much like Jahar. The boys occasionally looked at the news on their devices—there was something about a cop shot at MIT, but no information on whether Jahar was really Jahar; Azamat made an attempt to do his homework, without moving from the couch. When the movie ended, a bit after midnight, Dias and Bayan retired to Dias's bedroom. Azamat and Robel turned the television set to the news but soon dozed off.

Azamat woke up around two o'clock and looked at the video of the FBI press conference again. It still looked like Jahar. He watched it one more time. And one more. Then he started watching Fox News on his computer, then CNN. Both seemed to be showing the same thing.

"Where yu looking?" he messaged Dias at 2:26. Over in the bedroom, Dias had also been watching the news.

"I think they caught his brother," Azamat messaged at 2:28. Tamerlan had been dead nearly an hour, but some news outlets were reporting that the older and bigger suspect was in custody. CNN had already reported that the suspects were believed to be brothers—and both Dias and Azamat had met Tamerlan. Which mattered if the surviving bomber was indeed Jahar.

In the bedroom, Dias and Bayan started discussing the news. He told her that he had taken a backpack from Jahar's room that contained emptied-out fireworks and a half-full jar of Vaseline, and that he suspected that Jahar had used these in making the bombs. Bayan took this information badly. "It could be evidence," she said. "I don't want it in the apartment!" This must not have occurred to Dias—nor did it occur to either of them now that they should take the backpack to the police, who were chasing after someone who appeared to be Jahar: they just realized that they had come too close to a bad sort of trouble. Dias walked out of the bedroom and either informed his friends that he was now going to dispose of the backpack or consulted them on this matter—later this would be much discussed in court. He removed the laptop from the backpack—there was no talk of getting rid of a perfectly good Sony VAIO just because it might belong to America's most wanted man of the moment—took a half-full black garbage bag out of the kitchen trash can, stuffed the backpack inside, cinched the bag, and walked out of the apartment to toss the backpack with the fireworks and the Vaseline jar into the apartment complex dumpster.

"No more backpack," he reported to Bayan when he returned.

"Where is it?"

"Far away."

WHEN AZAMAT next woke up, Dzhokhar's name was written on the television screen. A couple of hours earlier, after seeing a picture that was even more clear than all the previous ones—the resolution kept going up—and looked ever more like Jahar, Azamat had Googled "Dzhokhar," "Dzhakhar," "Dzhokhar Tsarnaev," "Djahar Tsarnaev," and other spellings he could imagine for his friend's name, and perhaps felt reassured by not finding the name linked to the words "Boston bomber." But now it was, on television, and now Azamat believed it. He smoked pot for what may have been the first time in his life. He woke up Robel, who was now panicking, too. Robel said he had changed his mind about staying the weekend at the Carriage Drive apartment—and that he urgently needed Azamat to drive him to campus to drop off his backpack. He was afraid the police would now come to search the Kazakh students' apartment and discover Robel was carrying marijuana.

Azamat and Robel came to UMass Dartmouth a little after nine in the morning, just as dozens of police vehicles were pulling up to campus, which was about to be evacuated. Robel still managed to drop his backpack in a friend's room. Back at Carriage Drive, he frantically texted another friend, asking to be picked up—and within half an hour, he left Azamat, Dias, and Bayan, none of whom had lived in the United States for more than two years, to wait for what seemed to him an inevitable encounter with law enforcement.

The FBI called in the early afternoon, through a friend—probably because the people at 69A Carriage Drive still had no regular telephone service on their "family plan" and the friend knew to text the Kazakhs first so they could Skype back. Azamat dictated the address, and the three teenagers started waiting for the FBI to come. Azamat Skyped his father, the most powerful man among all their parents.

"The FBI are coming here," said Azamat.

"Why?" asked Amir, his father.

"Because one of the Boston bombers was our friend."

"The Chechen?" Amir was beside himself. He had always thought Chechens were trouble—and he certainly did not send his son to the United States so he would make friends with one of them. "Did you have anything to do with the bombing?"

"No."

"All right, in that case we are not getting a lawyer—that will show that you have nothing to hide. Now show me the apartment."

Azamat lifted his MacBook to give his father a panoramic view of the place. It looked like a dungeon: they had drawn the blinds and were huddling like three scared kids as they waited.

"Open the blinds!" Amir barked. "You need to give the FBI a clear view inside the apartment so they won't shoot."

The kids did as they were told and sat down at the dining table to wait again. Azamat's family was now looking at them through the Skype window in the laptop perched on the table. After a couple of hours the wait grew tedious; it was now nearly five in the afternoon in New Bedford and four in the morning in Kazakhstan. Amir said he did not think the FBI was coming after all, and said good night to his son and his friends.

Just after he signed off, Azamat looked down at his chest and saw more than a dozen red spots—for the number of gun sights trained on him. The apartment was surrounded by several score law enforcement officers in SWAT gear. Since that morning, a large part of Greater Boston had been in virtual lockdown—residents had been asked to "shelter in place," meaning not to leave their homes—and police and FBI had been searching for Jahar house by house in Watertown. He seemed nowhere to be found, and that elevated the possibility that he was simply at his best buddies' apartment. The troops had come here prepared to fight him, or perhaps his allies.

The three Kazakh students were ordered out of the apartment, searched—the boys were directed to remove their shirts—and placed in police vehicles.

"This is the biggest thing since nine-eleven," Robel had said, ill-advisedly, to Azamat at some point on Friday morning. Massachusetts state authorities and media, the FBI, and the police apparently thought something similar—although, if one measured "big" in loss of life, bigger things, meaning bigger acts of sudden violence, had certainly happened, including the Virginia Tech shooting, which took thirty-three lives in 2007, and the 2012 Aurora, Colorado, shooting, in which twelve people died during a midnight show at a movie theater. Those, however, fell into the "angry white man" category of crimes, which FBI investigators believe they understand well. (In 2009 there was also the Fort Hood shooting, in which an Army major killed thirteen people on a military base, but because the shooter was a Muslim, the crime was seen as belonging to a different category—and a Senate report called it "the worst terrorist attack on U.S. soil since September 11, 2001.") The Boston Marathon bombing, it seemed immediately apparent to investigators, did not fall into the "angry white man" category, if only because the brothers were two, and not exactly white, by virtue of being Muslim. They therefore approached the crime as an attack in progress, as September 11 had been when that investigation first got under way. Following policy and practice established at least fifteen years before September 11, 2001, investigators focused on the suspects' networks among aliens, presuming these networks to be both extensive and dangerous—in other words, they pursued a lot of dead ends.

Early Friday morning, a neighbor called Larry Aaronson, screaming into the phone: "They are fucking us!" Aaronson thought he was aware of the facts contained in that statement, however one interpreted the syntax. "You don't think I'm following the news on Facebook?" he asked.

"You don't understand," the neighbor shouted. "They went to Rindge and Latin, they live next door, they are fucking *us*!"

Just then Norfolk Street was starting to fill up—with the FBI and the police, all in SWAT gear, and the media. Chris LaRoche's husband shook him awake after a friend had called saying, "Your street is on TV." Chris had seen the suspects' pictures the previous evening, but he had not recognized the brothers. Now, as he tried to wrap his not-yet-awake mind around the information, someone pounded on the door: "FBI!" The residents were hastily herded up the street and corralled in the garage where condo owners rented parking spaces. They stood there exchanging bits of information and answering questions from reporters who floated up from Norfolk Street every few minutes. Everyone had different impressions of the Tsarnaevs. Someone thought that Tamerlan looked like a good father. Chris had assumed the family had fled conflict in the Balkans, probably Kosovo. Rinat Harel, the art teacher, seemed to be the only one who thought the family was from Chechnya. She caught herself thinking that now, after all these years, she could start using the front entrance to her building again, and immediately felt ashamed. After about an hour, the residents were allowed to leave the garage, but not to return to Norfolk Street. A group went to Dunkin' Donuts, because it was open. Then Chris and his husband walked to a friend's house in Porter Square, a couple of miles away. It was eerie: a beautiful sunny morning, and the two of them the only people on the streets in all of Cambridge and Somerville.

ABOUT AN HOUR after law enforcement raided the Carriage Drive apartment, the shelter-in-place request was withdrawn and tens of thousands of people stepped out for the first time that day, tens of thousands of pairs of eyes scanning familiar landscapes for anything that seemed different. Very soon, a Watertown homeowner reported seeing blood on the side of a boat he had stored in the backyard and what he thought was a body inside the boat itself. Jahar was hiding in the covered boat; he might have been there the eighteen hours that the police had been searching for him. The house-by-house search of the neighborhood had missed this house, along with a number of others. Law enforcement once again assembled a SWAT team to take the prisoner. They tried to smoke him out with tear gas, scare him with gunfire, and coax him with words. Finally, an officer approached the boat and barked at Jahar to get down from it. The terrorist responded with a childish "But it's going to hurt": it was a seven-foot drop off the edge of the boat, which sat on a wheeled platform. The officers helped him down indelicately.

PART THREE

AFTERMATH

Nine

HOW MUSA KHADZHIMURATOV FELL OUT OF LOVE WITH AMERICA

This is a catastrophe," the woman told me. "It is a catastrophe for us Chechens."

She said she knew right away. In fact, she had always known. The woman had been eight years old when the first war in Chechnya began—she had grown up being a target. So when her own eight-year-old daughter here, in suburban Boston, asked if it was true that the bombers were Chechen, the woman said, "No!" and turned off the television: the word CHECHEN had been right there on the screen, beneath a picture of the younger brother. Turning off the television did not help any more than turning off bad news has ever helped anyone. The girl soon heard it at school and at the playground, and her best friend was not allowed to come over to play anymore.

The woman would not let me use her name, but she talked to me while she cooked—traditional rough Chechen bread in large square loaves, and cake: the family was expecting a visitor from Chechnya. They had been living in Boston for about seven years at the time of the bombing, and life had been pretty good. They came as refugees—a relatively privileged status that entitles new arrivals to seek both employment and public assistance—because the brother and father of the woman's husband had both been disappeared by the Russians. Her husband worked in construction, and she was staying home with their three children, two of them born in this country. They had a house in a middle-class neighborhood, next door to another Chechen family. They socialized primarily with other Chechens; this was a traditional house, where the woman would set the table for the men and stay out of the room while they ate and talked. She knew the wives, but since Tamerlan never brought his wife to their house, she knew nothing of the Tsarnaevs except that the older brother sometimes played soccer with her husband and the other men. She had never seen Dzhokhar—until she saw him on television on April 19, 2013.

Two days later, they came for her husband, just as she knew they would. It was the woman's mother-in-law who called Almut Rochowanski, the New York City lawyer who had started an organization for Chechen refugees: "The FBI has taken my son." Rochowanski arranged for a lawyer from the Massachusetts branch of the American Civil Liberties Union to step into the FBI's interviews as the man's representative, and the FBI soon seemed to lose interest in the man, but for his mother, Rochowanski told me, "It was just repeating what had happened to her other son and husband in Chechnya."

A short while later, Rochowanski and the ACLU put together a one-page Russian-language memo on how to act when the FBI comes to your door. Most important point: "You don't have to let them into your home." Other most important point: "You don't have to go with them." But, sighed Rochowanski, "most are too intimidated not to let them in."

. . .

ROCHOWANSKI HAD TRAINED as a lawyer in her native Austria, then continued her studies at Columbia and ended up spending many years working in and around the North Caucasus, which boasts some of the world's highest concentrations of uniforms per square kilometer, but she had never spent time dealing directly with law enforcement. "It's the first time I became intimate with this," she told me. Up close, it was not pretty. "You don't want to think that they take a kid in their early twenties and interrogate him for eight hours without giving him a drink of water. Which probably amounts to torture. But then you hear about it and you think, 'Right, this is how law enforcement works: it breaks people down.'"

Rochowanski is wrong, legally speaking: these coercive interrogation practices used by the FBI in the course of the War on Terror would probably not be considered torture if an international court were to review them. A possible exception, according to legal scholars Philip Heymann and Tom Lue, is the prolonged withholding of medical treatment, which has been a part of the interrogators' repertoire. In 2003, the United States Supreme Court took up the question of coercive interrogation practices in the case of *Chavez v. Martinez* but was unable to render a majority decision. Six separate opinions resulted. The question of whether it is constitutional for law enforcement to employ such techniques as sleep deprivation, the withholding of treatment, and hooding remained open.

After the attacks of September 11, 2001, the United States declared the War on Terror. "Terror, like fear, is an emotion, so declaring war on an emotion is hardly a strategy conducive to success," snapped terrorism scholar Louise Richardson in a 2006 book. President George W. Bush's 2002 National Security Strategy narrowed the focus of the so-called war, but only slightly: "The enemy is terrorism—premeditated, politically motivated violence perpetrated against civilians." Unlike terror, terrorism is not an emotion but rather a phenomenon, or even an instrument, but that does not make it any easier to fight. And as Heymann has pointed out, declaring war against an enemy who is not a state or a person or a group of people makes it impossible to determine when the war has been won—or lost, or otherwise ended.

President Barack Obama's National Security Strategy, published in 2010, retrospectively redefined the War on Terror as "a war on al-Qa'ida and its affiliates" and responded to Heymann's criticism: "This is not a global war against a tactic—terrorism [*sic*] or a religion—Islam. We are at war with a specific network, al-Qa'ida, and its terrorist affiliates who support efforts to attack the United States, our allies, and partners." This may have sounded more specific, but the basic political and legal problems of the war, by then nine years old, remained unresolved. What laws govern an American war against something that is not a state or even a circumscribed entity? And considering al-Qaida's loose structure, how are the generals and soldiers of this war to define the enemy? A lack of clarity persisted on the issue of the objective, or the end point, of the war: When would it be over? When there are no more attacks on U.S. soil? But for over ten years following September 11, there were no attacks that were attributed to al-Qaida. When there are no more attacks on Americans anywhere in the world? When there is no one left who is capable of launching such an attack? The War on Terror—or on terrorism, or on al-Qaida—remained a shapeless and an endless one.

It is in the nature of terrorism to engender an outsize response. "A little bit of terrorism goes a long way," writes Heymann.

> Even small-scale terrorism possesses an almost magical ability to produce fear, anxiety, anger, and a demand for vigorous action in a sizeable portion of a country's population. A handful of terrorists led Canadian Prime Minister Pierre Trudeau to declare a state of emergency in Quebec province [after the kidnapping of two government officials in October 1970]. Belgium responded powerfully to a similar concern flowing from an equally small group [following the 1981 bombing that killed three and injured 106 people outside a synagogue in Antwerp]. The Red Army Faction, which preoccupied Germany for more than two decades, rarely had more than a few active members. Even the Provisional IRA at its most active in Northern Ireland involved only hundreds, not thousands, of armed opponents of the British government.

And a nineteen-year-old kid escaping on foot compelled the governor of Massachusetts to put the state's largest city on virtual lockdown—what seemed like a reasonable safety measure at the time but was also one of the most extraordinary curtailments of liberty experienced by Americans in living memory.

Perhaps it is just too frightening for most people to believe that a small group—or just a pair—of ordinary people using means most of us could have at our disposal and following a plan that spanned barely an afternoon could inflict so much pain and suffering on so many. Behind such great fear, surely there must be an equally great threat.

Using the language of war when talking about terrorism enabled the Bush administration to draw on the practices of war as well. The legal waters were murky, particularly because much of what was being called war was taking place on U.S. soil, and the enemy was ill-defined. Immediately following the September 11 attacks, the president claimed the right to detain anyone, including United States citizens on American soil, indefinitely without charges. And since this was war, the president also wanted detainees who were not U.S. citizens—but who may have been longtime legal residents—tried by military tribunals, which would have extraordinary powers and whose proceedings would be closed to the public. Some of Bush's more far-reaching measures were rolled back over the following few years, but the practice of targeting noncitizens—"investigative profiling on the basis of immigration status," in Justice Department terminology—persisted. This happened in part because, unlike such extraordinary measures as the indefinite detention of citizens, the indefinite detention of noncitizens in practice required no change in the law. For the majority of the more than twelve hundred aliens detained in the wake of September 11, visa violations or other immigration-status irregularities could be found to justify detention. For the rest, a novel way of applying an existing statute was introduced: simply by being noncitizens they became, in the eyes of the law, witnesses who might not be available to testify unless detained. An untold number of people were deported after being detained. Testifying before the National Commission on Terrorist Attacks Upon the United States, in December 2003, Heymann pointed to this cycle—detention, closed hearing, deportation—as one of the greater threats to liberty contained in new antiterrorist policy and practice, calling it "what amounts to a claim of a right to make individuals disappear from American society on executive orders and without the public openness that is necessary for trust in the legitimacy of your government."

The practice of targeting aliens long predated Bush's counter-terrorism policies, however. In 1986, amid that era's fears of international terrorism, President Ronald Reagan issued a secret directive establishing the National Program for Combatting Terrorism, which in turn created the Alien Border Control Committee, charged specifically with finding ways to quietly deport suspected members of the Palestine Liberation Organization. The best-known case to have resulted from the ABCC's activities was that of the L.A. Eight, six student-visa holders and two long-time permanent residents who were arrested in 1987 and held in maximum-security cells without ever being charged with a crime. The L.A. Eight tried to sue, but the government turned itself into a moving target, continuously switching what was presented as grounds for detention and deportation: the arsenal of rules and regulations of what was then called the Immigration and Naturalization Service made that eminently possible.

Bush's counterterrorism reforms created the vastly powerful Department of Homeland Security, which subsumed the Immigration and Naturalization Service. Aliens remained the target. In the case of the Boston Marathon bombing, following established policy and practice to focus on noncitizen immigrants from Chechnya seemed the obvious thing to do. Never mind that the brothers themselves were not from Chechnya, that there was no indication—only the assumption—that they were part of a larger network, that Dzhokhar was a United States citizen, and that one of the last things Tamerlan is known to have said is, "I am a Muslim American."

IF CHECHEN IMMIGRANTS were the obvious focus for the FBI investigation, then Musa Khadzhimuratov was the obvious first suspect. He had been a fighter in the Chechen insurgency—indeed, he was chief bodyguard to one of its leaders in the 1990s. He owned firearms. He lived in New Hampshire, where Tamerlan had apparently purchased the fireworks used in making the bombs and where he had gone to a shooting range. Tamerlan had visited Musa at his house less than three weeks before the bombing. From Musa's point of view, he was just as obviously beyond suspicion: he came from an earlier, secular generation of Chechen resisters, as foreign to the proponents of an Islamic state as the Russians themselves; owning guns is the norm for a Chechen man, and since New Hampshire places no restrictions on the purchase or possession of firearms, it should not, Musa figured, make him subject to scrutiny; and most to the point, he was so obviously and profoundly disabled. Though after several years in the United States he could drive a car and lift himself in and out of it, he needed help stowing his wheelchair in the trunk and removing it. More generally, in order simply to live he needed the around-the-clock care of his wife, who helped deal with everything from his persistent petit mal seizures to his procedure for emptying his bowels.

Just a bit less obviously but even more crucially, the Khadzhimuratovs were deeply aware of the precariousness of their good life. They had everything—the credenza, the chandelier, the crystal glasses from which they had never removed the tiny oval paper stickers, the used car—but all of it had been bought on credit, all of it paid off by scrimping enabled by a most powerful desire to build a normal life in peace. They now had friends here, and their kids had friends, and the kids were using Americanized names at their American school—fourteen-year-old Ibragim was calling himself Abraham—but they themselves had been teenagers when the first war in Chechnya began, and they knew how life could change drastically and irrevocably. When they came to the United

States, they made the unspoken new-immigrant pledge: though nothing in their lived experience had taught them to put their trust in a state, or in the future, they did—they chose to believe that the United States would shelter them and care for them. The country met them partway. They came bearing refugee "white cards," entitling them to public assistance, but after a couple of years only Madina and the two kids got their permanent-resident green cards; Musa was rejected for having been part of the insurgency, which, in the post-9/11 era of Russian–American cooperation, made him an accessory to a terrorist organization in the eyes of not only the Russian but also the U.S. government. Musa could continue to live in the United States as a refugee, but unlike the rest of his family, he would never be entitled to apply for citizenship and his status would remain forever temporary, subject to being revoked by the authorities. More important to his everyday life, as a noncitizen he would be entitled to medical help from the state for a maximum of seven years—and that time had just run out when the bombs went off at the Boston Marathon.

They came for Musa. Two FBI agents questioned him in his apartment. "They wanted to know why I didn't go to the authorities to say that I know him. I said, 'I was waiting for you to come to me.' I guess that response kind of got to them." It probably did. It was a dumb thing to say, too, because it was not exactly true. Like some other immigrants who came to the United States in the Internet era, the Khadzhimuratovs left Chechnya without leaving it: they were constantly, for hours on end, on Skype with Madina's older sister in Grozny, and while they followed the news, they got it by way of the Caucasus, reading the websites that covered their native region. The Caucasus was not interested in the Boston Marathon bombing—the Caucasus was not exactly impressed by a bomb that killed three people, well below the weekly average for that region—until the suspects were identified as Chechens. By that time, the names of the Tsarnaev brothers were known and Tamerlan was dead. There was nothing to do but wait for the FBI to come with its questions.

When the FBI came again, the agents took Musa to a local office for questioning. It was a typical FBI interrogation room: windowless, lit with a flickering fluorescent light. And it was a typical FBI questioning session—no audio or video equipment was used. The FBI records its interrogations only if the subject is in the Bureau's custody, but Musa, like most of the Chechens, submitted to the questioning voluntarily and without engaging a lawyer, not only because he knew himself to be innocent but also because he thought that this way his innocence would be all the more obvious.

"It turned out they thought I was the mastermind," he discovered. "Because I keep guns at home. And also because I'm into sports and so I would have chosen the Boston Marathon as a target. I said, 'If I'd had anything to do with it, do you really think I would have gone out and bought guns under my own name, or let him come for shooting practice right here, under my nose?'"

Several hours into the interrogation session—by this time Musa had been without food, water, or medication for eight hours, so he was beginning to slip in and out of consciousness—he was hooked up to a polygraph machine.

"Let's see how you are going to lie now," he remembered one of the agents saying.

"Look at the wall!" he remembered one of the agents shouting. Musa was having difficulty holding his head up and his eyes open. "Lift up your head and look at the wall when we ask you questions!"

"Did you help the Tsarnaev brothers plan the bombing?" he remembered one of the agents asking.

"I freaked out," he told me a couple of weeks later. "I tore the wires off me and said, 'You can't treat me like a criminal. This is the last time I set foot in this building. You can arrest me if you want, you can never give me a green card if you want, but I'm going home now.'"

"You can't," he remembered an agent saying. "Your apartment is being searched right now." He also remembered being told that his refugee status would be revoked and he would be deported. At this point, Musa felt that he no longer cared: he wheeled himself out of the FBI office.

MUSA, like other Boston-area Chechens, and like Almut Rochowanski, who was trying to help them, was just beginning to discover how, exactly, law enforcement casts a wide net in the age of the War on Terror. "This is what they [the FBI] do," Rochowanski told me. "The policy priority is to get as many of them [aliens] out of the country as possible. You would think you'd want to keep them where you could watch them, but I don't know, I'm not a policy expert for Homeland Security."

Indeed, for nearly thirty years the main threat American law enforcement has used against aliens suspected of supporting terrorism has been deportation. It has remained the weapon of choice even in the dozen years since the September 11 attacks showed clearly that a terrorist attack on the United States could be planned and directed from overseas. From a policy or strategic standpoint, deporting suspected terrorist supporters to countries that are themselves suspected of supporting terrorism makes no sense. But it suits the bigger imagination of the War on Terror, in which terrorists are larger than life and have America under siege.

Ten

THE STRANGE DEATH OF IBRAGIM TODASHEV

On May 1, 2013, twenty-four-year-old Reni Manukyan landed at JFK Airport in New York. She had been traveling for a while: a two-hour flight to Moscow from a southern Russian city where she had been visiting cousins, then the ten-hour flight to New York, and now she had to recheck her luggage for the final leg to Atlanta. But before she could get her bags, the Homeland Security officer at passport control instructed her to follow another officer to a room off the giant baggage hall. The room is large and windowless, and at any given time three or four officers are seated behind metal desks there, talking to passengers who have just arrived from some foreign country, while other similarly inconvenienced passengers wait their turn in stiff plastic chairs. The space is eerily bright and still; the optimistic din of the arrivals hall disappears the moment an officer shuts the heavy door. The use of any electronic devices is forbidden. People spend their time waiting with nothing to distract them from the dread of not being allowed to enter the country.

A few minutes after Reni was led in, the door closed behind a woman wearing a hijab, and Reni knew why she was here: "What, are you taking all the Muslims off their flights?" she snapped at the officers. Reni herself was wearing a tracksuit and a simple black-and-white-patterned scarf on her head—she liked to be comfortable when she traveled—but in her passport picture, taken soon after she converted to Islam in the summer of 2010, she was fully covered. That must have been what drew the officer's attention, because nothing else about Reni could arouse suspicion. She was born in Russia but had lived in the United States since she was a teenager; her mother was serving in the U.S. Army; Reni herself had a good steady job as an assistant housekeeper at a big chain hotel in Atlanta; and she traveled back to Russia to visit relatives with some regularity.

It was not too long before one of the officers motioned Reni over to his desk and started asking questions. He wanted to know where she had been. Reni had gone to Russia for a cousin's wedding—she had left Atlanta on April 16. Over the course of the next twenty minutes, the officer asked a great many detailed questions about her mundane and limited travels in Russia during the previous two weeks. Then he asked her if she knew Tamerlan Tsarnaev. Reni said she did not. The officer insisted that she knew him, and she equally adamantly insisted that she did not.

"Who is Ibragim Todashev?" the officer asked then.

"Why? Did he do something?" Reni asked back.

"What do you mean?" the officer asked. "What could he have done? Why did you ask that? What do you think he would have done?"

Reni had asked the question because she was not taking any of this very seriously. It was not until later that she realized that "you should never joke with them." Ibragim Todashev was her husband. They had married in July 2010, after knowing each other for a couple of months—this was why Reni had converted to Islam. Ibragim had moved from Boston to Atlanta to live with her, but after a bit less than a year she grew tired of supporting him while he did nothing but the "brainless sports" in which he competed, namely mixed martial arts. They moved to Orlando together, thinking that the Chechen community there would make it easier for him to find a job, but there they split up and Reni moved back to Atlanta, although subsequently they had made up and split up and maybe made up again, eventually settling into a comfortable pattern of talking on the phone every day and spending every other weekend or so together.

So what bad things could Ibragim have done? He could have cheated on Reni. He could have gotten into a fight—that had happened a few times, and once, a couple of months before they met, he had been arrested in downtown Boston for attacking a driver who he thought had hurled an insult that mentioned Ibragim's mother. Reni was not all that surprised by these fights: as she saw it, Americans and Russians—especially Russians from Chechnya, where Ibragim was born—just drew the line between acceptable and unacceptable behavior in different places. Chechens saw an insult as no less a transgression than a blow, and as far as a Chechen was concerned, an American who shouted an obscenity was spoiling for a fight. Sometimes Reni thought Ibragim might have been better off staying home and mooching off her than roaming the streets and getting into fights with Americans, who were liable to call the police, who in turn were liable to think a loose cannon like Ibragim—a professional martial artist to boot—should be kept under lock and key. Reni, who was not Chechen and who had spent the last two weeks with relatives in Russia, had no idea of the hold the very idea of a Chechen martial artist had taken on the American imagination in that time.

Reni spent five hours in that room, answering questions that made little sense to her. Her plane had left by the time she came out. She dialed Ibragim, who explained that Tamerlan Tsarnaev was his friend Tamerlan from Boston. Reni had never met him, but Ibragim had mentioned him and she had talked to him once or twice when she answered Ibragim's phone.

"Tell them what you know," Ibragim instructed her. "Don't try to hide anything. I'll tell you more when I see you."

The next morning two FBI agents were waiting for Reni when she came to work. They had another circular conversation. A week later, Ibragim came to visit: he drove up on Thursday and back the following day. He told Reni that all the Chechens in Boston and Orlando were getting dragged in for questioning. The day he left, the FBI agents came again. This time Reni decided she had something to say about Tamerlan.

"If you ask me, I'm going to tell you, I don't think he did it." She really was starting to think that maybe, like some of the American Chechens were saying, the Tsarnaev brothers had been set up. People were starting to point out some inconsistencies in the FBI's story—but even more, the ongoing siege of the Chechen community made it feel like they were the ones under attack.

After Reni said she did not think Tamerlan did it, all hell broke loose. "That's when it started with the curse words," she told me. "He says, 'So you fucking think it's right to kill people?' And I say, 'Don't put words in my mouth.'"

Reni was starting to get scared of the FBI. They could do anything—they could even get Ibragim deported. He had booked a ticket to travel to Chechnya on May 24: he had just gotten his green card, and this would be the first time he would visit his parents and eleven younger siblings. Now Reni was begging him to cancel the trip because she was afraid he would not be allowed to return. She spent all day May 21 calling and texting him, trying to get him to cancel. Ibragim relented, and Reni, who had booked the ticket for him herself, logged onto Expedia.com to return it. By the time Reni texted Ibragim to tell him she had canceled the ticket, it was around six-thirty in the evening—the end of Reni's shift at the Hilton, one of her two hotel jobs.

She rode her motorcycle home. She felt her phone vibrating like crazy as she rode, but she did not look at it until she got home: it was her younger brother Alex, whom she had helped get a job at the Hilton, calling to say that the two FBI agents had shown up there again. She had Alex pass the phone to one of the agents, and then she told them to come to her apartment. They came at seven-thirty. While Reni was waiting for them to arrive, she called and texted Ibragim, finally writing in Chechen: "Why aren't you answering me?" When they first got married, Ibragim had said he would want their children to speak Chechen, so Reni, who found languages easy, learned this one. Whatever was going on now, it seemed like a good time to switch to a language few other people would be able to understand.

The two FBI agents left a bit after nine, after another circular and unpleasant conversation; as usual, one of them had asked most of the questions while the other took notes. Reni looked at her phone: still no response from Ibragim. She went to bed. When she woke at five and her phone's screen was still blank, she grew worried. She dialed his number. *I'm going to wake him up,* she thought. *He is going to scream at me.* There was no answer.

ELENA TEYER THOUGHT it was only slightly odd when her daughter converted to Islam. That is, covering herself was a strange choice for a beautiful young woman with long thin legs. Riding her motorcycle in that getup could not have been comfortable, either. Other than the dress, converting seemed to have been easy. Reni explained to her mother that the basic "Thou shalt not kill" and "Thou shalt not steal" from the Bible—roughly the sum total of her familiarity with the Christianity into which she was born—underlay both religions. It had also seemed logical: Reni had been in search of an identity ever since they moved to the United States, and if she had now found one through the love of a good man, so much the better.

Elena's own story contained perhaps too little love, too few good men, and too much change. She was one of those Russian women who rely on no one but themselves. The Soviet Union collapsed while she was still in college, making her one of the millions who had to make their way without their parents' help or guidance. Elena became a restaurant manager. She did well, raising two kids on her own. In the early aughts she moved from southern Russia to Moscow to help open and run a hotel restaurant there. In 2004, she started corresponding with an American man, who soon came to visit and then soon came to visit again, and within two years thirty-five-year-old Elena and her children moved to Atlanta to live with him. The marriage lasted less than six months before Elena moved out with her kids. She wanted to go back to Russia, but three tickets would have cost nearly three thousand dollars and she could not imagine getting that kind of money. A local Orthodox church helped her rent a tiny basement apartment. Elena started working—first as an on-call waitress for a catering business, then she worked her way up to maître d' at a fancy hotel restaurant. Two years after arriving in the United States, she was making enough to pay rent on a good apartment and cover expenses, but she had no health insurance. Plus, her permanent-resident status, for which she had qualified as the wife of an American citizen, could be revoked now that she was no longer married, which would make it illegal for her and the kids to stay in the country. Elena was no stranger to hardship, but the uncertainty was starting to feel like too great a burden.

Someone mentioned that the U.S. Army was hiring. After fighting two wars for years, the military was perpetually short on personnel. She failed the test administered at the recruitment office: her English was not up to par. But the recruitment officer gave useful advice on how to study for the test and—even better—told her that an English-language course for prospective recruits would be opening up soon.

Elena left the kids in Atlanta and went to a base in Texas for the course. It was like English-as-a-second-language basic training. The students had to rise at four in the morning, dress in uniforms, and stand in formation in the quad—before spending the day studying English. Elena discovered that she loved it. It might have had something to do with having grown up a military brat, but that was not the crux of it. This was difficult—giving up your personal freedom at the age of thirty-eight is hard, as is getting up at four every day—but things had been difficult her whole life. What they had not been was fair. The Army offered a clear, transparent, and fair deal: Elena gave over her mind and body in exchange for training, job security, medical insurance, and American citizenship for her and her kids. Both partners paid up front. Then she would be set: there would be retirement benefits, too. Honesty and openness are inherently seductive qualities, especially for people who have rarely encountered them. Elena became a patriot of the United States.

She completed the English course, then eight weeks of basic training, followed by vocational training—she had decided she wanted to work at an on-base drugstore—in San Antonio. She served in Fort Jackson, South Carolina, for two and a half years, and then was transferred to Germany. When she went overseas, only her son, Alex, went with her. Her daughter was twenty by then, too old to be dragged around by her mother. Elena wished she had commenced the dragging around a bit earlier, in fact: Alex, who was eleven when they came to America, was doing very well. He was growing up American, while his sister, Nyusha (in her case a diminutive for Evgenia), seemed to be struggling to figure out who she was. While Elena was away for her initial military training, Nyusha went and legally changed her name to Reniya Manukyan, taking the last name of a family friend of Armenian descent who she believed was her biological father, despite Elena's denials. Reni stopped considering herself Russian, began referring to herself as Armenian, and even taught herself the language. She had the ability and perseverance for these kinds of feats.

Although Elena continued to call her daughter Nyusha, she got it: the girl was looking for somebody to be. The conversion to Islam was the product of the same need and actually made a bit more sense to Elena because it was not an abstraction—her daughter was in love with Ibragim. Nyusha took things a bit far when she tried reprimanding her mother for her insufficiently modest dress; Elena was not one to be told what to wear, except when she was at work in the Army. But Elena liked Ibragim. He was gentle, and he had been through a lot: fleeing the war in Chechnya with his family as a child, growing up in Saratov, a Russian city on the Volga, an ethnic Other, returning to Chechnya when it was still in shambles. Ibragim had gone back to Saratov to attend college—he had studied to be a translator from English—and had come to the United States on a work-study program before what would have been his last year of college. He had stayed, getting political asylum. His family back in Chechnya was doing well—his father had a high-level job with the new administration—but most of the prospering had come after Ibragim left. Elena saw him as a boy alone in a strange country, and she had a pretty good idea of what that felt like. She was happy to accept him fully into her family, as long as he finally got a job and stopped relying on her daughter, who worked two.

Elena herself felt like she was finally settling into a good life. After two years in Germany she requested a transfer to Georgia: she had spent only a few years in Atlanta, but she felt like the city was home, both because Nyusha was there and because it was where Elena first landed as a Russian mail-order bride. She and seventeen-year-old Alex returned to Georgia in March 2013. She was now based at Fort Stewart, 230 miles southeast of Atlanta, and Elena immediately set about house-hunting in Savannah, the beautiful historic town about forty minutes away, toward the coast. A month later, she was closing on her first house. The date was April 15.

ELENA DID NOT BEGIN to grasp the impact of the Boston bombing until two weeks later, when her daughter was detained at the airport on the way home. Reni-Nyusha told her mother that Ibragim had been called in for questioning and said that the FBI was following him everywhere he went. On May 10, during a visit to Reni, Ibragim came down to see Elena in Savannah. Reni had asked him to run some things of hers from Atlanta to her mother's house. Ibragim struck Elena as depressed. She was also surprised to see he was still limping, ostensibly a consequence of a knee operation back in March. It might in fact have been the result of a fight he had had in an Orlando parking lot a few days earlier.

Around seven-thirty in the evening on May 21 someone knocked on Elena's door. It was two FBI agents. "What's our fools' psychology?" she ranted to me a year later. "If we haven't done anything wrong, we fear nothing. I even kept telling them they were doing good for the country." Obviously, she let them into her house.

"They spent two hours asking me the same questions over and over again: Did they sleep together? Did they sleep on the couch together when they spent the night at my place? How religious was he? Did he abuse her? I told them that if anyone had so much as touched my baby in a bad way, I would have killed them. That's exactly what I said." That is easy to believe. Elena is a large, shapely woman with long blond hair—the very image of an all-powerful Russian matriarch, as well as of the ideal Russian mail-order bride, and the very opposite of her own daughter, who is slight, dark-haired, and soft-spoken.

After a couple of hours of circular questioning, Elena asked the agents to leave. She called her daughter.

"I just had a visit from them," said Elena.

"So did I."

Elena tried calling Ibragim, but he did not pick up.

AFTER TRYING IBRAGIM unsuccessfully at five in the morning, Reni got ready for work and jumped on her motorcycle. As she left her apartment complex, she noticed a car. Everything about the car was conspicuous: the way it was parked, across two spaces, the man at the wheel, who was white—an unusual sight in this neighborhood—and the fact that he was sitting at the wheel of a parked car in the wee hours of the morning. Ibragim had mentioned being followed by the FBI, but Reni did not yet realize that overt, menacing surveillance is a typical FBI tactic that was being applied to several of Tamerlan's friends. She did know that the man at the wheel had to be an agent. She raised the face shield of her motorcycle helmet and gave the guy a stare she hoped conveyed the depth of her disdain for him, and rode away. The car followed her, but she lost it easily and rode to the Holiday Inn, where she was working the morning shift. The FBI car, as it turned out, went to the Hilton, where she was supposed to work that afternoon and evening.

At seven o'clock Reni's phone rang; it was a former supervisor with whom Reni had stayed friends. He was also a biker, and he, his wife, and Reni often took weekend riding trips together.

"What's your husband's last name?" he asked. "It says in the paper that a guy named Ibragim has been killed in Orlando."

The thing about working at a hotel is that there is always a newspaper at hand early in the morning. Reni grabbed a copy of *USA Today* off the top of a stack and found the headline. The FBI agent called from the Hilton just then; she told him where she was, and he said he was coming. It took him forty minutes to get there. Meanwhile, Reni kept dialing her mother.

Elena had a training session that morning. She could not pick up when her daughter called or when an unknown number began showing up on her phone every few minutes. She finally picked up when the training ended, around seven-thirty in the morning.

"Hello. We were at your house last night."

This was when she lost her cool. "You are going to start calling me at work now? I told you everything yesterday. I have nothing else to say to you."

"We have something to tell you. Ibragim Todashev died of gunshot wounds this morning."

Elena hung up and called her daughter. Reni was screaming into the phone: "Mama, they've killed him!"

"Then I knew that they weren't kidding," Elena told me. She rushed to do the paperwork for an emergency leave; her commanding officer was understanding, but bolting from work at an Army base still requires a lengthy bureaucratic procedure. Meanwhile, the two FBI agents from the evening before came.

"You don't have to worry about your children," said the one who usually did the talking. "Your family is safe."

"Why? Why?" Elena remembers screaming, meaning, *Why was Ibragim killed?*

"He became aggressive," the agent told her.

"What are you telling me that my children are safe for when you just killed one of them? Look at me—I'm being aggressive now, too. Are you going to kill me?"

What Elena remembers the FBI agent doing next is this: "He placed his foot up on the chair right next to where I was sitting, and he hiked his pant leg up. He had a gun strapped to his shin. He said, 'If you touch my gun now, my partner can kill you. He has that right.' The gun was just about level with my face. It's a good thing I didn't reach for it then. Or I wouldn't be talking to you today."

WHAT EXACTLY Ibragim Todashev did to get himself killed was not clear then and is not clear now. By the day of his death, he had been what the FBI called "interviewed" three times. The first time, on April 20, began with Ibragim on the ground on the condo complex's bucolic lawn, with armed men crowded around him: this was the manner in which the FBI first ID'd him, though he was never arrested and all his conversations with the FBI were, technically, voluntary. From that point on he was under constant overt surveillance. In addition, the FBI took all of his electronics—but returned them a day later. At least at some points, the FBI appears to have had a drone follow him. And on May 16, his girlfriend, Tatiana Gruzdeva, was arrested.

The other women in Ibragim's life seem to have had varying levels of awareness of Tatiana's existence: Elena thought Tatiana was Ibragim's roommate, and Reni thought she was the girlfriend of Ibragim's best friend, Khusein Taramov. In any case, Tatiana was arrested for alleged visa violations, leaving Ibragim living in the apartment alone.

On May 21, Ibragim got a call from the FBI agent he had seen a few times over the preceding month. He said that a group of agents from Boston had come to Orlando and wanted to talk to Ibragim—and that this would be the last interview. Ibragim still did not want to make the trek downtown to the FBI offices, so the agents agreed to come to him. He wanted to meet at a hookah bar; they eventually settled on talking in his apartment. Ibragim was apparently scared of the FBI at this point: he asked Khusein, who was also from Chechnya, to come to his place and stay there during the interview.

The team from Boston consisted of one FBI agent and two state troopers. A Justice Department report later described them as a homicide team. They were in Orlando to investigate the triple murder in Waltham in September 2011, the one in which Tamerlan's best friend, Brendan Mess, and another Rindge and Latin graduate were killed. Khusein was not allowed to be in the apartment; a Florida FBI agent kept him in the parking lot, talking. Ibragim lived in one of those Orlando planned communities that look like they have been airlifted from a place that never existed. The condos are small vertical affairs, but each has its own entrance and two levels. The facades are a combination of cheap texture paint and equally cheap siding, but the backs feature double-height windows and sliding doors that open onto a lake with bridges and a fountain. Khusein and the Florida FBI agent stayed in the working-class front; Ibragim spent his last hours sitting by the sliding door, looking out onto the aspirational back. At seven-thirty in the evening, the homicide team from Massachusetts began questioning Ibragim, just as the FBI agents in Atlanta and Savannah began questioning Reni and Elena. After the interviews in Georgia ended, the one in Florida went on—and on.

According to the report, around ten-thirty Ibragim slowly began confessing to having been Tamerlan's accomplice in the triple murder. In another hour, he agreed to write a statement about it. Around midnight, one of the state troopers went out to the parking lot to get Ibragim's phone from Khusein. While he was out of the building, something happened. Early reports had the remaining two officers saying, variously, that Ibragim had grabbed a broomstick and charged the officers with it, and that he had run to the kitchen area to grab a knife. The final official report said that Ibragim jumped up from the mattress on which he had been sitting composing his confession, threw a coffee table up in the air, knocked the FBI agent out of his chair, ran into the kitchen area, grabbed a metal utility pole, raised it over his head with both hands, and charged the trooper, who raised his hands to his face to protect it. The FBI agent fired seven shots at Ibragim, killing him.

IT WAS *THE BOSTON GLOBE* that first reported that law enforcement seemed to be investigating Tamerlan's possible connection to the September 2011 triple murder. The newspaper's source was a relative of one of the victims, who had been questioned by police following a months-long lull during which the investigation seemed to have gone dormant.

In the spring of 2011, after nearly a year of marriage, Reni had demanded that Ibragim find a way to make money. He went to Boston that summer and worked as a van driver for an adult-care center. According to the law enforcement narrative that eventually emerged, he left the city immediately after the killings.

Reni told me Ibragim had actually left Boston earlier and was not there on September 11, the day the three men were murdered. She said she could see that from the records of their joint checking account: the charges Ibragim was making using his debit card showed he was elsewhere. Reni has the kind of memory and attention to detail that make her quite certain of things like this. But the bank, she said, had already deleted records for 2011 by the time she tried to get proof of Ibragim's alibi.

Nearly a year after Ibragim's death, the confession he did not finish writing would be leaked to the media. Written in slanted Russian-style cursive on a pad of white ruled paper, it said:

> My name is IBRAGIM TODASHEV. I wanna tell the story about the robbery me and Tam did in Waltham in September of 2011. That was [illegible] by Tamerlan [illegible] went he [illegible] to me to rob the dealers. We went to their house we got in there and Tam had a gun he pointed it [illegible] the guy that opened the door for us [illegible] we went upstairs into the house [illegible] 3 guys in there [illegible] we put them on the ground and then we [crossed out] taped their hands up

This short description contains four details that are inconsistent with what little is known about the murders. First, it was clearly not a robbery: five thousand dollars in cash and even more in marijuana had been left behind. Second, if Tamerlan had a gun, why did he not use it to kill the men instead of slashing their throats? Third, two of the bodies had signs of struggle, while this confession seems to describe them as lying down on the floor and allowing themselves to be immobilized without resisting. Finally, the men were not found with their hands taped up—nor were they found all together: the bodies were laid out in separate rooms and their blood had pooled there, suggesting that those were the rooms in which they were killed.

There may be explanations for all of these discrepancies. Tamerlan may have, for example, initially told Ibragim that the crime he was planning was a robbery. Indeed, he may have done this in order to persuade Ibragim to help. It is conceivable that Tamerlan had a gun he could not or did not want to fire, for reasons either technical or conceptual. The struggles may have occurred when the men were being taken to different rooms. And the killers may have removed the tape after the victims were dead. Alternatively, the confession may have been written, or dictated, or both, by someone who lacked specific information about the murders.

Two things are certain. One, Reni is quite sure that the handwriting is Ibragim's: the document is genuine. And two, Ibragim is dead and so is Tamerlan, which means it is virtually impossible that the facts of the Waltham murders will ever be fully known.

WHEN SHE WAS at last able to leave the base, Elena had to drive to Savannah to change into civilian clothing. Then she drove the two hundred fifty miles to Atlanta, straight to the Holiday Inn. Reni was in one of the hotel rooms with the FBI agents and her manager; she was afraid to be alone with the agents. "I kept saying to them, 'Show me what you say he wrote with his own hand,'" Reni told me. "They kept saying, 'We don't have anything here.'"

That afternoon Elena drove her daughter the four hundred–plus miles down to Orlando. Reni's phone kept ringing, and she kept trying to tell people what she knew but finding herself unable to speak. She'd cried and screamed so much that morning that she still had not regained her voice. She phoned Ibragim's mother, whom she called Mama. "Mama, they have killed him."

In Orlando, they met up with Khusein, who told them what he knew. They drove to the medical examiner's office. "When I asked them how many bullets," Reni told me, "I sure didn't expect to hear that kind of number. I fell facedown on a table and I wailed. I said, 'I want to see the body.'—'Are you sure?'—'I'm sure.' They wheeled him in on a gurney, he had a sheet covering him up to his neck. They had us standing on the side where you couldn't really see the wounds. His eyes were still open, and they were this murky gray color. His upper jaw looked clenched but the mouth was slightly open. And I started saying, 'Mama, why isn't he getting up? When has this ever happened that we are all standing around him and he is not getting up?' It was like I knew everything but I couldn't believe anything."

Then began a month of paperwork. Reni did not cry anymore. She had to take her husband's body home to Chechnya, and the process required so many steps, each of which required so many documents that she really did not have to think of anything but getting the right letters and certificates to the right people. The original death certificate indicated that Ibragim was to be buried in the USSR, a country that had been defunct for twenty-two years. The certificate had to be reissued. The new version had Ibragim's mother's maiden name where Reni's last name should have been; it had to be reissued again, and Reni began to suspect that all of this was being done on purpose. Delta Airlines, which operated the only direct flight from Miami to Moscow, refused to take the body on board. Reni was terrified of flying with a layover because she was convinced something would go wrong. She called a Delta supervisor to beg and argue. The explanation she was given, she told me, had to do with Ibragim's alleged association with Tamerlan. Eventually, the Russian carrier Aeroflot agreed to fly the casket. Ibragim's father, Abdulbaki, came to Orlando to fly back with Reni and the body. At boarding, Reni was taken aside and subjected to a complete body search.

It was just before takeoff that it all hit Reni: "He and I had talked about going home together one day. And here we were, he and I, flying home. Except I'm in the passenger cabin and he is in baggage. I'd been working all month to bring this about, but it's like it wasn't seeping in. I hadn't slept all month. And now it all came, the tears and everything."

THEY CHANGED PLANES in Moscow and flew another couple of hours to Grozny. A group of men met them at the airport. Jamal Tsarnaev was among them: it seemed appropriate for the Tsarnaev family to be present, but it had not been clear if the Todashevs would want Anzor there.

The plane was late—it was almost four in the afternoon when they landed. It was the time of year when days are longest, but the men still thought they should hurry in order to bury Ibragim before sundown, in accordance with Muslim tradition. Tradition actually requires that people be buried by sundown on the day of death, and this was June 20, nearly one month later. With the coffin in a boxy Russian-made van, the men drove in a caravan to the Todashevs' house to drop off Reni; women do not attend Muslim burials. Ibragim's mother ran out of the house barefoot and rapped on the van door. One of the men let her in and she threw herself on the coffin, trying to grasp it in an embrace.

"Let me see him!" she wailed.

The men had discussed this earlier and decided that the coffin should stay shut to avoid traumatizing any of the women. The gunshot wound on Ibragim's head had been stitched up, but they worried about the condition of the body after nearly twenty-four hours in transit.

"Then I want to be buried with him!" screamed his mother.

The men would open the casket later, at the cemetery, out of sight of the women—and later they would report that Ibragim looked fine, and even the smell of the embalming solution struck them as pleasant.

I MET RENI in July 2014. She was living in a village about three hours outside the city of Volgograd (once called Stalingrad), in the desolate Russian countryside, the land of hopelessness and depopulated villages. In Volgograd itself, there was a lot of new construction: the city was slated to host the European soccer cup in another four years, and stadiums and hotels were going up. I stayed at a brand-new Hampton by Hilton. Reni walked into my hotel room and scanned it with a professional's skeptical eye: "I see. An electrical teakettle in place of a coffeemaker. The pad and pen are missing. Otherwise, not bad."

She was out of the hotel business, though, and out of the United States. After the funeral, she did not return. "I'm never setting foot in America again," she told me. "Everyone is getting either deported or killed. I'm sure I have a mark next to my name and if I went back I wouldn't be able to find a job." Nor, she said, did she want to live in America. The realization must have come to Reni when she was already in Russia, because she asked me to take a few things back to the States for her, including a key to the car her brother was now driving in Atlanta. A friend, the bike-loving former supervisor who had called her with the news of Ibragim's death, had sold her motorcycle for her. Khusein, who had a green card, had not been allowed to return to the United States after a visit to Chechnya, and Tatiana had been deported. Reni waited out her year of mourning and remarried; her new husband's name was Ibragim, and he was Chechen. She now lived with his family in the Russian village and spent her days helping with the difficult day-to-day of a farm, looking after cattle and milking. She stayed in touch with Zubeidat Tsarnaeva, who gave her updates after each of Dzhokhar's weekly Wednesday phone calls: he generally reported he was doing well. "I don't want to tell her this, but I don't believe they're going to let him live," Reni said to me. Like Zubeidat, she was sure of the Tsarnaev brothers' innocence—they were "set up," both women kept saying. "At least I know Tamerlan is in heaven," she said, meaning he had been innocent and he had been murdered, just as Ibragim had been.

A lawyer with an organization called the Council on American-Islamic Relations, with offices in Orlando, was, more than a year after Ibragim's death, still working on a report and a possible lawsuit to be filed on the family's behalf. In Russia, the Todashev family had also engaged a young Chechen Moscow-educated lawyer named Zuarbek Sadokhanov. I met with him in Grozny the day after the funeral; he was simultaneously jazzed and heartbroken at the prospect of going up against the FBI and the U.S. government itself. "When the state acts unlawfully, this destroys democracy," he told me earnestly over espressos in a café in a city that had long been the capital of lawlessness in a profoundly lawless country. But this was precisely Zuarbek's point: "I'm sad. I feel like I'm watching the last perfect justice system in the world destroy itself."

ON MARCH 25, 2014—ten months after Ibragim Todashev's death—the Justice Department's Civil Rights Division and a Florida state attorney, Jeffrey Ashton, released separate reports, both of which concluded that the FBI agent who shot Ibragim had acted in self-defense and in defense of the state trooper, and that his actions had been justified.

The 161-page Florida report included detailed interviews with the FBI agents and the Massachusetts policemen as well as neighbors who had noticed something going on in Todashev's apartment during the wee hours of the interview. The image of Ibragim that emerges from the report is radically different from the image of the gentle, innocent man painted by Elena: in the document he is frightening. More to the point, the officers were frightened of him. Before traveling to Florida they had viewed five videos of Ibragim's fights, studied the physical traces the fights had left on his body—his broken nose and the "cauliflower ears" deformed from being repeatedly boxed. The fights they watched are indeed scary: filmed in poor lighting, from below, they show lithe, extremely muscular men attacking each other in a cagelike ring. The men wear shorts, boxing gloves, and nothing else, and what they do to each other looks as fierce as a street brawl, and as regulated as one. In one of the videos, Ibragim is knocked to the ground at the very beginning, then pounded by his opponent, but around minute three gets up as though possessed of some superhuman power—and the fight goes on for a couple of minutes more, until he loses.

The officers also viewed a video of the May 4 fight in the Orlando parking lot that had led to Ibragim's arrest, his second. Ibragim had already been under surveillance for two weeks. The Florida FBI agents filmed him beating up two men until the police arrived. Ibragim, for his part, knew he was being watched, if not filmed. The agents who showed their Massachusetts colleagues the video also explained that they had interviewed people at the gym where Ibragim trained and had been told that "they thought he might be retarded, ah, because of the level of force and, ah, injuries that he was taking and he wouldn't submit."

The officers were scared going in, but the interview went better than they could have expected. The report included text messages sent and received by one of the state troopers.

"He signed Miranda. About to tell is [sic] his involvement," he wrote at 10:28.

"Amazing," someone responded a minute later. An hour and twenty minutes later—four and a half hours into the interview—the trooper grew positively giddy.

"Okay he's writing a statement now in his apt," he wrote at 11:53.

And two minutes later: "Whos your daddy."

And immediately after: "Whos your daddy."

And: "???"

And half a minute later: "Getting confession as we speak."

In seven minutes, his mood shifted drastically. He texted the FBI agent and the other trooper: "Be on guard. He is in vulnerable position to do something bad. Be on guard now. I see him looking around at times."

In another minute, whatever it was that happened that night began happening. Ibragim had stopped writing the confession and had gotten up. The trooper, who had gone from giddy to worried, was now apparently so terrified that he fumbled with his holster. The FBI agent shot Ibragim three times, and he went down. Then the trooper saw exactly what he had seen in one of those fight videos: Ibragim, wounded and bleeding, rose again, like some sort of deathless monster. The FBI agent fired four more shots, one of them hitting Ibragim in the top of the head and three of them hitting him in the back.

The Florida report included a screenshot of the trooper's phone with the text messages, but the messages following his warning one—"Be on guard"—were redacted, covered with rectangular bars applied to the graphic. A blogger then did what most people with a computer could do: he removed the bars to reveal the messages. (Several journalists successfully repeated the trick.) The next message the trooper sent to his fellow officers—the other trooper and the Massachusetts FBI agent—went out the evening of May 22, nineteen hours after Ibragim died:

"Well done this week man well done joy some time at home and in will talk soon."

A minute later: "That was supposed to say well done men we all got through it and are now heading home. Great work."

The un-redacting of the report also revealed the name of the FBI agent who shot Ibragim—and *The Boston Globe* then meticulously verified his identity. He was Aaron McFarlane, he was forty-one years old, and he had been with the FBI since 2008. Before that, he had been a police officer in Oakland, California. While there, he was accused of falsifying a police report, and the Oakland Police Department was sued twice by former suspects who claimed he had physically assaulted them. The Oakland police settled each of the lawsuits for $32,500, and McFarlane left in 2004, with a lifetime annual pension of $52,000.

OF COURSE *they sent a killer to interview Ibragim*, thought Elena. *And look at those text messages in which they congratulate each other for killing him!* Her view of America had changed radically in the months that passed between Ibragim's death and the publication of the text messages and information about FBI Agent McFarlane.

Elena returned to Fort Stewart in late June 2013, after Reni finally left for Chechnya with Ibragim's body: Elena's emergency leave had lasted a month. On June 26, she told me, she was at a doctor's appointment on base when two sergeants from her unit came to fetch her. "They took me somewhere. A woman came out and, without introducing herself, started to search me and told me to hand over my phone and keys. She said, 'You can't take anything with you if you are going inside.' I said, 'I'm not planning to go anywhere, at least not alone.' One of the escorts, a female sergeant, said she'd go in with me, so she was also frisked. When we went in, I saw one of the agents who came to my house before. He said, 'We have received information that you are planning to buy a gun and shoot FBI agents.' I said, 'Tell me, is it illegal to have a gun in the house?'—'No.'—'Okay, that's the only question I have for you, and I have no answers for you anyway.'" The agent did not try to keep her in the room.

Elena told me she had never owned a gun and had no desire to have one.

Three weeks later, the agent called again. Elena hung up as soon as he introduced himself, then recorded his number in her phone as "Terrorist." He did not call again, though.

In another month, Elena's commanding officer summoned her to inform her, apologetically, that the FBI had flagged her as being under investigation. As she understood, that essentially meant she was being placed on indefinite paid leave: she could neither carry out her work duties in the military nor be reassigned or promoted as long as she was so "flagged." The next day, Elena accepted a medical discharge from the Army. She was now forty-four, retired, and, she felt, a lot wiser than she had been a few months earlier.

America's promise of fairness, openness, and honesty had turned out to be a ruse, she concluded. It was not a better country than Russia; it was just a better liar. Elena had grown up and begun raising her own children in a country that was capable of anything:

bombing its own cities out of existence, as it did with Grozny in 1995 and 1999; blowing up more than three hundred people in order to secure an election, as it did in 1999; killing its own citizens abroad and endangering dozens of lives in the process, as it did with a former secret agent in London in 2006. America had said it would be different—its laws were firm, its courts were fair, and its respect for human life was absolute. Nothing in Elena's lived experience had taught her that a country could really be like that, but as both an immigrant and a new Army recruit, she had accepted the premise enthusiastically.

But the minute she heard her daughter screaming into the phone—"Mama, they killed him!"—she knew she had been fooled. The same rules applied in this country as in the old one. The secret police killed people when they wanted to; a reason could always be found later. The secret police could and would engineer tragedies to their own ends, or to the government's; someone to blame could always be found later.

In May 2013, someone who claimed to be a resident of the Watertown neighborhood where the gun battle between law enforcement and the Tsarnaev brothers occurred posted a video on YouTube that, he wrote, showed the apprehension of Tamerlan—alive—by the police and his saying *"podstava,"* the Russian word for "setup," as he was detained. I watched the video several times—it was darkness, flashing lights, sirens—but I was unable to discern someone being detained or to hear anyone say *"podstava."* If Tamerlan had indeed said that word at any point, it could have meant anything from "I was set up" to simply a rueful interjection, as though life itself had engineered the setup. But the interpretation of the video became gospel among followers of the numerous "Free Jahar" groups on social networks: here was evidence that the brothers themselves believed they had been set up.

Elena became part of the online community of Jahar's defenders. The many online groups, with a combined membership in the thousands, were an odd conglomeration of left-wing doubters, right-wing conspiracy theorists, young women with crushes on Jahar, and middle-aged women aghast at the too-apparent barbarity of keeping a young man alive in order to kill him after a trial the outcome of which was preordained. Early on, the movement had been dominated by energetic young people intent on exposing a truth that departed dramatically from the official version of events. In the summer of 2013, for example, I interviewed a thirty-one-year-old Truther with a shaved head and tattoos on most of his exposed skin who had moved to Boston from Las Vegas to conduct his own investigation. Over time, men like him switched their focus to other government conspiracies, and middle-aged women driven primarily by compassion gradually took over. Elena fit in well among them, and the story of the killing of Ibragim naturally became the centerpiece of the movement's narrative of the obstruction of truth and the lack of justice. Elena now devoted herself to the movement fully.

In December 2014, she flew to Boston, barely scraping together enough money for the ticket and one night in a hotel, to attend Jahar's final pretrial hearing—the first time he would be brought to court since pleading not guilty in July 2013. As the brief proceedings were wrapping up, she shouted out in Russian: "Dzhokhar, there are people here who love you! We pray for you and support you! We know you are innocent!" She told me later she had decided ahead of time she would scream in Russian "so he would know it wasn't someone mocking him." As the U.S. marshals moved in to usher Elena out of the courtroom, she screamed at them, too: "I am an American citizen and I have the right to say what I think!"

Eleven

EVERYONE IS GOING TO JAIL

After he pulled off his shirt, as instructed, outside the apartment door, Azamat was frisked, handcuffed, shackled, walked a few paces through a thicket of men in SWAT gear, and shoved into the backseat of a police car. A few moments later a man in civilian clothes thrust his head into the car. He was in his forties, broad-shouldered, with close-cropped gray hair and plain white good looks.

"Where the fuck is Jahar?" he shouted.

"I don't know," said Azamat. "The news says he is in Watertown."

"Don't you fucking lie to me!" barked the agent. Afterward, he shouted something else about Jahar's life being over and Azamat's being in danger.

After about an hour just sitting in the cruiser while men in SWAT gear ran around and in and out of the building, shouting and radioing, Azamat was driven a short distance in New Bedford. He no longer knew where Dias and Bayan were. An officer got him out of the car, unshackled him, and told him to stand next to the vehicle. Azamat stood. People in uniform and in civilian clothes continued to run in and out of the building. They had arrived at the state police barracks, where the FBI had temporarily set up shop that afternoon, nearly certain that Jahar would be captured at the Carriage Drive apartment. It was another hour before someone led Azamat into the building, into a tiny, windowless room that was almost completely empty—even the shelves against one of the walls were barren, save for a recording device that sat on one of them. The device, however, would not be used, because the FBI records interviews only with subjects who are in custody, which Azamat was not.

There were two agents in the room, an olive-skinned man and a pale woman. They were both small—they did not tower over Azamat like the man who had shouted at him. Although Azamat was still handcuffed and shirtless, he must have felt a bit less scared—Special Agent Sara Wood later testified that he was relaxed and smiling. He asked to go to the bathroom. The agents said he could not, just yet. He said he was bursting and would go in his shorts if they did not let him use the bathroom. One of the agents said that he could go if he signed a form first. The form said that Azamat was agreeing to talk to the FBI voluntarily and was waiving his right to an attorney. Azamat signed—he would have signed that anyway—and then Special Agent Farbod Azad, the olive-skinned man, took him to the bathroom.

When Agent Azad brought Azamat back, they began talking. It was just before eight on Friday evening. It was almost half past four in the morning on Saturday when Azamat got home. In the intervening hours, Agent Wood, the pale woman, asked most of the questions, and Agent Azad took notes. Azamat answered questions about Jahar, who not long after the questioning began was found in the boat in Watertown, though Azamat would not know about this until later. Sometimes one of the agents would leave the room for a while. At one point Azamat was so cold that he begged the agents to find him a shirt. Agent Wood went to look for one but returned empty-handed. Apparently, in the entire police barracks filled with people many of whom had come in from other cities (Agent Wood herself had driven up from New York that morning), no one had a spare shirt, T-shirt, sweater, or jacket to lend to Azamat. Agent Wood later testified that Azamat shook violently but not from the cold: it was nerves. She said that the shakes began when the questioning brought them to Thursday night and the friends' visit to Jahar's dorm room. Azamat told the agents that they had taken a computer, his own Beats headphones, and a backpack. He also told them that in the morning, once he learned that Jahar had been identified as one of the bombers, he had told Dias that he needed to remember where he had disposed of the backpack.

"Why?" asked Agent Wood. She later testified that Azamat shrugged in response.

"Why did you throw out the backpack?"

"I don't know." In Russian, even more than in American culture, "I don't know" can mean many things other than simply pleading ignorance—including "I don't know what to say" and "I don't know how to explain it to you."

"Between his shaking and indicating that they threw the backpack out, it was clear we weren't getting the full story," Agent Wood later told a jury in federal court. "As I began to confront him, he continued to say, 'I don't know.' Finally, he didn't respond, but his shoulders slumped and his body language changed. I lowered my voice and leaned across the table. 'What was in the backpack?' He responded, 'The stuff you use on New Year's.'"

Agent Wood did not understand.

"Petarda," said Azamat, trying a Russian word. No match.

He tried to use a translation app on his iPhone, as he had several times during the conversation, but it did not know the word, either. He gestured with his hands and tried to imitate the sound of fireworks: "Wee, wee, wee, boom!" Agent Wood finally got it.

On the fourth iteration, Azamat's list of things removed from Jahar's room included: the laptop, the headphones, the backpack with hollow fireworks, and a brown ashtray, which he also had not mentioned earlier. He succeeded in omitting what he most wanted to conceal, which was the bag of marijuana. And he still did not know where Dias had thrown the backpack.

Before Azamat mentioned the fireworks, but after he had handed the agents his phone and told them the password and gone through and translated for them the text messages he had exchanged with Dias, he asked if he should speak to his consulate. Agent Wood got the number of the Kazakh consulate and let Azamat use the landline, but it was half past ten at night and he got voice mail.

A bit after midnight, the agents told Azamat that he was free to go. He had no idea how to get home: Dias had also been taken into custody, and at any rate, Azamat had no phone service. He put his head on the lone desk in the little room and fell asleep.

The person who roused him was the big man from the previous afternoon. He was Agent John Walker, and he was directing this part of the investigation.

"I'm beginning to think I am being held here against my will," said Azamat.

Agent Walker told him it was nothing like that—he was free to go. In fact, Agent Walker would drive him. When they arrived at Carriage Drive, Dias was there with two other FBI agents. They assembled around the table—the one at which Dias, Azamat, and

Bayan had sat twelve hours earlier waiting for the FBI. Now it was the FBI, Dias, and Azamat, standing. The laptop, the ashtray, and the baseball hat sat on the table. One of the agents spotted the red hat.

"Is that Jahar's?" he asked.

The boys nodded.

"We want that hat," said the agent.

"I don't know, I kind of like the way it looks on me," said Dias, grabbing the hat and putting it on his head.

Azamat quickly tore the hat off his friend's head and handed it to the agent.

The agents searched the apartment—Azamat had signed a consent form for that, too—and left, taking with them what they had found of Jahar's stuff. When they were gone, Azamat asked Dias where he had thrown out the backpack.

"In the dumpster," said Dias.

"You idiot," said Azamat.

ROBEL DID NOT SEE the men in SWAT gear lay siege to 69A Carriage Drive, and he did not see his friends being led out of the building at gunpoint, in handcuffs and shackles. He had known to get as far away as possible from that place. After Azamat drove him to campus so he could dump his bag with the marijuana in it and they returned to Carriage Drive, Robel said, "The media are going to be here soon," and got to work finding a ride out of New Bedford. He got hold of Quan Le Phan, a former roommate. He probably did not have to explain why he had to get away from the Kazakhs' apartment: by this time, all of UMass knew that Jahar had been identified as one of the bombers. Quan had to leave campus anyway because the dorms were being evacuated, but Robel bombarded him with messages urging him to hurry until, less than half an hour later, Quan took Robel with him to his parents' house in Worcester, about seventy miles to the northwest.

Just after three in the afternoon, Robel got a text from Azamat: "Policemen are coming to our apartment . . ." and less then a minute later: "They are looking for you . . ." Robel responded, "Tell them we left because of campus lockdown and are coming back when they tell us to."

Robel's strategy must have been to try to make himself invisible while also appearing cooperative. He knew the police would come to Carriage Drive, but he figured that if he avoided being spotted by them and especially if he made it inconvenient enough to try to get him, maybe the police would forget about him. There is, however, no such thing as being too inconveniently located for FBI agents conducting an investigation. Two officers—an FBI agent named Dwight Schwader and a county police detective named David Earle, who was also assigned to the Joint Terrorism Task Force, one of a hundred such interagency groups run by FBI offices around the country—drove to Worcester. They asked Robel, Quan, and Quan's roommate Jim Li, who had gone with Quan and Robel to Quan's house from Dartmouth, to meet in the Price Chopper parking lot. The boys came and then took turns walking across the lot from their car to the officers' SUV, getting in, and answering questions. Before letting them into the vehicle, the officers, who were wearing SWAT gear, stood each of the boys against the SUV and patted them down thoroughly.

Robel's interview lasted a couple of hours, and just another two hours later, he was already feeling cavalier about it.

"It was kind of funny," he texted at 1:53 in the morning to a friend named Elohe Dereje, an aspiring actress and model in

Maryland. "They asked me what I was doing all day when I was hanging out with people. I told them smoking on so many occasions that they just started to laugh."

A minute later, he added, "They grilled me for 2 hours straight." Elohe responded:

> LMAOO WHAT?? YOU DID NOTTT . . .
> LIKE WHERE THEY INTERROGATE YOU?

> THEY HAD TO TAKE YOU?

> I'M NOT PLAYING, THEY INTERROGATED
> ME IN A PARKING LOT IN THEIR CAR

> THESE GUYS ONLY CARED FOR
> THE BOMBS AND GUNS

> WOW, SO DID YOU FIND OUT
> WHY THEY DID WHAT THEY DID?

> WHY HIS BROTHER BOMBED
> THE MARATHON?

> NOPE, NOTHING SO FAR.
> THEY SAID IF THE GUY DOESN'T TRY
> TO PLEAD NOT GUILTY MORE PEOPLE
> WON'T INTERROGATE ME

It was less than twenty-four hours since the brothers had been identified, but the narrative had already taken hold: it was the older brother who had bombed the marathon.

Later, when the officers who interviewed Robel were cross-examined in court, it would become clear that the interview had not been all that funny. At one point, Agent Schwader asked for Robel's phone, and Robel placed it on the center console of the car. The agent went through his text messages, including the ones he had gotten from Dias the evening before: "Come to Jahar's!" and again "Jahar!" But Robel kept saying that he did not remember anything about going to Jahar's room, and his repetitive recollections of his numerous pot-smoking sessions served as his explanations both for how he had spent the day and for why he did not remember anything but the smoking. Agent Schwader thought he was stonewalling. Among other things Agent Schwader yelled at him was, "Maybe you are their bitch and you stayed outside," when Dias and Azamat went in. Robel still insisted that he did not remember going to Jahar's room.

It was not until after the officers allowed Robel, Quan, and Jim to go back to Quan's parents' house that the agents at the New Bedford police barracks got Azamat to talk in detail about Dias's search of Jahar's dorm room. So a couple of hours after Robel had relaxed enough to start bragging in text messages about his interrogation, the agents showed up at Quan's house. They said they needed to talk to Robel. It was four in the morning.

They talked for about forty minutes. They studied his phone again. Robel still insisted that he did not remember going to Jahar's.

The next day, Robel got a call from Michael Dukakis, the almost eighty-year-old former governor and 1988 Democratic presidential candidate, with whom Robel's mother was on friendly terms. The old man said Robel's mother had called him, worried sick because she had not heard from her son in two days. So Dukakis tried calling, perhaps hoping that Robel would answer out of respect—or because he was avoiding only his mother's calls. And indeed, Robel answered. He told Dukakis that he was so confused he was not even sure what he had told the investigators so far. Dukakis must have told him to go home, because on Saturday both Robel and Jim, whose parents also lived in Boston, left Worcester and returned to their families.

BACK AT CARRIAGE DRIVE, Dias and Azamat assessed their situation. They seemed to be out of the woods. They had not been arrested, they had given the FBI Jahar's things except for the backpack, and with Jahar himself having been caught, maybe the FBI did not need the backpack anymore. Dias and Azamat did not know where Bayan was, but they assumed the officers must have let her go early: after all, she had not gone to Jahar's with them, and anyway, she was a girl. They could sleep—they had not done much of that in a while.

They came for Dias and Azamat in the afternoon. Both were told they were being arrested for visa violations. "This may be the first time Immigration makes a house call over a student-visa violation," one of Azamat's defense attorneys, Nicholas Wooldridge, would later say at trial. "And the FBI is with them! This may be the first time the FBI makes a house call over a student-visa violation." Wooldridge was almost certainly wrong; with arresting people on visa-violation grounds having become one of the most important law enforcement tools after September 11, there had probably been many such joint "house calls."

When Azamat saw Agent Walker, he rushed to tell him what he had found out—that Dias had thrown the backpack in the dumpster. He also said he remembered that the garbage had been picked up the previous afternoon.

Dias and Azamat were taken to Boston, to the Thomas P. O'Neill, Jr., Federal Building, a 1980s stack of glass and concrete bands that houses a variety of government agencies, including a number of Homeland Security offices. Dias and Azamat were questioned again. Then they were booked and taken to county jail. They still did not have lawyers.

AZAMAT HAD CALLED his father, Amir, as soon as the FBI agents had left in the early morning—it was the middle of the day in Kazakhstan. "Everything is fine," Azamat told him. "We've been released." It was late at night in Kazakhstan when he called his father again: "They are taking us again, it's about the visas." This was when Amir started looking for a lawyer and booking a ticket to Boston.

Amir Ismagulov (in the Kazakh tradition, the eldest son takes his surname from the grandfather's first name, which is why Azamat and Amir have different last names) is the kind of man who may not believe in the system but is certain of his ability to work the system. Amir became famous in Kazakhstan in 2011, after he addressed the country's authoritarian president, Nursultan Nazarbayev, publicly asking that authorities stop gratuitous inspections of businesses, and immediately received personal assurances for himself and his enterprise. Later that year, two bombs went off in Atyrau, the Kazakh oil capital, where Amir had a house; a radical Islamist group took credit for the bombings. Amir played a role in the ensuing shake-up of the city and received a government medal for his role in the fight against terrorism. Not only did Amir have money, expertise, and connections that always made him feel safe and confident, he even had proof that his family was on the right side in the War on Terror.

By Sunday, April 21, Amir had engaged a large Chicago law firm that had done work for Kazakh oil and gas companies. He expected VIP service from it. It took only a few days to get a visa, and on Thursday Amir landed in Boston. A Russian-speaking representative of the law firm—a junior partner, not a flunky—greeted him at the airport. Then he informed Amir that the firm had decided to drop the case: "It's too high-profile for us." It was also the wrong profile; the firm did not generally handle criminal cases. But Amir was now certain it had something to do with the fact that the firm's senior partners were Jewish. The junior partner recommended a Boston-based immigration firm, with which he had already made the preliminary arrangements. The immigration lawyers assured Amir that there was nothing to worry about; they had handled hundreds of visa-snafu cases. While the immigration lawyer was preparing for the arraignment, the criminal defense lawyer who was representing Dias recommended lining up an experienced criminal attorney as well, and had an acquaintance of his come up from New York to start familiarizing himself with the case. Amir hired everybody.

On the morning of May 1, both Dias and Azamat were scheduled to appear at an immigration hearing. They had been in jail for ten days; their fathers, who were both in Boston, had not yet been allowed to see them. But when Amir got to the courtroom, his son and Dias were not there: each of them in turn appeared on a video screen through an uplink from the jail, and the judge informed them that their cases were continued for a week. Reassured by his son's new immigration lawyer, and by seeing his son on the screen, Amir left the court certain that Azamat would be free in a week's time.

At four o'clock that afternoon, Azamat and Dias were brought to the federal courthouse. The FBI had filed a criminal complaint against them. The document, which named both Azamat and Dias, described their alleged crime as follows:

[They did] willfully conspire with each other to commit an offense against the United States, to wit, 18 U.S.C. § 1519, by knowingly destroying, concealing, and covering up objects belonging to Dzhokhar Tsarnaev, namely, a backpack containing fireworks and a laptop computer, with the intent to impede, obstruct, and influence the criminal investigation of the Marathon bombings, in violation of 18 U.S.C. § 371.

An accompanying affidavit by Special Agent Scott Cieplik explained that Dias, Azamat, and Robel had "collectively decided to throw the backpack and fireworks into the trash because they did not want Tsarnaev to get in trouble." Although the criminal complaint concerned only Azamat and Dias, the affidavit stated that there was probable cause to charge Robel with lying to investigators.

Amir got on the phone with the Kazakh consul in New York, Yerlan Kubashev. Amir had had enough of the slick American lawyers who seemed to think their job was to take his money and issue reassurances in exchange. "Find me a Russian-speaking lawyer!" Amir demanded. Kubashev thought it was a bad idea. Amir clarified: "Find me a good Russian-speaking lawyer!" The conversation lasted two hours, and in the end Kubashev helped Amir make contact with Arkady Bukh, a forty-one-year-old New York City criminal attorney given to wearing long velvet jackets and red bow ties. Bukh had immigrated to the United States from Azerbaijan in the early nineties and was admitted to the bar in 2003. He had represented a long line of Russian cyber-criminals, including hackers, spammers, and child pornographers. His website called him "Top New York Criminal Defense Lawyer" and implored: "Stop being a victim of the circumstances. Trust your freedom to No-one [sic] but Bukh." Amir hired him. By this time he was out about seventy thousand dollars, between the bulk of the retainer that the big Chicago firm had kept and the fees he had paid the immigration lawyer and the criminal lawyer, both of whom he had taken off the case almost as soon as they entered it.

Amir's belief in his ability to work the system might have been shaken, but his faith in his son remained firm: Azamat was innocent, and he was a good young man. Amir finally got to see him on May 3—two weeks after the arrest, two days after the arraignment—and Azamat told him everything. He said that lots of students had gone to Jahar's room that evening—it just so happened he and Dias and Robel were the only ones who got in. He said that he and Dias had both told investigators the truth, and if there had been any obfuscation at all, it concerned the marijuana. He said that he had not even realized that the FBI was interested in the fireworks. He also said that he would never snitch on Dias; he would never agree to testify against him. And in any case, no one had ever intended to do anything bad, except smoke pot.

It looked like the classic game-theory setup known as the prisoner's dilemma: Bonnie and Clyde are held separately and pressured to testify against each other. If either testifies, he or she will get a reduced sentence, while the other is put away for a long time, but if neither testifies, both have a chance of going free. Just as Azamat would never snitch on Dias, father and son were sure Dias would not give Azamat up either; the young men had been brought up with similar concepts of honor and friendship.

AFTER A FEW DAYS back in Cambridge, Robel had started to feel safer. Dias and Azamat had been jailed—they were probably getting deported—but he was home. Although the FBI had called, Robel remained a free man. By April 22, he was even feeling cocky again about having come that close to real danger.

"I was the last person to see the terrorist!" he texted a friend in Ethiopia. "I got questioned by the FBI detectives and I got followed for a day."

"Are you lying??? Did you know him personally?? they didn't hurt you or anything?" The friend was suitably impressed and worried. And a few minutes later the friend texted again: "Did he ever say anything to you about it?"

"He was one of my oldest friends," was all Robel would say.

Then the FBI wanted to talk to him again. Robel made childish excuses on the phone: he did not have a good way of getting to downtown Boston (a twenty-minute subway ride from Cambridge). The FBI sent a car.

At eleven in the morning on April 26, Robel was delivered to a Homeland Security office in Boston. It was another windowless room, barely large enough for the desk and two chairs that were there. This time Robel talked to Special Agent Michael Delapena, a twenty-four-year veteran of the FBI who favored what he called "building rapport" over yelling and threatening as interviewing techniques. He asked about Robel's drug use, his classes, his family: he learned that Robel had been raised by his mother, an Ethiopian immigrant, and had never known his father. He established that they, Robel and Agent Delapena, were both Americans, and he said, "We have been attacked."

At first Robel insisted that he remembered getting Dias's text—"Come to Jahar's!"—and nothing after that. Agent Delapena told him he needed to choose sides: "You need to be part of Team America." The other guys were playing for the other team, he said, and as long as Robel could not remember anything about being in the room, Delapena said, he was "on the bench." He then instructed Robel to close his eyes and imagine being in the room—as a mental exercise, to try to break through the amnesia. Robel said he still could not remember. "That's not an answer," said Delapena.

A couple of hours into the interview, Robel remembered being in the room and seeing Jahar's roommate there. Delapena stepped out of the room—to brief other agents on the progress he had just made, but also perhaps to let Robel's distress intensify. When he returned, Robel was terrified. Was he going to be arrested? Were the other agents, whom he had glimpsed outside, going to be mad that he had not told them what he was telling Delapena now?

"There are wolves out there," confirmed Delapena. Then he got up and locked the door. "It's just you and me in here." All Robel had to do to enjoy Delapena's continued protection was produce a written statement.

The resulting document, a bit more than one single-spaced page, eventually became evidence in the case against Robel.

> On Thursday, April 18th, at approximately 9 pm, I received a text from my friend Dias. The text asked me to go to Jahar's room. As requested, I went to the room, where Dias and Azamat were waiting in front of the door.

The timing of the text message is off by an hour, but that is understandable. More important, according to the testimony of at least three other people—Lino Rosas, in whose room Robel and Azamat were playing FIFA when the message arrived; Azamat; and Andrew Dwinells—Dias had entered the room first and had been rummaging through Jahar's things for about ten minutes by the time Robel and Azamat arrived, together.

> Dias has free access into the room unless the door is locked, which it was not.

Robel had lived in the same dorm, so he knew that the door locked automatically when closed and required a key card to open.

> One of the items was a dark backpack, possibly with one red stripe.

It was a plain black backpack.

> He opened the bag, at which point I observed approximately seven red tubular fireworks, approximately 6 to 8 inches in length.

None of the fireworks was red.

> I know that Jahar has a black SONY laptop, but I do not recall Dias taking it. It is possible that it was in the backpack.

The statement contains no other references to the laptop. Why would Robel include the assertion of lacking any recollection of a fact that was probably relayed by the interviewing agent? Something similar happens at the end of the penultimate paragraph:

> At one point that evening, around 11:00 pm, the three of us had a discussion about what to do with the backpack and fireworks. Dias asked, in words I can't exactly recall, if he should get rid of the "stuff", which I took to mean the backpack. I said in response, "do what you have to do." I was concerned how it would look if the Police found us (Jahar's friends) with a backpack with fireworks, given what had happened. I took a two hour nap, and when I awoke, the backpack was gone. I do not know for sure who took it from the apartment. I am aware that there is a dumpster about 80 or 90 yards from their apartment.

The statement hardly reads like a spontaneously produced recollection of the facts known to Robel. It reads rather like it was dictated or even written by someone else and then given to Robel to sign. The last paragraph reads:

> In retrospect, I should have notified the Police once I knew Jahar
> was the bomber. Further, I should have turned over the backpack
> to the authorities. I regret these decisions. I make this statement
> without any threats or promises made to me.
> *Sincerely,*
> *Robel Phillipos*

The charges proposed in the criminal complaint against Azamat and Dias added up to a maximum sentence of twenty-five years—five for conspiracy and twenty for obstruction of justice—but Robel, who would now be accused of lying to investigators, was looking at a maximum of sixteen. And because Robel was a United States citizen, he spent less than two weeks wearing an orange jumpsuit: on May 6, he was released on bail.

AZAMAT AND DIAS left county jail, too: they were transferred to a federal facility and placed in solitary. They saw each other again after a few weeks, when they, Robel, and all of their lawyers came together in a large conference room with the prosecution's team and Bayan and her lawyer. They were there to videotape Bayan's deposition before she left for Kazakhstan. Such were the terms of her immunity deal: she would tell the truth, and she would leave the United States. The story she told was essentially similar to what Dias and Azamat had by now told the investigators; she even admitted to being the one who demanded that the backpack be removed from the apartment. But she told the story first.

"Bayan's father was the smart one," Amir admitted later, during Azamat's trial. "He got a lawyer right away."

ABOUT HALFWAY THROUGH Azamat's trial, Amir asked me over a lunch of oysters at a waterfront restaurant near the courthouse, "Do you think our lawyers are talking too fast? Is the jury having trouble following them?" It was July 2014. Amir had been living in the Boston area since he flew in at the end of April the previous year—he had gone back to Kazakhstan only once, for a month, to renew his visa. Azamat's mother and toddler sister had temporarily moved to Boston as well. Amir wanted his other son, who was a year younger than Azamat, to come join the support team, too, but the young man's application for a visa was rejected. Amir had even yanked him out of Cambridge University to intern at Chevron's Kazakhstan operation for half a year—he had figured a recommendation from an American employer would get his son a visa. He figured wrong.

Living in America was hard. Amir started out driving the boys' BMW, the one he had paid for, but every few days he would be chased by several unmarked cars at once, stopped with great fanfare, made to get out of the car and submit to a search, so that each time it was a couple of hours before he was allowed to continue on his way. After a few weeks, with no sign that this pointless ritual was going to end, Amir ditched the BMW and started alternating between cabs and rental cars. Then there was the issue of housing: Amir had to change apartments every month or two, because every renewable short-term furnished-apartment lease had a way of becoming not so renewable once the landlord learned why Amir's family was in Boston. Arkady Bukh's people would find Amir a new place, negotiate the option of renewing the contract every few months—and in a few weeks the cycle would be repeated. Amir racked up more than half a dozen Boston neighborhoods in just over a year.

Hiring Bukh had been a good idea: it was by far the highest-profile case he had ever handled, and he threw everything he had at it. Seven of his people rented a house together in a Boston suburb, and, when they were not busy apartment-hunting for Amir, they were cramming for the trial. They went to see every person with whom Azamat had been friendly in college; most of them refused to talk to the lawyers, a few explained that the FBI had told them not to talk to anyone, and not one person agreed to testify for the defense. The legal team reconstructed every FBI interview and interrogation, finding numerous inconsistencies and digging into them. Since they had no witnesses, they would mount a defense based solely on attacking the government's case.

They did it like it's done in the movies—in fact, while I was reporting on the trial, I enticed two of my own family members to come watch on two separate days, promising them a cable-series-worthy spectacle, and they were not disappointed. Cross-examining Special Agent Sara Wood, defense attorney Nicholas Wooldridge asked whether Azamat had been allowed to use the bathroom on request—and after Agent Wood asserted that he had been, and denied that he had been told he needed to sign his waiver of rights in order to be allowed to pee, the defense showed a video of Azamat being taken to the bathroom several minutes after the time recorded for his signature on the form that said he had agreed to talk to the FBI without a lawyer. Agent Wood had not merely denied coercion: she had claimed that Azamat signed the form after he returned from the bathroom. What made this cross-examination particularly cinematic was that the lawyers had been able to establish that the clock on the wall at the police barracks had not been set forward to daylight saving time, so a video that at first glance appeared to show an innocuous sequence of events was revealed to tell a different story.

After that day, which came about halfway through the two weeks of testimony, I could not imagine the jury convicting Azamat: the FBI agent who had conducted the first and most important interview with him had just been caught lying on the stand. That, I thought, served to discredit her report—the only existing record of the interview—and without the report, the government's case would seem to fall apart. Later, Wooldridge caught Wood's partner, Agent Azad, in the same fib, cementing what I thought was a victory for the defense. Perhaps even more important, the government's case was not so much about facts, which were not in dispute—Dias, Azamat, and Robel had certainly gone to Jahar's room, they had driven away with the backpack holding the fireworks, and Dias had thrown it in the trash—as it was about intention. Did they, as the charges alleged, "willfully conspire," and did they have the "intent to impede, obstruct, and influence" the investigation? The prosecution repeatedly pointed to Azamat's obsessive surfing of news sites as proof that he was trying to track the manhunt in order to help Jahar get away. The defense was arguing that Azamat kept checking the news because he was confused, scared, and incredulous. The government's only witnesses who could testify to Azamat's state of mind before he knew that Jahar had been caught were the FBI agents who had interviewed him then—and the jury had now seen that they could not be trusted.

But Amir, who did not speak any English—the court provided simultaneous translators, but they had some trouble keeping up

with the defense—had picked up on cues to which I was not pay-
ing attention. The New York lawyers were indeed talking too fast.
They also looked too good: their suits fit too well, and Wooldridge's
hair actually shone. The government's lawyers—the men in their
baggy suits, the lone woman in her boxy outfits—and their speech,
which struck me as occasionally hokey, and broad Massachusetts
accents, had a much better connection with the jury.

The jurors took a day and a bit to return a verdict, but as I
found out later, that had been an illusion of deliberation: one of the
jurors had simply been ill on the first day. In fact, the jury's unanimous decision had been nearly instant. Azamat never had a
chance.

Azamat and Dias were in solitary for the first six months in
federal prison. Then they were placed together for a few months,
then separated again—and placed in solitary—before Azamat's
trial began. Once they were in separate cells, each was offered a
deal: a reduced sentence in exchange for pleading guilty and
testifying against the codefendants. Azamat told Amir he had
turned the deal down. Amir told me that Dias's father had told him
that Dias had said no as well—indeed, he did not testify at Azamat's trial.

Dias was scheduled to face trial two months after Azamat, in
September. A month earlier, at what was scheduled as a pretrial
hearing, Dias pleaded guilty. In exchange, the government asked
that he be sentenced to no more than seven years behind bars.

THE SENTENCING was scheduled for 2015. If Bayan's father, by
being first to hire a lawyer, proved that he was the smart one, now
it looked like Dias's father, who had had his lawyer cut a deal with

the prosecutors, was not so dumb either, while Amir, who had spent a million dollars on lawyers and uprooted his family to come to Boston to try to move mountains for a year, was enough of a fool that his son was staring at twenty-five years in prison. Amir instructed the lawyers to look for a deal: it was a question of survival now, not of honor. At Robel's trial in November, Azamat was a witness for the prosecution.

Azamat's head was shaved now. He was prison-pale, the kind of pale that results from spending twenty-three hours a day in a tiny locked room. Amir must have bought him a new shirt for this trial—he was well used to the routine of exchanging a laundered white shirt for a soiled one through a special window at the courthouse—but he made a mistake with either the size or the style: the cutaway collar of the shirt spread out over the collar of Azamat's navy English-cut suit, making him look like he was wearing someone else's clothes.

When Assistant U.S. Attorney Stephanie Siegmann asked Azamat to tell the jury of his agreement with the prosecution, he said, "As long as I tell the truth, it may help with my sentencing." He had been given no promises.

Azamat had not testified at his own trial, so now he told the story in court for the first time. Answering the prosecutor's questions, he ran through it step by step: Dias texted him, they went to Jahar's room, it was locked, later they got in, he and Robel watched *Project X* while Dias searched the room, they left, they ate, some of them smoked, they watched *The Pursuit of Happyness*, they slept, and then Dias emerged from the bedroom. "He wanted to throw the backpack," testified Azamat. "I agreed with him." When the prosecutor asked him what language he and Dias used to talk about the backpack, Azamat said it had been English. When Robel's defense attorney pointed out that Azamat had not said this in earlier interviews and interrogations, Azamat said that he did not remember.

The question of whether Russian or English was spoken that morning in the apartment was essential to Robel's defense. His lawyers' strategy rested on two assertions: Robel was too stoned to remember anything, and he did not understand what Dias said about the backpack because Dias and Azamat spoke Russian to each other. The prosecution, basing its case in large part on the strange statement Robel had signed in April 2013, in that little room Agent Delapena had locked, promising to keep the "wolves" out, insisted that the conversation had been conducted in English—and Robel had even said, "Do what you have to do," which his defense now denied. In other words, in the prosecution's narrative, Robel and Azamat had played identical roles in the story: neither of them had touched the backpack or the fireworks, and both of them had passively acquiesced to Dias's intention to dispose of them. Indeed, they had been together every step of the way, from eight in the evening on April 18 to nine in the morning on April 19. They had watched *Project X* together while Dias searched Jahar's room, and they had both napped together while Dias and Bayan had words about the backpack. Unlike Robel, Azamat had never denied going to Jahar's room. So why was Azamat charged with conspiracy and obstruction of justice while Robel was charged only with lying to investigators? The prosecutors would not answer that question, but when I asked Robel's defense attorney Derege Demissie, he suggested the government chose the lighter charge for Robel because "they could make it stick."

Why could the heavier charge be made to stick to Azamat and not to Robel? It was obvious: Robel was not a foreigner or a Muslim. Demissie used every opportunity to point out the distinction, stressing that Dias, Azamat, and Jahar "shared a language and a religion" that were foreign to Robel. At one point, Judge Douglas Woodlock instructed the jury that it would be "inappropriate" to take the defendant's religion into consideration—but he allowed Demissie's remark to stand.

Demissie even got former Governor Dukakis to take the stand. He admitted that he had no direct knowledge of the events in question, but his testimony demonstrated that Robel was one of Massachusetts' own. That was evident even before he came to court, causing a minor news sensation. The local media, which had only briefly acknowledged Azamat's trial and Dias's guilty plea— there had been a day or two when I was the only journalist in the courtroom—turned out in force for Robel's trial. *Boston Globe* columnist Yvonne Abraham published a piece titled "Robel Phillipos Made Stupid Mistakes That Any Kid Could Make." In it she asked, "Is it absolutely necessary to bring the full force and power of the federal government down on him?" The following day, Abraham was a guest on a public-radio talk show, and listeners kept calling in to affirm her view: Robel seemed like a regular kid, he could be one of their kids, and he should not go to prison.

LOST IN THE DISCUSSION of just how stupid a mistake Robel had made was a simple question: How much damage had the three friends' actions done? When Azamat was on the stand during Robel's trial, prosecutor Siegmann asked him to explain to the jury why he had been convicted. "Because I took the stuff, it blocked the investigation," he said.

Once the FBI learned of the backpack and its having been thrown in the dumpster, it appointed Special Agent Kenneth Benton, a twenty-six-year veteran of the agency who specialized in white-collar crime and public corruption, to look for it. Benton assembled a team of twenty-five agents who, dressed in hazmat suits and armed with rakes, spent a day and a half sifting through trash pulled up by an excavator at the landfill where a garbage truck had taken Carriage Drive waste on Friday afternoon. The agents produced a number of false-hope backpacks before they finally got one with the JanSport logo on the outside and an eight-and-a-half-by-eleven sheet of ruled paper inside, with some of Jahar's ethics homework. It also contained the emptied-out fireworks containers and the Vaseline jar. Between assembling a team of agency volunteers, cordoning off a section of the landfill, and a bad-weather delay, the agents did not start digging through the garbage until Thursday the 25th and did not find the backpack until the afternoon of Friday the 26th. Jahar had been in custody for one week. Robel was just signing the confession with the inaccurate description of the backpack.

Robel was charged with "knowingly and willfully making a materially false, fictitious, and fraudulent statement." The key word here is "material"—meaning that it had a substantial impact on the investigation, or, as Azamat said, "blocked" it. But Robel knew less than the investigators learned from Dias and Bayan almost as soon as they were detained—before Robel was interviewed for the first time, in the Price Chopper parking lot. Even if he had instantly spilled everything he had known about the fireworks and the Vaseline, it is difficult to imagine that the information could have influenced the course of the investigation. What if the investigators had learned of the backpack and the dumpster even sooner than they got to Robel, say, as soon as they laid siege to Carriage Drive? The garbage truck had already come and gone, so the FBI might have been spared a little time and expense but none of the humiliation and filth of the landfill search.

And what if Dias had not taken the backpack at all? That would not have aided the process of identifying Jahar: by the time investigators arrived at Pine Dale Hall, his name had been known for hours. Nor did the government ever claim that the contents of the backpack helped determine where or how the Boston Marathon bombs were made.

IN ROBEL'S CASE the jury was out for four days. Longer deliberations bode better for the defendant. But the jury returned with a verdict of guilty on two counts of making false statements, which left him vulnerable to the maximum sixteen years for that crime.

IN MAY 2014, a year after Amir moved to Boston, some young women from the boys' informal support group happened to catch a cab with a Russian-speaking driver from Central Asia. They asked him for his number so that they could give it to Amir: not only did the guy speak Russian but he drove a minivan—handy for when Amir was going to visit Azamat in jail with family and friends, or members of the defense team. A day or two later, Amir called the cabbie to drive him and several others to the federal prison.

Khairullozhon Matanov, Kair for short, said he knew about the case—he understood whom Amir was going to see—but that is not what they discussed on the way. Kair was an ethnic Uzbek from Kyrgyzstan: he left in 2010, when mobs were attacking Uzbeks and setting fire to Uzbek-owned businesses throughout Kyrgyzstan. He had family back home—he had been sending them money from his work as a cabdriver, but now he had his green card and wanted to set up something more permanent and lucrative, like perhaps some sort of an export-import business with

Kyrgyzstan. He asked Amir which he thought would be better to ship to Central Asia: clothes or cars. Amir was in favor of cars. "The profit margin is the same," he said, "but there is less busy-work. But you have to take care to have a customer lined up for every vehicle you ship—then it will work." This was the kind of conversation Amir would have liked to have with one of his own sons. He decided he wanted to know Kair.

That was on a Wednesday. On Friday, Amir needed a ride, and he called Kair. Or maybe he just wanted to talk to Kair and needing a ride was an excuse, because Amir kept calling. There was no answer.

THE INDICTMENT against Kair was filed on May 29, 2014—the Thursday between the Wednesday he drove Amir and others to the jail and the Friday when Kair himself was arrested. The timing may have been a coincidence—or Amir's acquaintance with Kair may have been the indirect cause of Kair's arrest. Like other immigrants who had known the Tsarnaevs, he had been tracked by the FBI for months, but unlike all the others, he failed to stay as far away as possible from anyone else affected by the case. He was charged on two counts—obstructing justice by destroying evidence, like Dias and Azamat, and "making materially false, fictitious, and fraudulent statements," like Robel.

Indictments are written by grand juries, groups of sixteen to twenty-three people who, unlike trial juries, are appointed in proceedings that are closed to the public and who are sworn to secrecy in perpetuity. Federal grand juries consider prosecutors' requests for indictments, hear from witnesses—predominantly, though not exclusively, FBI agents—and decide whether there is probable cause to charge a person with a crime. Their decisions do

not have to be unanimous, and far more often than not, they agree
with the prosecution and the federal agents who make the case
that charges should be brought. There is no standard of "reasonable doubt" in the work of a grand jury, because it does not determine guilt; the question the grand jury is answering is: "Do we
suspect this person of having committed a crime?" The indictments, then, are usually accurate reflections not only of the story
the FBI is telling about a crime or a person, but of what makes us
suspicious. In Kair's case, the narrative began after the eleven
points of the indictment that rehearsed the story of the marathon
bombings:

12. Khairullozhon Matanov is a citizen of Kyrgyzstan who
    entered the United States lawfully in 2010, has lived in
    Massachusetts since then and has worked, among other
    jobs, as a taxicab driver.

13. While in the United States, Matanov met Tamerlan
    Tsarnaev and became friends with him, and he also
    knew Tamerlan Tsarnaev's brother, Dzhokhar Tsarnaev.
    Matanov participated in a variety of activities with Tam-
    erlan Tsarnaev, including discussing religious topics and
    hiking up a New Hampshire mountain in order to train
    like, and praise, the "mujahideen."

14. In the hours and days following the bombings, Mata-
    nov contacted and attempted to contact Tamerlan and
    Dzhokhar Tsarnaev by cellphone and saw Tamerlan in
    person at least twice.

15. About forty minutes after the bombings, at approxi-
    mately 3:31 p.m. on Monday, April 15, 2013, Matanov
    called Tamerlan Tsarnaev and invited him to dinner
    that night. Tamerlan accepted. That night, Matanov

bought Dzhokhar and Tamerlan Tsarnaev dinner at a restaurant.

16. After Matanov returned from dinner with the Tsarnaevs following the bombings on Monday, April 15, Matanov spoke with Witness 1 (whose name is known to the Grand Jury). When Witness 1 told Matanov that Witness 1 hoped that the Boston Marathon bombers were not Muslim, Matanov initially responded that the bombings could have a just reason, such as being done in the name of Islam, that he would support the bombings if the reason were just or the attack had been done by the Taliban, and that the victims had gone to paradise.

17. In the days following the bombings, Matanov continued to express support for the bombings, although later that week he said that maybe the bombings were wrong. He expressed sympathy for the victims' families, although he continued to explain away the significance of the victims' deaths on the ground that everyone must eventually die.

18. On Wednesday, April 17, 2013, Matanov called Dzhokhar Tsarnaev at approximately 5:04 p.m., but did not connect. Within a minute or so, Matanov called Tamerlan Tsarnaev and talked for almost one-and-a-half minutes. He then placed a call to Dzhokhar Tsarnaev around 5:35 p.m. that did not connect. At around 6:53 p.m. Matanov called Tamerlan Tsarnaev again, and talked for about a minute. Matanov made another call to Dzhokhar Tsarnaev that did not connect on April 17, 2013, a few minutes later, around 6:57 p.m. At some point later that night, Matanov visited Tamerlan Tsarnaev at his residence in Cambridge, MA. Around 9:35 p.m. the same

night, Matanov made another call to Dzhokhar Tsarnaev that did not connect.

Paragraphs nineteen and twenty describe the release of the suspects' photographs by the FBI. According to the indictment, Kair looked at the pictures shortly after they were released by going to the CNN website on his laptop. At 8:16 in the evening he called Jahar's cell phone and did not get an answer. New, higher-resolution pictures were released at two in the morning, and Kair looked at them again shortly afterward. At 7:17 in the morning he called Jahar's cell phone again and did not get an answer.

The next section of the indictment is called "Matanov's Cover-Up."

Early in the morning on Friday, April 19, Matanov, visibly upset, woke up Witness 1. When Witness 1 asked Matanov why he appeared upset, Matanov answered that pictures of the bombers had been released and he knew the bombers.

In other words, Kair had gone through the same process as Dias, Azamat, and several others: the knowing and not knowing, going back and staring at the grainy photos over and over, then knowing and not believing, and finally being unable to maintain denial once the bombers had been named—and going into a panic. So what did he cover up? "Matanov falsely told Witness 1 that he did not know whether Tamerlan Tsarnaev held any extremist views," states the indictment.

It is not illegal to lie to one's friends or roommate—and judging from the fact that Kair talked to Witness 1 when he returned from dinner and that he woke up Witness 1 early in the morning, Witness 1 was probably his roommate. By seven in the morning Kair was in his cab, driving a regular client, and telling him that the person they were talking about on the radio was someone he knew—and that he even recognized the address the reporter mentioned. The client, referred to in the indictment as Witness 2, asked whether Kair had visited the place on Norfolk Street, and "Matanov falsely claimed that it had been a while, when in fact he had been at Tamerlan Tsarnaev's apartment less than 2 days previously." This lie did not break any laws, either. The episode itself hardly qualifies to be included in the section of the indictment called "Matanov's Cover-Up": if he was covering up, he was not doing a very good job.

After dropping off his client, Kair went to see Witness 3, whom he had once introduced to Tamerlan.

Matanov then asked Witness 3 to take some cellphones which were in Matanov's possession because, Matanov said, they were illegal and might be found if the FBI searched his apartment.

What he was covering up here was the possession of either contraband or stolen cell phones, much as Robel and the others had tried to cover up their marijuana use.

It was still Friday morning. Kair picked up Witness 2, his regular client, again and, it would appear, asked him for advice on the best way to report to the authorities his relationship with the Tsarnaev brothers. He was under no legal obligation to do this: even though the FBI was imploring anyone with information about the brothers to come forward, such cooperation with the authorities is voluntary and failure to heed such calls cannot be punished. Witness 2 tried dialing a police officer acquaintance on Kair's behalf, and when he could not reach him, the two—the cabbie and his client—went to the nearest police station together. This happened to be in Braintree, a suburb on the opposite side of Boston from where the brothers had lived and staged their bungled escape.

Kair was interviewed by a Braintree police officer—and, according to the indictment, though he gave the officer some information about the brothers, including their phone numbers, he also told some lies. He said, for example, that he had not seen photographs of the brothers released by the FBI: he was apparently trying to justify not having gone to the police earlier, most likely because he did not realize that the law did not require him to.

> Matanov also told the detective that he mostly knew the Tsarnaevs through a common place of worship and through playing soccer, which Matanov intended to be false, misleading, and to conceal the fact that Matanov was Tamerlan Tsarnaev's friend and had seen him twice that week on occasions unconnected with soccer and worship.

There is no indication, however, that the detective asked Kair when or under what circumstances he had last seen Tamerlan. In fact, when Kair's defense attorney got a transcript of this interview, he discovered that the detective had interrupted Kair's story of his relationship with Tamerlan.

> Matanov also told the detective that he knew that Tamerlan Tsarnaev had a wife and daughter but claimed not to know whether they lived with Tamerlan, which Matanov intended to be false, misleading, and to conceal the fact that Matanov knew that Tamerlan Tsarnaev lived with his wife and daughter and that Matanov had even exchanged greetings with Tsarnaev's wife and played with his daughter while he visited the Tsarnaevs' residence less than two days previous.

In fact, as defense attorney Edward Hayden pointed out in court a few days after the indictment was filed, the transcript shows Kair saying that he was not sure that Tamerlan's wife and daughter would still be at Norfolk Street now that Tamerlan was dead.

> Matanov also told the detective that he had not "participate[d] with" Tamerlan Tsarnaev at a house of worship since 2011, which Matanov intended to be false, misleading, and to conceal the fact that Matanov had been at a house of worship with Tamerlan at least as recently as August 2012.

That is the last of the lies Kair ostensibly told the Braintree police officer. Then he went home and asked Witness 1 to take some of the illegal cell phones off his hands. The person refused. Then Kair deleted most of the video files he had on his laptop as well as its Internet cache. By doing so, claimed the indictment:

> Matanov obstructed the FBI's determination of his Internet activity during the night of April 18 and the day of April 19, 2013, and the extent to which he shared the suspected bomber's philosophical justification for violence, among other topics of interest.

There is no allegation in the indictment that Kair was in any way involved with organizing the bombing or with trying to help the brothers evade law enforcement—or that he knew anything that might have altered, influenced, or sped up the investigation. Sharing violent beliefs is not a crime, and neither is trying to hide one's beliefs. It is also possible that Kair was trying to cover up the fact that he, like most Russian speakers on the planet, watched pirated video.

The FBI did not contact Kair until Saturday afternoon. Over

the course of several interviews he told the FBI everything he could recall, including the contents of his conversation with the brothers over dinner the evening of the bombing. Tamerlan had pointed out that no one had taken responsibility for the bombing and this probably meant that it was not al-Qaida, which always made its claim of responsibility within two hours of the act—a patently false assertion. The indictment accused Kair of making a series of contradictory statements in his conversations with the FBI: he had at first omitted the fact that he drove the brothers to the restaurant that night, though he admitted right away that dinner had been his treat. He also made muddled statements about when he finally and fully realized that the Tsarnaevs were the suspects, but the grand jury was certain that he knew when he first looked at the pictures on Thursday evening.

In sum, Kair's crime appears to amount to having been confused and perhaps scared, and trying to conceal his own petty illegal activity—after voluntarily going to the police with information about the brothers.

IN APRIL 2013, the FBI placed Kair under "overt surveillance"—like Ibragim Todashev, he knew he was constantly being followed and watched. He got a lawyer. In early May, Kair apparently decided to see if he could drive crazily enough to shake his FBI tail. The following day, his lawyer relayed the FBI's request to drive more carefully; Kair complied. Just before the Fourth of July, the lawyer relayed the FBI's request that Kair stay away from any celebrations ("The city was on edge," Special Agent Timothy McElroy offered later in court by way of explanation); Kair complied. Just before Patriots' Day 2014, the lawyer relayed the FBI's request that Kair leave the city for the holiday; Kair complied. But once the anniversary of the bombing had passed, things appeared to get back to normal: Kair began making plans for his new export-import business, and he even let his relationship with his lawyer lapse. Then he gave Amir a ride to the federal prison. Two days later, he was in jail himself.

He was wearing an orange jumpsuit when he was led into a courtroom at the federal courthouse in Boston for his detention hearing and arraignment on June 4, 2014. A bailiff removed Kair's handcuffs once he had waddled over to the defense table; the shackles stayed on. His court-appointed defense lawyer, Edward Hayden, ran through the indictment, pointing out the inconsistencies, the absurdities, and most important, the absence of a description of anything that could be construed as a crime.

The prosecution stressed that Kair was facing up to twenty-eight years in prison—eight for lying and twenty for obstructing justice—and this made him a flight risk. Kair speaks seven languages and has "significant ties outside the country," making it even more likely that he would flee, argued Assistant U.S. Attorney Scott Riley. Plus, he said, the defendant would probably be deported if convicted—all the more reason to try to leave the country before trial if he were released on bail.

The judge noted that Kair could not actually be deported to his country of origin because the United States had granted him political asylum. At least one of the prosecutor's arguments was thus rejected out of hand. It began to seem possible that this was that rare—perhaps unique—occasion when a noncitizen in a terrorism case would be released on bail. Maybe all the defense attorney had to do now was ask for it.

"At this point I cannot find reason to argue against detention," said Hayden instead. "I don't see any place for him to go." Kair had been behind bars for less than a week, but his life had fallen apart: his landlord had already evicted him and his employer had fired him, revoking his lease on the cab. With no home, no job, and no family in the United States, Kair was now committed to "voluntary detention without prejudice" in county jail.

In a few weeks, the women of the Free Jahar movement organized a place for Kair to stay in the Boston area—and if the judge would allow him to leave the district, Elena Teyer had volunteered to house him in Savannah indefinitely. But the judge rejected this proposal, and Kair's detention stopped being "voluntary." He was scheduled to face trial no sooner than the summer of 2015.

Twelve

WHAT WILL WE KNOW?

W hy are you writing this book?" Mohammed Gadzhiev, Tamerlan's friend and deputy head of the Union of the Just, asked me. We had spent most of a day talking, and the conversation had taken a few twists. Gadzhiev had been by turns condescending, engaged, and intimidating. Now, in the evening, we were drinking black tea at a large wooden table outdoors at a roadside café on the outskirts of Makhachkala, and Gadzhiev signaled it was time I came clean about my agenda. Specifically, he wanted to know why I had asked comparatively few questions about the celebrity martyrs whom Tamerlan had been rumored to have tried to contact in Dagestan. Because, I said, I saw no credence to the rumors—an impression my interlocutor clearly shared. I had asked him many detailed questions about his own time with Tamerlan and conversations they had had, and what he was asking me now was this: If I was not chasing the story of the great Dagestan-based terrorist conspiracy that radicalized Tamerlan Tsarnaev, then what story was I writing?

I told him I had been a reporter at both of the wars in Chechnya and had covered their aftermath, and he was mildly impressed. I told him that a few years back I had spent time at a university studying with people who strove to understand the nature of terrorism. I told him that I had been a teenage Russian-speaking immigrant in Boston—and at this point I sensed that Gadzhiev had lost interest.

"So you are one of those people who think social injustice is to blame," he said, his voice brittle with disappointment. "Why can't you believe that he simply objected to U.S. foreign policy and that's why he did it?"

In fact, I can and do believe that not only Tamerlan but Jahar as well could have made a rational choice—that is, a choice consistent with their values and their understanding of causal relationships—and, as a result of that choice, set off bombs that killed three people and injured at least 264. The story I was trying to tell was not one of big conspiracies or even giant examples of injustice. The people in key roles in this story are few, the ideas they hold are uncomplicated, and the plans they conjure are anything but far-reaching. It was the hardest and most frightening kind of story to believe.

The dominant understanding of terrorism in American culture, which has driven both media coverage of terrorism and law enforcement response to it, rests on the concept of "radicalization." Radicalization theory has its roots much more in the FBI, whose staff psychologists and behavior specialists have developed it, than in the academic study of terrorism, whose representatives briefly became talking heads on American television after September 11 and still stalwartly try—and fail—to explain to the civilian branches of government what they have learned. According to radicalization theory, a person becomes a terrorist by way of identifiable stages of adopting increasingly radical ideas, until he or she is finally radicalized into terrorist action. This theory has shaped policy, behavior, and lives, though it remains highly controversial among terrorism scholars. Common sense and human experience show that only a small minority of people who subscribe to radical ideas—even the kinds of radical ideas that justify and promote violence—actually engage in violence. Research also shows that some terrorists do not hold strong political or ideological beliefs. In other words, knowing what someone believes can help neither to predict terrorism nor to explain it. Still, the bulk of the FBI's efforts in the War on Terror have concentrated on tracking routes to presumed radicalization, ferreting out ostensibly radicalized individuals, and cracking down on networks that supposedly facilitate radicalization. At first it was assumed that where there is radicalization, there is a network, but in recent years the FBI has been proposing the "lone wolf" terrorist model to explain the apparent absence of such networks in some cases. The radicalization hypothesis itself, on the other hand, has held steady in the face of a glaring lack of evidence.

In the wake of the Boston Marathon bombing, both law enforcement and the American press corps focused their efforts on finding out who radicalized Tamerlan or both of the Tsarnaev brothers, and when and where. The possibility that their actions were driven by simple ideas acquired without any concerted outside help, that, as Gadzhiev said, Tamerlan "simply objected to U.S. foreign policy" like hundreds of thousands of other people but, unlike the overwhelming majority of them, decided to use a bomb to express his opposition—this terrifyingly simple idea was never on the table.

For anyone inclined to feel sympathy for the brothers, or at least to attempt to understand them—that is, for their friends and family, and the friends and family of anyone caught up in the investigation—Gadzhiev's simple explanation is also too painful and counterintuitive to entertain. The fallout that has so direly affected this group seems to demand a larger, more dramatic explanation. So people as different in background, social status, and relationship to the events as Zubeidat, Amir, and some of the Tsarnaevs' American friends have come to subscribe to one of any number of variants of a single conspiracy theory.

THE FIRST COHERENT conspiracy theory took shape within a month of the marathon bombing. In May 2013, in London, I met with Akhmed Zakayev, the last surviving member of the 1990s pro-independence Chechen leadership who was still fighting that fight. He had no doubt that the bombing had been organized by the FSB, the Russian secret police. "Putin and his cohorts are the only ones who benefited from this bombing," he said. How? Russia was preparing to host the Olympic Games in Sochi in 2014. Some politicians and media in the West had questioned the wisdom of giving the Olympics to Russia, because Putin's law enforcement could not be trusted to ensure the safety of visiting athletes, dignitaries, and the public. Russia had seen dozens of terrorist attacks every year of the past decade—suicide bombings, car bombs, and several hostage-takings—so many, in fact, that they drew public attention, even inside Russia, only when the attacks occurred outside the embattled regions of the North Caucasus. In November 2009, a high-speed train going from Moscow to Saint Petersburg crashed, killing twenty-eight people and injuring more than ninety; law enforcement classified the disaster as a terrorist attack. In March 2010, two explosions in the Moscow Metro killed forty people and injured more than a hundred; a pan-Caucasian insurgent organization with roots in Chechnya claimed credit. In January 2011, a bomb went off in the arrivals hall of a Moscow airport, killing thirty-seven people and wounding 180. Add to this history the many attacks, large and small, in and around

Chechnya and Dagestan; the fact that Sochi is geographically close to the region; and the Olympic Games' unfortunate history as a terrorist target: the 1972 hostage-taking at the Munich Olympics, where eleven members of the Israeli team, one German police-man, and five of the terrorists were killed after a long standoff and a bungled rescue, was one of the attacks that launched the current era of international terrorism.

According to Zakayev's logic, Putin and his secret police, faced with growing concern about Russia's ability to provide adequate security during the Olympics—and knowing just how well-founded this concern was—hatched a paradoxical plot. They en-ticed two Chechen-Americans, the Tsarnaev brothers, to set off bombs at the Boston Marathon. This would reposition Chechen terrorism as an international threat—something Russia had long claimed but lacked evidence to back up—as well as shore up American support for a continued Russian crackdown in the Cau-casus and preemptively disarm any critics of what might prove to be an imperfect security effort in Sochi. After all, events would have ostensibly shown, the Americans had proved unable to pro-tect their own sporting events against the Chechens.

Zakayev based his arguments on the known facts. By this time the FBI had acknowledged that back in 2011 the FSB had alerted it to Tamerlan's existence, as part of a regular exchange of informa-tion on suspected terrorists. In Zakayev's view, this showed that the FSB was already tracking Tamerlan. When Tamerlan traveled to Dagestan in 2012, Zakayev was convinced, it was at the FSB's instigation. Once the young man was indoctrinated and trained, the FSB sent him back to the United States with instructions to set off a bomb at the next big sporting event.

No wonder Putin was uncharacteristically fast to react to the Boston bombing, becoming one of the first world leaders to express his condolences and stress the importance of international cooperation in the fight against terrorism. The Russian president, reasoned Zakayev, had planned the tragedy—and the reaction—himself.

Then there was the opposite theory, or perhaps the same theory but with a different cast of characters. A number of people, many of them far outside the usual-suspect circles of conspiracy theorists, became convinced that the FBI was behind the bombings. The FBI certainly had greater opportunity to commit the crime than did the FSB. The FBI had access to Tamerlan, it had had Tamerlan on its radar at least since the FSB alerted it to his existence in early 2011, and the FBI has been known to engage people in elaborate imaginary terrorist plots in order to identify potential attackers. But what would have been the FBI's motive? This is the weak part of the theory: most of the proponents to whom I have spoken suggest that the FBI enticed Tamerlan Tsarnaev to bomb the Boston Marathon in order to test the agency's ability to impose martial law in America.

Part of what has kept people engaged with the FBI-conspiracy theory, and has even kept new adherents streaming in, is the impressive list of inconsistencies a slew of self-styled investigators have identified in the law enforcement narrative of the bombing. Many of the criticisms of the FBI story are nitpicky and hardly bear repeating, and some are imaginary, but a few seem significant enough to consider. Any conspiracy theorist, for example, will tell you about the backpack: in the available photographs of Jahar taken at the marathon, he is seen walking in the crowd, carrying a gray backpack easily on one shoulder. Another set of pictures shows a backpack that has been ripped apart by the device that exploded inside it. The backpack in the second set of photos is black. Of course, the most likely explanation for the discrepancy is that there were two backpacks, a gray one carried by Jahar and a black one carried by Tamerlan. But the indictment in Jahar's case says that both bombs were concealed inside black backpacks. And the conspiracy theorists also have pictures of a third person—someone whose general demeanor and outfit make the theorists believe he is an officer of some sort of military or militarized organization—with just that kind of black backpack with a white square on its handle that can also be seen in the second set of photographs. (In the available photos of Tamerlan, he is carrying a black backpack, but one without a white square on the handle.)

There may be a variety of explanations for this—two people at the giant event could have had the same backpack, or any or all of the photographs may be inauthentic—but the conspiracy theorists point to other holes in the story: Danny, the owner of the hijacked SUV, made contradictory statements about the timing and sequence of events; police officers' accounts of the manhunt and the shoot-out are full of incredible assertions—cars turning around on a dime on narrow streets; individual cops being in three places at once, or on what appear to be thirty-six-hour shifts, or both—and the explosive device that was supposedly thrown by one of the brothers in the middle of a tiny residential street harmed no one and damaged nothing.

The inconsistencies in stories told by police officers are likely to have logical explanations, paramount among them the fact that the police were sleep-deprived, scared, and genuinely confused by the disarray in the ranks of law enforcement. The general human tendency to misremember details would have been exacerbated. If any of them had things to conceal, these probably concerned matters peripheral to the question of whether the brothers were guilty of the bombing. But they serve as a reminder to consider what evidence was available when American public opinion convicted the brothers, long before any proof was presented in a court of law.

Members of the investigative team originally picked out Jahar and Tamerlan on surveillance videos because their behavior appeared different from that of the rest of the marathon spectators. When the first blast sounded, the two did not panic or run. By all accounts, before the FBI released the surveillance photos and asked for help identifying the suspects, the brothers acted normal, showing no signs of distress or intention to escape—until they became the objects of a manhunt. At that point the very fact that they were running away served as affirmation of their guilt.

Later, other evidence was said to emerge. A few days after Jahar was captured, Massachusetts governor Deval Patrick and several media outlets citing sources in law enforcement said that there existed another video, in which Jahar could be seen setting his backpack down on the ground at the spot where the second explosion occurred. Then, according to these sources, he could be seen walking away—and acting calm when the first explosion sounded. The video was not released to the public.

While Jahar was hiding in the boat, he scrawled a note on its interior wall. It was quoted in the grand jury indictment, and later a larger portion was included in one of the prosecution's filings in the case:

> I'm jealous of my brother who ha[s] [re]ceived the reward of jan-
> nutul Firdaus[1] (inshallah) before me. I do not mourn because his
> soul is very much alive. God has a plan for each person. Mine was
> to hide in this boat and shed some light on our actions. I ask Allah

---

1. In Arabic, the "highest part of paradise."

to make me a shahied (iA)[2] to allow me to return to him and be among all the righteous people in the highest levels of heaven. He who Allah guides no one can misguide. A[llah Ak]bar!

The US Government is killing our innocent civilians but most of you already know that. As a [illegible] I can't stand to see such evil go unpunished, we Muslims are one body, you hurt one you hurt us all. Well at least that's how muhhammad (pbuh[3]) wanted it to be [for]ever, the ummah[4] is beginning to rise/ [illegible] has awoken the mujahideen, know you are fighting men who look into the barrel of your gun and see heaven, now how can you compete with that. We are promised victory and we will surely get it. Now I don't like killing innocent people it is forbidden in Islam but due to said [illegible] it is allowed. All credit goes [illegible].

Stop killing our innocent people and we will stop.

At some point someone managed to snap a picture of the note—or a picture was leaked by law enforcement—and ABC News published it. It appears to show that the quoted version in the filing omits the following sentences: "I bear witness that there is no God but Allah and that Muhammad is his messenger. [bullet hole] actions come with a [me]ssage and that is [bullet hole], in'shallah."

This note, which the media often called a confession, certainly makes it seem that the brothers were the marathon bombers, but it does not say it—at least the portion known to the public does not. It contains no information on where, when, or how the brothers made the pressure-cooker bombs and whether anyone helped

---

2. Martyr (inshallah).
3. Abbreviation for "Peace be upon him."
4. Nation; community; a people.

them, how and when they transported them to Boylston Street in Boston, where and when they planted them, and who detonated them. In other words, it contains none of the kinds of specific information that generally constitutes a confession. If the court of public opinion could be held to the standard of reasonable doubt, then someone would have to ask its jury this question: *Is it conceivable that the Tsarnaev brothers were not the marathon bombers but, once they knew they were the suspects, they decided to run?* The answer would have to be, *Yes, it is conceivable.* The evidence available to the public before the trial began in January 2015 included nothing that directly linked the Tsarnaev brothers to the bombing or explained its mechanics or the brothers' motivation.

THIS BOOK is not an impartial jury. Like the American public, it assumes from the start that Tamerlan and Jahar Tsarnaev are the Boston Marathon bombers. The difficulty with making sense of their story occurs sometime before Jahar's non-confession confession and has only a little to do with the lack of a clear picture of the steps they took to manufacture and plant the bombs. What is truly lacking from the story is a clear and accessible explanation for how two young men who appear to be very much like hundreds of thousands of other young men came to cause carnage in the center of their own city.

On the Friday after the bombing, when Tamerlan was already dead but Jahar was still on the loose, Maret Tsarnaeva, Anzor's older sister, spoke to reporters in Toronto. Soon after, she would tell people that she was certain the bombing was a secret-police plot and that she was in danger. And then she would disappear— American friends assumed that she moved back to Chechnya. But that day, she was still seeking to make herself heard, in fluent, idiomatic, if heavily accented, English. "For me to be convinced that these two nephews of mine did this cannot be taken lightly," she said. Journalists shouted questions, struggling to be heard over one another's voices and the incessant clicking of shutters. "Why are you asking question, 'Do you believe?'" Maret finally snapped. "If they have done this, I have to believe."

It was just very difficult to believe. Friends and other relatives argued that it was impossible: the brothers were normal, acted normal, and loved their friends and family. But terrorists are normal. As far back as 1981, Martha Crenshaw, a pioneer in the study of modern terrorism, wrote, "The outstanding common characteristic of terrorists is their normality." This observation has since been echoed and further substantiated. Scott Atran, an anthropologist who has traveled the world talking to current and perhaps future members of jihadi groups, has identified several other characteristics that his subjects seem to share. They are usually in their early twenties, they are often immigrants, they have usually been educated in secular schools, often with an emphasis on science, they are usually married, and their socioeconomic background is usually middle-class but marginalized. They tend to form most of their connections in small circles of family and friends; they socialize within them, marry within them, and their terrorist networks are for the most part limited to them.

Crenshaw points to political conditions that enable terrorism—a group has to be excluded from the political process. And she suggests one other personality trait required of a terrorist: a high tolerance for risk. Growing up in and around war zones and in high-crime environments will inure a person to risk and violence. So the Tsarnaev brothers fit the profile perfectly. But most disaffected immigrants from unstable countries, most immigrants who never make it out of the struggling lower rung of the middle class and beyond the bounds of a suffocating social circle, even most angry Muslim young men without a religious education but with a high tolerance for danger, do not build bombs and kill people.

The imagination demands something distinct, huge, and immediately recognizable to explain the leap between an ordinary life and the path of a terrorist. In December 2013, *The Boston Globe* published a near-book-length exposé based on almost eight months of reporting by a team of journalists, and this team's conclusion was that Tamerlan suffered from schizophrenia. He apparently heard voices that told him to do terrible things. The evidence for this newspaper diagnosis was this: it would seem that Zubeidat once said something about Tamerlan's "voices" to Max Mazaev's wife, who, years later—after the bombing—relayed the conversation to her husband, who, in turn, mentioned it in a telephone conversation with a psychiatrist who had once treated Anzor but had never met Tamerlan—and the psychiatrist may have said the word "schizophrenia," among others. The diagnosis not only was based on ephemeral evidence but was actually counterfactual: terrorism experts broadly agree that a firm grip on reality is required to carry out a secret plot of any complexity. As for the "voices," Zubeidat most likely meant an inner voice that she felt, at that moment, was leading her teenage son astray.

But if it was not a giant mental disorder, was there a huge conspiracy that led Tamerlan and Jahar astray? Most of the media coverage hewed to the FBI's radicalization theory, and proposed a variety of characters suspected of having indoctrinated Tamerlan: first a man named Misha, who turned out to be a soft-spoken Armenian-born Muslim convert living in Rhode Island who had not seen Tamerlan in three years; then the Russian-Canadian Dagestani insurgent William Plotnikov and the teenage Dagestani fighter Mahmud Nidal; and, finally, Magomed Kartashov's Union of the Just. The problem with these theories is that either the supposed villains have no evident relationship to an armed struggle, as in the cases of Misha and Kartashov, or there is no evidence that Tamerlan ever met them, as in the cases of Plotnikov and Nidal.

SINCE SEPTEMBER 2001, U.S. courts have taken up an average of forty terrorism-related cases a year. More than five hundred people have been charged, and virtually all of them have been convicted and sentenced. Dozens of bombing plots have been revealed. In 2014, Human Rights Watch released a report that analyzed many of those cases. The researchers concluded that "all of the high-profile domestic terrorism plots of the last decade, with four exceptions, were actually FBI sting operations—plots conducted with the direct involvement of law enforcement informants or agents, including plots that were proposed or led by informants."

Since 9/11, the bulk of the FBI's efforts have centered on fighting terrorism, which became its top institutional priority and consumes forty percent of the agency's operating budget. Between 2001 and 2013, the number of terrorist attacks carried out on American soil by people connected to Islamic organizations numbered zero, but trumped-up terrorist plots numbered in the dozens, and the people who went to jail because of them in the hundreds. The Human Rights Watch report describes the work of the FBI (initially quoting from a former FBI agent, Michael German):

"Today's terrorism sting operations reflect a significant departure from past practice. When the FBI undercover agent or informant is the only purported link to a real terrorist group, supplies the motive, designs the plot and provides all the weapons, one has to question whether they are combatting terrorism or creating it. . . ." In many of the sting operations we examined, informants and undercover agents carefully laid out an ideological basis for a proposed terrorist attack, and then provided investigative targets with a range of options and the weapons necessary to carry out the attack. Instead of beginning a sting at the point where the target had expressed an interest in engaging in illegal conduct, many terrorism sting operations that we investigated facilitated or invented the target's willingness to act before presenting the tangible opportunity to do so. In this way, the FBI may have created terrorists out of law-abiding individuals. In these cases, the informants and agents often seemed to choose targets based on their religious or political beliefs. They often chose targets who were particularly vulnerable—whether because of mental disability, or because they were indigent and needed money that the government offered them.

In one case, it was the FBI informant who suggested detonating a bomb near a synagogue in the Bronx and using Stinger missiles to attack airplanes taking off from Stewart Air National Guard Base near Newburgh, New York. The informant assembled the group for the planned attacks and procured the weapons. Then the four men the informant had recruited were arrested. Federal judge Colleen McMahon, who heard the case in Manhattan in 2010–2011, said, "The essence of what occurred here is that a government, understandably zealous to protect its citizens from terrorists, came upon a man both bigoted and suggestible, one who was incapable of committing an act of terrorism on his own." The judge was referring to the alleged leader of the Newburgh Four, James Cromitie. "Only the government could have made a terrorist out of Mr. Cromitie, whose buffoonery is positively Shakespearean in scope," said Judge McMahon, and sentenced the defendants to twenty-five years behind bars, in accordance with mandatory-sentencing guidelines.

Most of the people I have heard arguing that the FBI was responsible for the Boston Marathon bombing were unaware of the agency's recent pattern of hatching terrorism plots. Some of them were basing their impression on their personal experience: "I am used to being set up," said Maret Tsarnaeva, referring to the life of a Chechen in the former Soviet Union. Others drew inferences from their knowledge of the Boston FBI office's track record.

When Jahar was indicted in federal court in Boston in July 2013, a major trial was under way in the courtroom next door: the notorious gangster James "Whitey" Bulger, captured after sixteen years on the run, was being tried for racketeering. Files made public during the Bulger trial showed that for at least fifteen years, the mobster had fed the FBI information about both rivals and associates, using the agency to eliminate obstacles and advance his business while the FBI ignored his crimes, which included numerous murders, in exchange for information and a cut of the proceeds.

Two years earlier, another high-profile case that was heard at the same courthouse brought to light what had long been rumored: a Watertown- and Waltham-based drug ring had for years, and to the tune of millions of dollars, enjoyed the protection of one or more members of the Watertown Police Department, who helped them avoid investigations and raids. The possible connection between this case and Tamerlan gave rise to some of the more complicated—and convincing—Boston-grown conspiracy theories.

The friends with whom Tamerlan dealt and smoked pot lived in Watertown—indeed, Tamerlan's stories about the town's crooked cops left an impression on his friend Mohammed Gadzhiev in Dagestan. Brendan Mess was almost undoubtedly connected to the Watertown drug ring. The murder of Mess, Erik Weissman, and Raphael Teken, which was never fully investigated, had been handled by the office of the Middlesex County district attorney, at the time Gerard Leone; Leone had also judged the Golden Gloves amateur boxing competition in Lowell that Tamerlan had won.

The list of coincidences continues. Less than three months after the Waltham triple murder, another person in the Boston area was killed in the same bizarre and barbaric manner, by having her throat slashed with such force that she was nearly decapitated. Sixty-year-old Gail Miles was found killed in her Roxbury apartment on December 3, 2011. Miles was a former Watertown police officer: she had made history by becoming the first black woman on the force, and then made history again sixteen years later, in 2000, when she sued the department for racial and gender discrimination. One of the men she accused of harassment was Jeff Pugliese, the officer who would later engage Tamerlan in the one-on-one firefight on Laurel Street in Watertown. No one was ever charged in her murder, and the crime itself has not surfaced significantly in the Boston media since the initial few days of coverage—a highly unusual lack of profile for the killing of a former police officer.

And then there are the CIA coincidences. Anzor's former sister-in-law Samantha Fuller, his brother Ruslan's first wife, was the daughter of Graham Fuller, a former highly placed CIA official whose areas of specialization included Russia and Islamic countries and communities. Both Samantha and Ruslan worked for U.S. government–funded programs in Kyrgyzstan and Kazakhstan, programs widely believed to have ties to the CIA. So in some conspiracy theories, it is the CIA connection that brings the Tsarnaevs to the United States in the first place.

There are enough connections and coincidences to spin any

number of narratives that explain not only how the Tsarnaevs got to America but also who is responsible for the Waltham triple murder, why it was not investigated, how the brothers got the idea to bomb the marathon, and why a Boston FBI agent killed Ibragim Todashev. Most likely all of these theories are wrong. The bulk of the contradictions and inconsistencies in this story can be explained by things much more pervasive and also often more dangerous than conspiracies: incompetence, ignorance, and fear. But some of these connections provide useful leads. Indeed, using only the known facts, it is possible to construct a plausible theory of what happened with the Tsarnaev brothers—and to point to the gaping holes that the investigation into the attack had, at least by the time Jahar's trial began, failed to answer.

THIS PART OF THE STORY begins in March 2011, when the Russian FSB sent the FBI a letter alerting the agency to the existence of Tamerlan Tsarnaev, a Chechen from Dagestan living in the Boston area who, the FSB claimed, had become radicalized. The FSB's approach to identifying suspected radicals abroad, for the purposes of continued cooperation with the FBI in the War on Terror, is exactly the same as at home: it considers all urban young Muslim men to be radical—and to be especially radical if they are of Chechen descent. The FSB's counterparts in the FBI know this and talk about the Russians "playing whack-a-mole" instead of fighting terror. They knew that they had received Tamerlan's name simply because the FSB happened to find it—and that happened probably because when Zubeidat and Anzor renewed their Russian passports, they had to put down the names and addresses of their children. Still, though the FBI knew that the FSB's intelligence on suspected Islamic radicals was generally useless, it had its own use for the name: Tamerlan fit perfectly the FBI's "investigative profile." He was young, an immigrant, lacked a steady income, and, as a Russian-speaking Muslim in Boston, was an outsider among outsiders. In fact, the FBI had followed this logic earlier, all on its own: the first time an agent came to Norfolk Street to interview Zubeidat was in 2002, the year the family arrived in the United States. The agency's visits were roughly annual after that—a perfectly ordinary occurrence for people from places the United States views with suspicion (my own first FBI interview, with the Boston field office, took place when I was sixteen; the agents did not bother to seek my parents' presence or permission)—but the FSB alert prompted the FBI to intensify its efforts.

In the spring and summer of 2011, FBI field agents interviewed Tamerlan at least three times, came to the house on Norfolk Street, and talked to members of the Tsarnaev household. Zubeidat says that the agents tried to recruit Tamerlan. After the bombing, FBI director James Comey, in response to a series of questions from Senate Judiciary Committee member Charles Grassley, a Republican from Iowa, denied that the agency had tried to recruit Tamerlan, but declined to elaborate.

In September 2011, Mess, Weissman, and Teken were killed. There are at least three possible explanations for why law enforcement failed to investigate the gruesome—and unusual—murders: (1) Tamerlan committed the murders, but he was already informing for the FBI or being recruited into one of its terrorist plots, and the FBI protected him from scrutiny as it had done with Whitey Bulger when he murdered people; (2) Tamerlan committed the murders, but he did so either on orders from or in cooperation with the Watertown police, which had its own long-standing interests in the local drug market; (3) the murders were committed by the cops themselves, which is one explanation for the similarity to the later killing of former policewoman Gail Miles.

In January 2012, Tamerlan traveled to Dagestan. The explanation given to Joanna Herlihy and others—that he was going there to renew his Russian passport—was a lie. At least by the time Tamerlan arrived in Dagestan, he had no Russian passport to renew. (Zubeidat told Joanna that he lost all his Russian documents when he got there, but it is unclear how he could have had a Russian passport at all, having lived in the United States for longer than one could have been valid.) He was going back for the same reason any of the Tsarnaevs ever went anywhere: to find a better place to be. He found it. But after six months, someone called him back to the United States urgently. He told people it had something to do with his documents, and this was probably true. Political asylees who do not yet have their U.S. passports are typically advised not to travel to their countries of origin; the very fact of such travel throws doubt on their claim that they face danger at home. In truth, though, people do it all the time and rarely get caught—but when they are caught, they may not be allowed to reenter the United States. It seems that Tamerlan rushed back to America because someone warned him—or, more accurately, threatened him—that he would not be allowed back in. Such a warning could have come only from the FBI. Either Tamerlan had been gone too long for the tastes of the agents to whom he had promised his services as an informant, or the agents had decided that it was time to use a threat to cement or jump-start the recruitment effort. Tamerlan hurried back to Cambridge, where he was a househusband with only the siren call of the FBI informant or recruiter and his friends in now faraway Dagestan for intellectual company. What happened then was most predictable.

The history of terrorism is full of recruits gone rogue—it is dominated by groups that switched or abandoned loyalties. Perhaps the only surprising aspect of the FBI's list of manufactured terrorist plots of the past dozen years is that all of them appear to have remained in the agency's hands. Until Tamerlan Tsarnaev, who had, from all available information, hardly given jihad a thought before being fingered by the FSB and targeted by the FBI, went rogue. And, in the way of many modern terrorists, teamed up with his brother.

ACCORDING TO FBI REPRESENTATIVES who have spoken publicly about the case, members of the investigative team first focused on the images of the brothers about thirty-six hours before they released the photographs—and the decision to release them was prompted by the threat of a media leak. So the agency called a press conference, showed the images, and asked for the public's help in identifying the suspects. The FBI could not use its facial-recognition software for the purpose because the surveillance camera that shot the video was mounted well above people's heads, distorting the angle. All the pictures shown at the press conference were indeed made by cameras looking down on the subjects. While that may work as a technical explanation, it cannot explain how members of the Joint Terrorism Task Force had failed to recognize an individual they had interviewed and had under surveillance just two years earlier—and whose entire family had been tracked by the FBI for more than a decade. One conceivable reason is incompetence: it is theoretically possible that agents who pinpointed the brothers on the surveillance video failed to take the obvious step of showing the pictures to every local agent who had recently interviewed people suspected of links to terrorist organizations. A more logical explanation is that the person or persons who were in a position to recognize the brothers were consciously concealing this fact in order to protect their own or the agency's reputation—either because it would look like the FBI had fumbled a solid investigative lead, causing tragedy, or worse, because the FBI had considered Tamerlan an informant.

Many people who recognized the brothers on television chose not to call the FBI hotline; but there were those who did call. At least one former high school classmate of Jahar's who had been on the wrestling team with him called. Maret Tsarnaeva, the brothers' aunt, called as well. By the time she talked to journalists, nearly twenty-four hours later, no one had contacted her in response to her call. Both of these calls appear to have been made before the MIT police officer was killed on Thursday evening.

In an October 2013 letter to FBI director Comey, Senator Grassley pointed to another odd set of circumstances:

> My office has been made aware of another instance following the bombing in which it appears that information was not shared. In the hours leading up to the shooting of Massachusetts Institute of Technology (MIT) Police Officer Sean Collier and the death of the older suspect involved in the bombing, sources revealed that uniformed Cambridge Police Department officers encountered multiple teams of FBI employees conducting surveillance in the area of Central Square in Cambridge, Massachusetts. It is unclear who the FBI was watching, but these sources allege that the Cambridge Police Department, including its representation at the JTTF, was not previously made aware of the FBI's activity in Cambridge.

Several months later, Boston reporters talked to a Cambridge police officer who described the town swarming with FBI that evening and concluded that the agency had been laying siege to the neighborhood in order to capture the brothers. By the time Senator Grassley's office released the letter, in October, both the head of the FBI's Boston operation, Richard DesLauriers, and Boston's police commissioner had resigned, but three days after the letter appeared, the FBI field office in Boston, the Massachusetts State Police, and the Boston police (but not the Cambridge police, which is separate) issued a joint statement denying that the FBI was watching the Tsarnaevs before the Sean Collier murder, or even the shoot-out in Watertown:

> Members of the Joint Terrorism Task Force did not know their identities until shortly after Tamerlan Tsarnaev's death when they fingerprinted his corpse. Nor did the Joint Terrorism Task Force have the Tsarnaevs under surveillance at any time after the assessment of Tamerlan Tsarnaev was closed in 2011. The Joint Terrorism Task Force was at M.I.T., located in Cambridge, Massachusetts, on April 18, 2013, on a matter unrelated to the Tsarnaev brothers. Additionally, the Tsarnaev brothers were never sources for the FBI nor did the FBI attempt to recruit them as sources. . . . To be absolutely clear: No one was surveilling the Tsarnaevs, and they were not identified until after the shootout. Any claims to the contrary are false.

Here, an explanation of incompetence strains the imagination: the FBI is claiming that it failed to follow up on leads identifying someone who was once considered a terrorism risk, even though these leads came in to its tip line set up specifically for this purpose, and in one instance from a woman—a lawyer—who claimed to have identified her own nephews in the pictures. It is also, bizarrely, claiming to have deployed personnel to pursue an unrelated matter in Cambridge on the Thursday after the bombing, despite an all-hands-on-deck order from the FBI director at the time, Robert Mueller. Another explanation in this instance makes infinitely more sense: The FBI was setting up an operation without notifying its local partners because it needed to ensure that no other law enforcement got to Tamerlan Tsarnaev before the FBI had captured—or killed—him. In other words, the explanation that best fits the facts is a cover-up.

TWO MYSTERIES REMAIN. Why did Ibragim Todashev die? Are Elena Teyer and Boston conspiracy theorists right to believe that his killing was planned—and if it was, then why did law enforcement want him dead? Logically, the assumption that Todashev was not involved in the triple murder in Waltham is at odds with the proposition that he was killed intentionally. If he knew nothing, there was no reason to get rid of him. If he did know something about the murder, it is still difficult to see why anyone would have needed him to die when he was already writing a confession. Of course, the confession is full of inaccuracies, but that in itself is neither unusual nor suggestive of Todashev's innocence. After all, Robel Phillipos signed an outrageously inaccurate confession describing actions he had actually witnessed or taken, and the FBI had no issue with presenting it as evidence in court. The court, in turn, found Phillipos guilty. Todashev's case, involving a Chechen immigrant with a criminal record, would have been even easier to prosecute, so the FBI had little reason to worry about the quality of its evidence.

Todashev's death almost certainly resulted from a combination of incompetence and fear. The FBI found Todashev terrifying. This comes across in the testimony of individual agents as well as in the institution's very approach to him: it sent seven armed officers to tackle Todashev in order to conduct its first "voluntary interview" with him. For his last interview, Todashev was to face four officers—the Orlando and Boston FBI agents and the two Massachusetts state troopers. One of the members of this team dropped out when the officers discovered that Todashev was not alone; the Orlando agent stayed in the parking lot with Khusein Taramov. Then the interview seemed to go much better than expected, the officers felt happy, lost vigilance, and one of the state troopers stepped outside, leaving only two armed men with the frightening martial artist, who was sitting on a mattress on the floor writing a confession. Whatever Todashev did when he stopped writing—whether he threw the coffee table, ran to the kitchen to rummage for a knife, grabbed a stick, or did all of these things—reminded the officers that they were facing a dangerously and perhaps superhumanly strong man. The fear caused the trooper to fumble with his holster and the FBI agent to shoot to kill. FBI agents are not generally instructed to try to make sure that an aggressive suspect survives, and the agency has exonerated its officers in every single internal investigation into such shootings, so there was no institutional incentive for Agent Aaron McFarlane to try to keep Todashev alive. His death virtually guarantees that we will never know who killed the three men in Waltham, and why.

The other mystery of the narrative of the Boston Marathon bombing is the buried lead of the story, the gaping hole in the investigation. Where did the bombs come from? The grand jury indictment postulates that the brothers read a bomb-making recipe in the al-Qaida–affiliated *Inspire* magazine and built them at home using pressure cookers, gunpowder from fireworks, and other materials. The *Boston Globe* exposé repeats this simple narrative:

> One article that both the Tsarnaev brothers apparently read closely, which appeared in the summer 2010 issue of *Inspire*, Al Qaeda's online English-language journal, was called "Make a Bomb in The Kitchen of Your Mom." The article provided detailed instruction on how to make a bomb in a pressure cooker using easily obtained flammable materials and shrapnel. The bomb is then attached to an electrical source with "the wires sticking out of the hole in the lid of the cooker." The article offers several final safety tips, including this: "Put your trust in Allah and pray for the success of your operation. This is the most important rule."
>
> And then the bomb is ready to go.

I talked to several explosives experts who assured me that "making a bomb in the kitchen of your mom" was probably an impossible proposition. In May 2014, after the initial and even the secondary wave of media attention had died down, U.S. Attorney Carmen Ortiz filed a motion that contained the following passage:

> The Marathon bombs were constructed using improvised fuses made from Christmas lights and improvised, remote-control detonators fashioned from model car parts. These relatively sophisticated devices would have been difficult for the Tsarnaevs to fabricate successfully without training or assistance from others.
>
> The Tsarnaevs also appeared to have crushed and emptied hundreds of individual fireworks containing black powder in order to obtain explosive fuel for the bombs. The black powder used in fireworks is extremely fine; it was therefore reasonable to

expect that if the Tsarnaevs had crushed the fireworks and built the bombs all by themselves, traces of black powder would be found wherever they had done the work. Yet searches of the Tsarnaevs' residences, three vehicles, and other locations associated with them yielded virtually no traces of black powder, again strongly suggesting that others had built, or at least helped the Tsarnaevs build, the bombs, and thus might have built more.

Of the five hundred people tried for terrorism and related offenses in U.S. courts in the past dozen years, Jahar Tsarnaev is the first to have set off a real bomb rather than a fake explosive provided by the FBI—and going into his trial, there was no indication that the FBI knew where and how the bombs had been made and whether anyone had helped make them. If someone had, it was not the young men who had been convicted as Jahar's accomplices.

THE STORY OF THE BOMBS, if it is ever known, may turn out to involve more people, and people with bigger ideas than the people named in this book—or it may not. As for the brothers themselves, theirs remains a small story, in which nothing extraordinary happens—or, rather, no extraordinary event is necessary to explain what happened. One had only to be born in the wrong place at the wrong time, as many people are, to never feel that one belongs, to see every opportunity, even those that seem within reach, pass one by—until the opportunity to be somebody finally, almost accidentally, presents itself. This is where the small story of the Tsarnaevs joins the large story of the War on Terror.

"The War Against Terror is another moment in this continuing saga of our species toward an unpredictable somewhere between

All against All and One World," writes Scott Atran, attempting to place terrorism in the context of the evolution of human identities.

> While economic globalization has steamrolled or left aside large chunks of humankind, political globalization actively engages people of all societies and walks of life—even the global econo-my's driftwood: refugees, migrants, marginals, and those most frustrated in their aspirations. For there is, together with a flat and fluid world, a more tribal, fragmented, and divisive world, as people unmoored from millennial traditions and cultures flail about in search of a social identity that is at once individual and intimate but with a greater sense of purpose and possibility of survival than the sorrow of here today, gone tomorrow. . . . Jihad offers the group pride of great achievements for the underachieving.

The rhetoric and actions of the U.S. government and its agents, in their outsize response and their targeting of specific communities, have probably done as much to create an imagined worldwide community of jihadists as have the efforts of al-Qaida and its allies. For Tamerlan, this vision offered a truer—and more realistic—path to greatness than boxing or keyboards could. And while Jahar may have envied his brother his place in heaven, he himself was getting ready to stand trial for doing exactly what he and his brother had wanted to do: for declaring war on a great power.

EPILOGUE

The winter of 2014–2015 in Boston was the coldest and whitest on record. One record-breaking blizzard accompanied by blistering cold was followed by another and then another, and then by the coldest days in living memory. Photographs of Bostonians skiing down once lively streets circulated in the papers and on the Internet, while in the city itself people watched life grind to a halt. Public transportation was suspended for days at a time, and then did not work with any regularity. Schools piled up snow days, stranding parents at home with children. At universities, some spring-semester classes never started. The roofs of dozens of businesses collapsed, and even where they remained intact, businesses lost money because neither workers nor customers could make their way through the snow. Ice dams formed when household heat melted rooftop snow, which instantly snapped frozen in the frigid air, making houses look like the Snow Queen's palace. "But for those of us living here, it's not a pretty picture," Cambridge journalist E. J. Graff wrote in *The New York Times* in February. "We are being devastated by a slow-motion disaster of historic proportions." The worst thing to happen to Boston since the Marathon bombing was in many ways its opposite: it was slow and quiet, and the full extent of the damage would be unclear for a long time.

"Where are the federal disaster funds, the presidential visit, Anderson Cooper interviewing victims, volunteers flying in?" wrote Graff. "The pictures may be pretty. But we need help, now."

Tamerlan had been dead for nearly two years, and Jahar had been in federal prison almost as long. Like some other inmates awaiting trial on terrorism charges, he was subjected to "special administrative measures," or SAMs, which create an extreme sort of solitary confinement. Inmates are usually banned from attempting communication with other prisoners. The exact restrictions imposed in specific cases are hard to ascertain, because SAMs subjects are forbidden to talk about them, but in Jahar's case, most of the SAMs provisions became part of the court record. Once the restrictions were imposed, in August 2013, he could communicate by phone only with his lawyers and immediate family members, and his interlocutors were banned from recording the conversations and from releasing any part of them to anyone else. All calls with family were to be monitored, recorded, and analyzed by the FBI for evidence of any attempt to pass messages. Aside from the legal team, only immediate family members could visit, and they were required to speak English to Jahar, while an FBI agent listened in. The visits with family could involve no physical contact: Jahar and the visitors used telephone receivers to talk through a glass partition. Correspondence was also allowed only with family members, only in English, and only at the rate of one three-page letter a week, addressed to a single recipient. Taken together, these restrictions meant that only Bella and Ailina could visit Jahar and that he could speak on the phone only to them and to Zubeidat.

The restrictions were imposed by order of U.S. Attorney General Eric Holder, who wrote: "I find that there is a substantial risk that his communications or contacts with persons could result in death or serious bodily injury to persons." Holder's memo gave two examples of the inmate's harmful contacts with the outside world: first, Jahar had asked Azamat, Dias, and Robel to hide evidence; second, Zubeidat had released portions of a May 24, 2013, phone call with him—the first time he had been able to speak on the phone after recovering from injuries to his vocal cords—"in an apparent attempt to engender sympathy for Tsarnaev." The memo added: "Tsarnaev has also gained widespread notoriety while incarcerated, as evidenced by his receipt of nearly one thousand pieces of unsolicited mail." By the time this document appeared, the government had collected all its evidence in the case against Dias, Azamat, and Robel, and it did not actually allege that Jahar had asked his friends to hide evidence. As for the portions of conversation publicized by Zubeidat, in which her son assured her that he was well, these "have little bearing on whether Tsarnaev will attempt to spread concrete actionable messages," argued the ACLU of Massachusetts in an amicus brief in support of the defense's attempt to have SAMs lifted. The court refused to lift SAMs—and even to allow the ACLU to file the brief.

AFTER THE INITIAL FLOOD of public attention—the news stories; then a *Rolling Stone* cover that drew fire because to some, the picture of Jahar, with tousled hair and the hint of a beard, made him look like a rock star, though the story itself could hardly be described as sympathetic or even sensitive; then the massive *Boston Globe* investigation—there was about a year of near silence. At least in part this was attributable to SAMs, which effectively restricted not only Jahar's but also the family's and the legal team's ability to communicate publicly.

After his arrest, Jahar appeared in public once, at his arraignment on July 10, 2013. He was wearing an orange jumpsuit, and he had what appeared to be a scab on his face—too fresh to stem from the wounds sustained almost three months earlier. He seemed to smirk. Or, some people thought, he might have been grimacing as a result of nerve damage caused by gunshot wounds.

The seventy-four-page indictment listed thirty counts, including "use of a weapon of mass destruction resulting in death," "bombing of a place of public use resulting in death," "malicious destruction of property resulting in personal injury and death," and a number of conspiracy and possession-and-use-of-a-firearm charges. Seventeen of the counts carried the potential maximum sentence of death.

It was a mob scene outside the courtroom that day. Only twenty journalists were allowed inside, followed by thirty-five victims and their companions, some wearing leg braces, some using crutches, many holding hands and looking scared. Twenty members of the public entered next, most of them Jahar groupies and conspiracy theorists. When an additional five journalists were allowed in, the rest of the press attempted to rush the courtroom. "Whoa, whoa!" somebody shouted. "Someone's going to get hurt!" Bella and Ailina, one of them carrying a baby, took seats at the front of the courtroom. A nurse in a white coat sat in the back. The courtroom became very, very quiet.

When Jahar was led in, one of the sisters began to cry loudly. Jahar's lawyers, on his behalf, waived the reading of the indictment, and the prosecutor listed the charges briefly, grouped by the maximum penalty each carried: death, life imprisonment, twenty-five years, twenty years, and less. The defendant repeated the words "Not guilty" seven times. Inexplicably, he spoke with a heavy Russian accent. In twenty minutes, the hearing was over, and Bella and Ailina cried audibly as their brother was led out of the courtroom.

Jahar had a sterling legal team: Miriam Conrad, the public defender for the district that includes Massachusetts; several people from her office, one of whom spoke Russian; Judy Clarke, a famous lawyer for hopeless cases who had succeeded in helping Ted Kaczynski (the Unabomber) and several others avoid the death penalty; and David Bruck, another death penalty heavy hitter. Before the arraignment, Clarke and William Fick, the Russian-speaking public defender, had traveled to Dagestan to meet with Anzor and Zubeidat for the first time. It did not go well. The lawyers could not promise that they could prevent a sentence of death, and this not only scared and disappointed the parents but also made them deeply suspicious. It did not help that the lawyers were being paid out of public funds—as the parents perceived it, by the very same government that was seeking to have Dzhokhar executed.

Kheda Saratova, a Chechen human rights activist who had been trying to help the Tsarnaevs in the weeks after the bombing and who was present during conversations with the lawyers, fumed to me a few days later: "If it happens, with this capital punishment, the parents will die for sure. And the U.S. will get so many new enemies that that terrorist attack will certainly not be the last one. There will be people who will want to avenge Dzhokhar." This was not usual human-rights-activist talk, but this human rights activist, most of whose international contacts were in Europe, was having trouble wrapping her mind around the idea of a civilized country that still used the death penalty. Even in Russia no one had been executed by the state in two decades. And America wanted to execute this kid?

AT JAHAR'S AGE, a year and a half is a long time. When he next appeared in public, in December 2014, he no longer looked like a gawky adolescent. His beard had come in dark and curly, if spotty. No trace of injury was visible, at least from a distance of a few yards. His mane of hair was disheveled. He was dressed for trial: a white shirt, a black pullover, gray slacks. He no longer spoke with a Russian accent as he affirmed to the judge that he was satisfied with his defense team.

Over the next couple of months he would not say anything else that was audible to the public. His look would gradually be tamed: he got a haircut, and the beard got a series of progressively closer trims. He would be brought to Boston's waterfront federal courthouse amid heavy security every day—traffic closed off for blocks, Coast Guard boats in the water—and sit at a large table, flanked by Miriam Conrad and a jury consultant, as the court interviewed 256 people in what at times appeared like a vain search for eighteen people who could constitute an impartial jury.

The process, originally planned for three weeks, lasted two months, albeit with many snow-related delays. Most of the potential jurors were middle-aged, almost all of them were white, and none of them could be seen as Jahar's peers. Very, very few of them seemed, on the face of it, suited to serve on this jury. On a detailed written questionnaire filled out before their interviews, sixty-eight percent had said they believed the defendant was guilty. Pressed by the judge to promise that they could set aside this presumption and listen to the evidence, most issued the promise easily, a few balked, and one, a psychologist, said, "I don't know that the brain works that way."

Some difficulties were inherent in seating a jury in a death penalty case: If it convicted the defendant, the same jury would have to reconvene to determine the penalty. People who are fundamentally opposed to capital punishment are disqualified from serving on death penalty juries, as are people who believe that all intentional murder should be punished by death. But finding people who have no strong views on the death penalty is a difficult proposition, and indeed, when the rare juror claimed that he or she had never given the issue much thought, it might have made one wonder how thoughtful this person was really capable of being. Members of the defense team also occasionally wondered whether potential jurors had been coached on answers that would make them likely to be selected—in order to write an eventual book, or to ensure that Jahar got the death penalty. For its part, all the defense needed was one juror who in the end would vote for life imprisonment: the defendant could be sentenced to death only if the decision was unanimous.

And so the process dragged on and on, some days yielding not a single suitable candidate. Jahar looked bored, even absent, most of the time: he leaned back in his chair and doodled on his legal pad. Only once did I see him actually look at a potential juror's file: this was a young Mexican-born political science professor who studied immigrants and immigration; his opposition to the death penalty disqualified him.

As the weeks wore on and the snow piled up, the number of reporters in the press room dwindled. The room reserved for members of the public who wanted to watch jury selection through a video uplink was often deserted. One day, a young Latino man with a close-cropped beard and equally short hair on his head was the only person there. His name was Luis Vasquez.

Luis's wife had woken him on the Friday morning after the bombing. She shook him, that is, until he was awake. Then she tried to say something, but words refused to form. She pointed at the television and said, "Look at the names." There were the same pictures the couple had seen on the screen the evening before, but now the suspects were identified. Luis had not recognized Tamerlan earlier because, frankly, the guy on television did not look like Tamerlan. "The Tamerlan I knew never wore a hat—his hair was far too good for that. He never wore sunglasses: girls loved his eyes. He was never clean-shaven, he always had a five-o'clock shadow going unless he had to shave for boxing. He was never stooped. The Tamerlan I knew was tall, he stood proud, he was a beautiful man." The man in the photos looked ordinary, even dumpy; Tamerlan and Luis had always been the opposite of that.

They had become friends at Rindge and Latin because they both shadowed a tight-knit group of ESL girls: Tamerlan was keeping watch over Bella, and Luis was trailing his girlfriend, Bella's best friend, who was Venezuelan. Now this girl, who had become Luis's wife, was pointing at the television set while Luis "felt like I was floating, like I was pulled out of my own body."

Then CNN called, and Luis became a star of its Boston bombing show. He did not know much—he realized how little Tamerlan had disclosed whenever they had run into each other in the years after graduating from high school—but compared with people who had been talking into microphones before him, Luis was an expert. He debunked the theory that the brothers "had been brought up to be terrorists," as he had already heard it put on the air. He stressed that they had been living in Cambridge for a decade. He mentioned that he had often seen Tamerlan in the library studying.

After high school their paths had been fairly similar. Both got married. Both became fathers: Luis's first son was born when he was nineteen. Luis had dropped out of the University of Massachusetts Boston as well as Bunker Hill. Both of them had been staring at hard and hopeless lives as working-class young fathers in an overpriced American city where they had been led to believe they could lead lives of meaning. About a month before the bombing, Luis had announced his candidacy for the Cambridge city council, the longest shot on a long list. And now he was on national television. He looked great. Strangers on Twitter began tagging CNN with calls for the network to hire him as an on-air personality. When it was all over, Luis applied to the competitive journalism department at Emerson College, and, with an over-the-top recommendation from CNN, he was admitted (he still lost his city council race). The college was not far from the courthouse, so Luis discovered the peculiar pleasure of spending some of his afternoons watching the interminable process of jury selection.

The week I met with Luis, a federal appeals court had heard the defense argue—as it had repeatedly in written motions—that the trial should be moved from Boston. Between the saturation publicity and what she called "the six degrees of connection," argued Judith Mizner, the public defender's appellate chief, justice in Massachusetts could not have the necessary "appearance of justice."

It was not a large state, and the Boston Marathon was a very large event in it: one after another, potential jurors had said that they knew someone on the witness list or someone who had been at the finish line or a first responder, or they worked for a company that sponsored the marathon or a hospital that treated some of the victims. As if to underscore the effects of saturation publicity, one of the judges had asked a prosecutor about "the video of the defendant placing a backpack at the site of the explosion." This was a video that, if it existed, had never been shown to the public—

a fact the prosecutor failed to point out. The following day, one of the prospective jurors also made reference to having seen this purported video.

To my surprise, Luis, who seemed to have perfected the political art of speaking with detachment about anything, waxed passionate against moving the trial. "It's an attempt to strip us of our dignity all over again," he said. "If someone has the audacity to hurt our community, they should have the *cojones* to face us back and to explain." Did he really think he would get an explanation from Jahar, who was not likely even to testify at his own trial? Luis admitted that he did not. After a few minutes, we circled back to April 2013. The afternoon of the marathon, Luis had been planning to go to the finish line with his family. He had not much wanted to, so they had been slow leaving the apartment. Luis had stepped back in to turn off the television—and on it, had seen the explosions.

I expected him to say that if he had been less reluctant to attend the marathon, he or any other member of his family might have died. But instead he said, "If I'd made it to the finish line, he would have seen me with my family. Would he have stopped? I just keep thinking of that small tiny chance that the whole thing could have been prevented just by being there."

On Friday evening, four days after the bombing, Luis was standing at CNN's temporary set in Boston's Copley Square talking with Anderson Cooper. He heard a producer say that the younger brother had just been captured, and he thought, "They are going to drop me now." Then he heard Anderson Cooper say that Jahar was in custody—and Luis was still there, at the very center of things, on the news. The crowd around them began chanting, "U-S-A! U-S-A!" What Luis really wanted to say was, "We got him, I'm going to Disney World"—he felt that much the winner at the moment. He might have failed, four days earlier, to prevent a tragedy by his mere presence, but now, by his mere presence, he had become intimately involved with bringing evil to justice. He did not give voice to any of that, but instead, with suitable grandeur, he did what Anderson Cooper had not done: he made a sweeping motion to include the chanting crowd in the shot.

This might have been what he had anticipated that morning, when he felt himself floating, like he had been pulled out of his body: his own moment of glory. And this was not only his moment of glory but, in the fervor of all those chanting people, the glory of his time, his place, his country, the vastness of all that it stood for, against the vastness of all that threatened it. "The one thing I hold dear and I cherish," Luis told me on a frozen afternoon in Boston nearly two years later, "is the chants 'U-S-A!' flooding the airwaves—and I forever got to be a part of that moment." No wonder he did not want to let it go.

Author's Note

Every nonfiction book is difficult in its own way. The difficulty with reporting this book was fear. People were afraid to talk to me because they had been questioned harshly by the FBI, because they believed they were in personal danger, because they feared bringing trouble to those they cared about, and because they had been disappointed by seeing their words quoted in simplistic, sensationalist, and misleading reports. I am grateful to those who placed their trust in my project in spite of these deterrents. This includes several people whose help was invaluable but who have asked not to be named in this book or to be acknowledged as sources.

In addition to them, and to those whose names appear in the book, I am thankful to the people who helped me grasp the context of the events I was describing.

In and about Dagestan: sociologist Alexei Levinson, anthropologist and my former colleague Konstantin Kazenin, the brave and inventive Dagestani journalist Zakir Magomedov, and especially Grigory Shvedov, human rights activist and editor of kavkaz-uzel.ru. Asya Tsaturyan and Nikita Bezrukov were my Moscow hosts extraordinaire: I got a room of my own and a set of Dagestan connections.

In and about Kyrgyzstan: my research assistant in Tokmok, Alexandra Ryabova; University of Colorado Boulder doctoral students Caitlin Ryan and Austin Cowley; and especially their teacher Elizabeth Cullen Dunn, now a professor at Indiana University. Elizabeth's expertise was invaluable, but her encouragement and understanding of this project were worth even more.

In and about Boston: Nick and Ruth Daniloff; Graham Fuller; ACLU Massachusetts staff attorneys Jessie Rossman and Sarah Wunsch and Privacy Rights Coordinator Kade Crockford, who has followed the Boston Marathon bombing case doggedly and seemed never to tire of explaining the intricacies to me. My Columbia MFA Writing Program intern Elina Mishuris systematized conspiracy theories and tracked down far-flung leads. Melissa Ludtke helped me with contacts and advice, as did Krystyna Colburn and Ellen Todres Gelfand, both of whom also gave me shelter. Svetlana Boym did what she does best, which was challenge everything I have to say and tell me to read Hannah Arendt. Julia Zagachin was the person who instructed me to drop everything and write this book.

Several journalists shared information with me generously: Alan Cullison of *The Wall Street Journal*, Simon Shuster of *Time*, Fatima Tlisova of the Voice of America, and the great Bruce Gellerman of WBUR.

I have been fortunate, at Riverhead, to work with the best team in all of publishing. I think that Becky Saletan might like me more than she likes deadlines, and I hope to God that never changes. My agent, Elyse Cheney, is the best advocate a writer could have.

Vera Shengelia tracked my every move when I was in Dagestan, and then handed this tedious task over to her husband, Ilya Venyavkin. In fact, they've had my back for years. And nothing I do would be possible without Darya Oreshkina, who gives me both my home and my freedom. She also made the maps for this book.

Selected Bibliography

Anokhina, Svetlana, and Polina Sanayeva, eds. *Byl takoy gorod: Makhachkala*. Moscow: Epokha, 2013.

Atran, Scott. *Talking to the Enemy: Faith, Brotherhood, and the (Un)Making of Terrorists*. New York: HarperCollins, 2010.

Avtorkhanov, Abdurakhman. *Imperiya Kremlya: Soevtskiy tip imperializma*. Moscow: Polifakt–Druzhba narodov, 1991.

Avtorkhanov, Abdurakhman. *Narodoubiystvo v SSSR: Ubiystvo chechenskogo naroda*. Munich: Svobodny Kavkaz, 1952.

Baiev, Khassan, with Ruth and Nicholas Daniloff. *Grief of My Heart: Memoirs of a Chechen Surgeon*. New York: Walker & Company, 2005.

Blum, Gabriella, and Philip B. Heymann. *Law, Outlaws, and Terrorists: Lessons from the War on Terrorism*. Belfer Center Studies in International Security. Cambridge, MA: The MIT Press, 2010.

Crenshaw, Martha. "The Causes of Terrorism." *Comparative Politics* 13, no. 4 (July 1981), pp. 379–399.

Helman, Scott, and Jenna Russell. *Long Mile Home: Boston Under Attack, the City's Courageous Recovery, and the Epic Hunt for Justice*. New York: Dutton, 2014.

Heymann, Philip B. *Terrorism, Freedom, and Security: Winning Without War*. Belfer Center Studies in International Security. Cambridge, MA: The MIT Press, 2003.

Human Rights Watch and Human Rights Institute, Columbia Law School. *Illusion of Justice: Human Rights Abuses in US Terrorism Prosecutions*. New York: Human Rights Institute at Columbia Law School, 2014. http://www.hrw.org/sites/default/files/reports/usterrorism0714_ForUpload_0_0_0.pdf.

Malashenko, Aleksei. *Islamskiye orientiry Severnogo Kavkaza*. Moscow: Gendalf, 2001.

Ploskikh, V. M., and M. K. Imakeeva, eds. *Deportirovanniye narody Kavkaza v Kyrgyzskuyu Respubliku: Sbornik dokumentov i materialov*. Bishkek: KRSU, 2010.

Post, Jerrold M. *The Mind of the Terrorist: The Psychology of Terrorism from the IRA to Al-Qaeda*. New York: Palgrave Macmillan, 2007.

Richardson, Louise. *What Terrorists Want: Understanding the Enemy, Containing the Threat*. New York: Random House, 2006.

Smith, Sebastian. *Allah's Mountain: The Battle for Chechnya*. London and New York: Tauris Parke Paperbacks, 2006.